LESSONS FROM
THE PAST

ANCIENT KNOWLEDGE, CONTEMPORARY ISSUES

Edited by Ken Feder

Central Connecticut State University

cognella®
academic publishing

Bassim Hamadeh, CEO and Publisher
Michael Simpson, Vice President of Acquisitions
Jamie Giganti, Managing Editor
Jess Busch, Graphic Design Supervisor
John Remington, Acquisitions Editor
Brian Fahey, Licensing Associate
Sean Adams, Interior Designer

First published in the United States of America in 2014 by Cognella, Inc.

Trademark Notice: Product or corporate names may be trademarks or registered trademarks, and are used only for identification and explanation without intent to infringe.

Cover image copyright © 2012 by Depositphotos / Beatrice Preve.

Printed in the United States of America

ISBN: 978-1-62131-225-3 (pbk) / 978-1-62131-226-0 (br)

academic publishing

www.cognella.com   800-200-3908

Contents

Section 1

THE PAST IS THE KEY
TO THE PRESENT

The articles in this section focus on how people in the past responded to the challenges presented by environmental change. The researchers and authors have investigated and reported on the impacts of climate change on the people of ancient Mesopotamia; the Harappan civilization of the Indus Valley, Egypt, Rome; the Han of China; and the Maya of Mesoamerica. The research presented in one of the papers even suggests that ancient people themselves contributed to climate change, showing, indeed, that there may be nothing new under the sun. A pessimist might recognize the depressing regularity with which human beings screw up their environment. The pessimist would be right.

In a world afflicted by poverty, oppression, inequality, warfare, terrorism, racism, and the threat of nuclear proliferation (even this incomplete list is depressingly long, isn't it?), an argument might still be made that climate change, sometimes referred to as "global warming," may represent the most significant challenge facing us in the modern world. As bad as the rest of the items on that list may be, if we fundamentally alter the environmental conditions that characterize our planet to the point where it can no longer sustain our current and growing human population and we descend into a chaos of literally billions of starving people competing for a diminishing planetary food base, well, the rest of that list becomes moot.

Today, most scientists recognize the existential challenge represented by climate change and the role played by human activity in contributing to that change. Whatever opinion you may hold on this topic, you must admit that the issue certainly attracts a great deal of attention in popular media. Newspapers report on climate change all the time, magazine articles discuss it, and it is a regular focus of cable documentaries. Vice president Al Gore's popular and award-winning 2006 documentary, *An Inconvenient Truth*, centered on climate change and its potential impacts on the planet including plant and animal extinction; sea-level rise and attendant inundation of coastal cities; desertification of areas today under cultivation; soil erosion; drought; raging pandemics; and, ultimately, starvation. The picture painted in *An Inconvenient Truth* was not a pretty one and, if even a fraction of Gore's doomsaying comes to pass, life on our planet is going to become significantly more challenging in the years to come. In the worst-case scenario, a lot of people are going to die.

How can archaeology contribute to the modern discussion of climate change? An often-repeated phrase extolling the virtues of studying the past comes from the pen of philosopher and essayist George Santayana: "Those who cannot remember the past are condemned to repeat it." Santayana may have been right, but I'm not convinced that there are any data to support the implication drawn by some that knowing the past inoculates people from making exactly the same mistakes their ancestors made. In other words, just because people are cognizant of the mistakes and missteps made in the past, just because they may "remember the past," doesn't mean they will necessarily wise up and successfully avoid those mistakes and missteps in the present or future. Of course, however, at least those who know the past may recognize recurring patterns and problems when they arise and they may warn people and encourage them to avoid those mistakes. In the pessimist's view, ultimately, those warning about the future may end up only being able to say "I told you so" when the same mistakes, despite the warnings, are made with predictably tragic consequences. And right after we issue those warnings gleaned from our study of the past, we'll starve to death along with everybody else who didn't see it coming. Granted, it's a minor victory, but it's something.

Here's where the selections in this section of *Lessons from the Past* fit in. Each of these articles makes the valuable point that climate change (primarily, but not exclusively, as the result of natural patterns or cycles) has challenged people in the past. People in the late twentieth and early twenty-first centuries are not the first to face local or worldwide mean temperature increases or decreases; we are not the first to experience long-term changes in precipitation, drought, and soil erosion; we are not the first to have to deal with the extinction of important plant and animal resources. And we are not the first to see, in very real terms, our way of life threatened by dramatic shifts in the environment. Each article that follows in this section reports on historical and archaeological evidence of how just such a dramatic shift was responded to by an ancient group of people. Hopefully, we denizens of the modern world will actually learn these "lessons" presented by these ancient responses of environmental degradation and attendant climate change.

Environmental Degradation and Early Mesopotamian Civilization

Charles L. Redman

EDITOR'S INTRODUCTION

The complex civilization of Mesopotamia—the "land between the two rivers," those rivers being the Tigris and Euphrates in Iraq—is one of the most ancient in the world. At the core of this civilization's evolution was the ability to harness the vast productivity of the agricultural soils in the double river valley in which it was located. As population increased, however, so too did the need to produce ever-increasing surpluses of food to feed more mouths and to support the lifestyles of the members of the growing elite classes. As archaeologist Charles Redman points out, the primary strategies employed by the ancient Mesopotamians to produce more food—including and especially, intensifying and expanding irrigation networks—worked in the short term, but, ironically, led to an overall decrease in soil fertility by overly concentrating salt in the soil. This lesson in unintended consequences is a valuable one for a modern world faced with feeding a burgeoning human population.

POINTS TO PONDER

1. How did the ancient Mesopotamians increase agricultural productivity? Why did they need to?
2. What were the unintended consequences of their strategies of increasing agricultural productivity?
3. What happened to the ancient civilization of southern Mesopotamia as a result of their effort to increase agricultural productivity?
4. What lessons can be learned from the Mesopotamian story?

Charles L. Redman, "Environmental Degradation and Early Mesopotamian Civilization," *Archaeology of Global Change: The Impact of Humans on Their Environment*, ed. Charles L. Redman, Steven R. James, Paul Fish, and J. Daniel Rogers, pp. 158-164. Copyright © 2004 by Smithsonian Books. Reprinted with permission.

T he development of cities in early Mesopotamia is an example of one of the great transformations in human history. People began solving the problems of living together in large social units, of producing goods on a massive scale, and of transporting and redistributing those goods so that many people in these newly founded cities could devote themselves to pursuits other than food production. Archaeologists have played a major role in recognizing these achievements. The relationship of these expanding early settlements to the surrounding landscape and the ways they manipulated it is at the center of the story of early cities. World-shaking inventions like the wheel, irrigation agriculture, and metallurgy, and the development of new food crops and improved strains of domestic animals were all part of the spectacular success of Mesopotamian civilization. Integral to this economic revolution were equally innovative organizational changes that relied on new concepts of ethics, ownership, religion, and government. All of these changes were refined over the centuries and many aspects of them were incorporated into subsequent civilizations, with a pervasive effect on modern social, economic, and government structures.

These brilliant innovations of early Mesopotamian cities were accompanied by some less positive developments: organized warfare, class-structured social hierarchies, and widespread degradation of the natural landscape. This chapter focuses on the last of these three legacies—environmental degradation. It begins with a brief discussion of the activities hypothesized in the introduction of this volume: social responses and environmental impacts associated with expanding settlement systems. It then turns to some of the general human-land relationships that have been suggested by other studies in the Near East and concludes with a case study of such relationships from the third millennium in southern Mesopotamia.

HUMAN-LAND RELATIONSHIPS IN AN EARLY CIVILIZATION

The basic assumption of this chapter is that as successful agrarian societies began to develop managerial and hierarchical social systems they set in motion forces that reshaped the decision-making process guiding human interactions with the environment. That is to say, as societies grew more complex, key decisions often rested not with the primary producers, but with individuals and groups facing different constraints and thus having a different view of risks and rewards. Furthermore, people higher up in the social hierarchy may not have had immediate access to information on the productive situation or a solid understanding of the actual alternatives. Anthropologist Roy Rappaport (1978) considered this type of inefficiency in the flow of information a "maladaptation" that exists in many complex societies and often undermines their continued survival.

People in positions of control in a complex society fashion institutional structures and promote belief systems that lead primary producers to make decisions that to us, as outsiders, appear illogical. The promulgation of these ideologies helps hold complex societies together. Their acceptance is fundamental to the support of the social hierarchy largely because ideologies are often designed to influence primary producers to generate a surplus and create rationales for it to be gathered and used to maintain nonprimary producers. Complex societies could not exist if agrarian producers only created enough goods to meet their biological needs. These goods could not be accumulated, transferred to others through peaceful exchange or violent theft, and transformed into elite goods that assume value through their restricted flow among members of the society.

To sustain itself, a complex society requires goods with a long "life," such as domestic animals and stored agricultural produce. Such goods not only constitute a form of wealth in themselves but they can also be converted into prestige goods and monumental constructions, and provide an economic basis for a military, bureaucracy, and cadre of elite. Hence it is in the interest of those who benefit from a complex social hierarchy to encourage increasing production and collection of agricultural surpluses, irrespective of the long-term environmental consequences.

It is useful to conceptualize the development of complex societies, as others have done, as a series of cycles of growth, stability, and decline over long stretches of history. These can be viewed as complex adaptive cycles, each of which passes through four phases: reorganization, expansion, conservation, and release (Holling 2001; Holling and Gunderson 2002). This approach helps us to measure the resilience of a social ecological system by focusing on interactions between participants that occurred at differing scales of time and space (Redman and Kinzig 2003). Events as they took place in Mesopotamia may therefore provide insight into other situations. The actual cycle can refer to the operation of the social-ecological system at a number of scales and can be measured in terms of population, energy consumption, other technological indicators, centralization of political power, changes in social organization, or agricultural productivity of the landscape. Many of these factors are in all likelihood interrelated through feedback mechanisms that act to limit excessive growth as well as regenerate over-depleted environments and hence give the appearance of cyclical behavior. The relevant questions that need to be addressed for the purposes of this volume are what suites of alternative decisions concerning means of increasing food production are faced by members of an early civilization, and how did the pathways taken affect their environment, particularly, its productive potential? The type of settlement system of interest here is one that relies heavily on the products of irrigation agriculture, as did many of the early civilizations of the world.

The four basic strategies for expanding food for urban centers are to (1) intensify production on current fields, (2) expand fields under cultivation, (3) centralize control of food-producing activities, and (4) increase reliance on goods imported from a regional system. Under favorable circumstances, each of these strategies may lead to increased overall food production, and most important, to increased available surpluses that could be used to support nonfood-producing urban dwellers. However, if these strategies are carried too far or if they are applied for too long, they may seriously degrade the environment and undermine the growing system. What is too far or too long depends on many factors including the soils, climate, productive activities, and social fabric of the society in question. Archaeological examination can provide the information required to understand what these balances are, how they are maintained, or how they are set off into a downward spiral. For example, intensifying production through shortening fallow periods and increasing the density of plantings can quickly multiply food yields, as many early civilizations discovered, but it also calls for increased labor and capital input—and over time can adversely affect soil fertility, thus making the system more vulnerable to disturbances. Expanding cultivation to more distant or less fertile fields can also increase the total amount of food produced, but at a significant additional cost in labor. As for the third strategy—centralizing the control of agricultural activities—it could involve enhanced coordination of irrigation construction and maintenance, adjudication of irrigation water allocation, and encouragement of specialization and exchange among producers. This coordination may bring big gains in production, but it also removes considerable decision-making authority from the local food producers and puts it into the hands of an urban elite. Investigation of early civilizations shows that most cities come to rely on food and other products from a regional system. Sometimes they depend on local villages only a short distance from the city and often held together by close kin ties as well as political authority, but as the cities grow sometimes the need for food extends to more distant sources whose sense of obligation is less certain and may fail in a time of crisis. Although each of these strategies may not be applied in every situation or may lead to differing results, the other chapters of this book strongly suggest they often do apply. One case study showing how each of the four strategies was attempted and what resulted is that of the Ur III Dynasty in the Near East.

THE NEAR EAST: UR III DYNASTY AS A CASE STUDY

Evidence of serious human impacts on the environment in the Near East seems to coincide with the introduction of agriculture and village life. It has been suggested that episodes of local deforestation and soil erosion were associated with the growth of village life, especially in the Levant (Falconer and Fall 1995; Rollefson and Köhler-Rollefson 1992). Numerous articles and entire books (Hillel 1991; Thirgood 1981) have been written about the general degradation of Mediterranean forests from anthropogenic activities. Helping to define the state of knowledge and guide subsequent research is a collection of 28 essays reviewing evidence from geology, zoology, botany, and archaeology to document human impacts in numerous localities (see Bottema et al. 1990). Some of these studies focus on the highlands of Anatolia and the Zagros Mountains, where Naomi Miller has found radical changes in the species of trees available to the occupants of Kurban Höyük in Turkey and Tepe Malyan in Iran as a result of having degraded their surroundings (Miller 1985, 1990; Chapter 6, this volume). Other studies in the highlands have focused on the effects on local forest cover of grazing animals, especially the goat, versus the pyrotechnological industries such as plaster, pottery, and metal (Wertime 1983). Although most of these studies have emphasized the deleterious effects of human use of the landscape, Karl Butzer (1996) reflects on the long duration of human occupation and suggests that in reality a successful balance has evolved that has allowed agriculturalists to have sustained use of the Levant region for almost 10 millennia. It is important not to focus unduly on the deleterious effects of expanding social units on their local environment, because in many localities human-environmental interactions were resilient over long periods of time. The key question to resolve is under what conditions and in what ways do these otherwise sustainable systems become vulnerable and eventually fail?

Most earlier studies have focused on problems of deforestation and soil erosion in the uplands of the Near East and in the dissected topography around the Mediterranean Basin. I am particularly intrigued, however, by what archaeology can tell us about a different set of human-land relationships—those of the alluvial plains where the great early civilizations arose. As early as 1958, an article published in *Science* spoke directly to the problems caused by salinization in lower Mesopotamia 4,000 years ago and what modern inhabitants of that region might learn from the past (Jacobsen and Adams 1958). Since then, papers on this subject have continued to appear sporadically (Dickson 1987; Gelburd 1985; Gibson 1974; Redman 1992), yet it is only recently that this approach has become more widely adopted (Balée 1998; Crumley 1994; McIntosh et al. 2000; Redman 1999). A number of textbooks (Nissen 1988; Redman 1978) point to salinization as a major cause of the reduced political importance of southern Mesopotamia despite considerable debate (Powell 1985) over the cultural context that led to this environmental "catastrophe."

The Ur III case study focuses on work that began in the late 1950s (Jacobsen and Adams 1958) and continued in subsequent decades (Adams 1978; Jacobsen 1982), and on the controversy surrounding it. Some have questioned whether the changes cited were as grave as suggested and whether the causes identified were in fact at fault (Powell 1985). The use of early textual accounts and incomplete archaeological investigations often leaves the most interesting interpretive models as hypotheses rather than confirmed facts. Whether or not subsequent studies show that this view of the Ur III situation holds true, it is likely that other Near Eastern civilizations experienced similar cycles of political and economic growth followed by environmental and subsequent social decline, both before Ur III (suggested by H. Nissen, pers. comm.) and after it (Adams 1978).

Four thousand years ago, the southern half of Mesopotamia was the site of one of the great early societies of the region, the Ur III Dynasty, which consisted of numerous cities, each inhabited by several tens of thousands of people and supported by an associated hinterland of farms and villages. Its prominent features were well-developed writing, a system of laws, extensive trade networks, ambitious builders, and strong centralized political control (Edzard 1967; Nissen 1988). The economic system relied heavily on irrigation agriculture, with vast field systems along the Euphrates River and canals leading from it. Winter-cultivated cereals were the main crop, although there were many secondary crops as well. Herding was also important, with contemporary records indicating that as many as two million sheep were being kept.

The interesting aspect of Ur III society for this discussion is the rapid rise in the centralized control of the political hierarchy and paradoxically its role in the region's declining agricultural productivity and environmental damage. Centralized control of the once independent city states was a logical objective of the Ur III rulers as their power increased. Centralization gave them greater access to labor pools, military conscripts, trade goods, and agricultural produce. Moreover, centralized control increased the potential for the production of food and other goods. Some of this increased productivity was achieved through increased specialization of production, but the majority resulted from centralized management of the construction and maintenance of waterworks and the allocation of water in the growing irrigation network that fed the Mesopotamian fields. It was therefore logical for Ur III rulers to decide to extend the land served by irrigation and increase the capacity of the existing canal system so more water could be brought to the fields. Another decision that would have seemed logical under pressure to produce more, would be to shorten the period of time fields were left fallow. But these same decisions that brought short-term increases in production, as evidenced in the high population density and great construction projects of the Ur III period, rapidly undermined the agrarian base and led to a long period of diminished productivity. The major scourge was salinization of the soils. Although there is general agreement that salinization was, as Hans Nissen (1988) says, "one of the greatest countrywide catastrophes," there remains considerable debate over the causes.

Salinization refers to an accumulation of salt near the surface of the soil. This salt is carried by river water from the sedimentary rocks in the mountains and deposited on the Mesopotamian fields during natural flooding or purposeful irrigation. In southern Mesopotamia, the natural water table comes to within roughly 2 meters of the surface. Excessive irrigation can bring the water table up to the root zone and capillary action can bring it to the surface, killing most plants (Gelburd 1985).

Written records of temple storehouses of the period allow scholars to reconstruct with some certainty the relative productivity of fields and the crops being planted. They indicate a long-term decrease in productivity between 2400 and 1700 B.C. At the outset of this period wheat was an important crop, accounting for at least one-sixth of the cereals produced. As salinization increased, people slowly shifted to the more salt-tolerant barley, so that by the end of the Ur III Dynasty in 2000 B.C., wheat made up only 2 percent of the crops cultivated, and by 1700 it appears that wheat was totally abandoned in the region (Jacobsen 1982). The end of this decline in wheat production coincides with a long period without centralized political control. Many cities were abandoned or reduced to villages, and the emphasis in agriculture shifted. During the height of Ur III control, the emphasis was on maximizing surplus production for central rulers, but during the subsequent political breakdown, it shifted to satisfying the needs of local populations in a more self-sufficient localized production mode.

DISCUSSION

The main point of this Mesopotamian example is that at least in this preindustrial state, short-term political stability and economic maximization were only achieved by weakening the adaptive capacity of the productive system to react to internal and external challenges, but this strategy undermined its long-term survival. State ideologies assumed at that time, as do many today, that everyone's interests are served when the interests of the central rulers are served. Clearly, however, most people may not share the rulers' objectives and not every segment of the population is likely to benefit equally from a particular productive strategy. The critical question, therefore, is the effective locus of decision making within the society, how its decision makers gain their information, and how they perceive their needs.

What does the bigger picture look like from here? Generalities begin to make sense when one compares other examples already in the archaeological literature with the case of southern Mesopotamia. Lowland irrigation settings, like Mesopotamia, are vulnerable to problems of salinization and siltation if major energy is not invested in maintaining the long-term productive potential of the landscape. The underlying cause of this mismanagement seems to lie in the hierarchical nature of complex societies. Whereas in a small-scale society the primary producers make the major decisions and are guided by a conservative, risk-minimization strategy, in complex societies the elites appear to demand a never-satisfied increase in surplus production themselves, frequent military activity, major construction, and the crafting of specialized prestige goods. Not surprisingly, to meet these demands the elite would encourage producers to allocate excessive amounts of irrigation water (especially during flood years), shorten fallow periods, extend cultivation to new areas (which would make herding more difficult), and cut down upland forests to provide fuelwood for newly emerging industries and a growing population.

Although textual records document a collapse of the central authority of the Ur III Dynasty, Mesopotamian society continued in the form of midlevel city centers and village settlements. Centralized, regionwide government did not reemerge for several generations, after landscapes had sufficiently regenerated, and when it did, the locus of power had moved to the north, Hence the ancient history of Mesopotamia can be be interpreted as a series of cycles of expansion, collapse, and reorganization from the vantage point of the political hierarchy, and as a more resilient, continuous system from that of the units at the lower levels of the social organization (Adams 1978; Redman and Kinzig 2003).

LITERATURE CITED

Adams, R. McC.
1978 Strategies of Maximization, Stability, and Resilience in Mesopotamian Society, Settlement, and Agriculture. *Proceedings of the American Philosophical Society* 122:329–335.
Balée, W. (editor)
1998 *Advances in Historical Ecology.* Columbia University Press, New York.

Bottema, S., G. Entjes-Nieborg, and W. Van Zeist (editors)

1990 *Man's Role in the Shaping of the Eastern Mediterrnnean Landscape, A. A.* Balkema, Rotterdam.

Butzer, K. W.

1996 Ecology in the Long View: Settlement Histories, Agrosystemic Strategies, and Ecological Performance. *Journal of Field Archaeology* 23:141–150.

Crumley, C. L. (editor)

1994 *Historical Ecology: Cultural Knowledge and Changing Landscapes.* School of American Research Press. Santa Fe.

Dickson, D. B.

1987 Cirurmcription by Anthropogenic Environmental Destruction: An Expansion of Carneiro's (1970) Theory of the Origin of the State. *American Antiquity* 52:709–716.

Edzard, D. O.

1967 Third Dynasty of Ur: Its Empire and Its Successor States. In *The Near East: The Early Civilizations,* edited by J. Bottero, E. Cassin, and J. Vercoutter, 133–176. Delacorte, New York.

Falconer, S. B., and P. L. Fall

1995 Human Impacts on the Environment during the Rise and Collapse of Civilization in the Eastern Mediterranean. In *Late Quaternary Environments and Deep History: A Tribute to Paul S. Martin,* edited by D. W. Steadman and J. I. Mead, 84–101. Scientific Papers, vol. 3. Mammoth Site of Hot Springs, South Dakota.

Gelburd, D. E.

1985 Managing Salinity, Lessons from the Past. *Journal of Soil and Water Conservation* 40:329–331.

Gibson, McG.

1974 Violation of Fallow and Engineered Disaster in Mesopotamian Civilization. In *Irrigation's Impact on Society,* edited by T. E. Downing and McG. Gibson. Anthropological Papers of the University of Arizona, No. 25. University of Arizona Press, Tucson.

Hillel, D.

1991 *Out of the Earth: Civilization and the Life of the Soil.* University of California Press, Los Angeles.

Holling, C. S.

2001 Understanding the Complexity of Economic, Ecological, and Social Systems. *Ecosystems* 4:390–405.

Holling, C. S., and L. H. Gunderson

2002 Resilience and Adaptive Cycles. In *Panarchy: Understanding Transformations in Human and Natural Systems,* edited by L. H. Gunderson and C. S. Holling, 25–62. Island Press, Washington, D.C.

Jacobsen, T.

1982 Salinity and Irrigation Agriculture in Antiquity; Diyala Basin Archaeological Projects: Report on Essential Results, 1957–58 *Biblioteca Mesopotamica* 14. Undena Publications, Malibu.

Jacobsen, T., and R. McC. Adams

1958 Salt and Silt in Ancient Mesopotamian Agriculture. *Science* 128:1251–1258.

McIntosh, R. J., J. A. Tainter, and S. K. McIntosh (editors)

2000 *The Way the Wind Blows.* Columbia University Press, New York.

Miller, N. F.

1985 Paleoethnobotanical Evidence for Deforestation in Ancient Iran: A Case Study of Urban Malyan. *Journal of Ethnobiology* 5:1–19.

1990 Clearing Land for Farmland and Fuel: Archaeobotanical Studies of the Ancient Near East. In *Economy and Settlement in the Near East: Analyses of Ancient Sites and Materials,* edited by N. F. Miller, 71–78. Masca Research Papers in Science and Archaeology. University Museum of Archaeology and Anthropology, University of Pennsylvania, Philadelphia.

Nissen, H. J.

1988 *The Early History of the Ancient Near East: 9000–2000 B.C.,* translated by E. Lutzeier. University of Chicago Press, Chicago.

Powell, M. A.

1985 Salt, Seed, and Yields in Sumerian Agriculture: A Critique of the Theory of Progressive Salinization. *Zeitschrift fuer Assyriologie una Vorderasiatische Archaeologie* 75(1):7–38.

Rappaport, R. A.

1978 Maladaptations in Social Systems. In *The Evolution of Social Systems,* edited by J. Friedman and M. J. Rowlands, 49–87. University of Pittsburgh Press, Pittsburgh.

Redman, C. L.

1978 *The Rise of* Civilization: *From Early Farmers to Urban Society in the Ancient Near East.* W. H. Freeman, San Francisco.

1992 The Impact of Food Production: Short-term Strategies and Long-term Consequences. In *Human Impact on the Environment: Ancient Roots, Current Challenges,* edited by J. E. Jacobsen and J. Firor, 35–49. Westview Press, Boulder, Colo.

1999 *Human Impact on Ancient Environments.* University of Arizona Press, Tucson.

Redman, C. L., and A. P. Kinzig

2002 Resilience of Past Landscapes: Resilience Theory, Society, and the Longue Duree. *Conservation Ecology* 7(1):14 (available at http://www.consecol.org/ vol7/iss1/artl4).

Rollefson, G., and I. Kohler-Rollefson

1992 Early Neolithic Exploitation Patterns in the Levant:

Cultural Impact on the Environment. *Population and Environment* 13:243–254.

Thirgood, J. V.

1981 *Man and the Mediterranean Forest: A History of Resource Depletion.* Academic Press, London.

Wertime, T. A.

1983 The Furnace Versus the Goat: the Pyrotechnologic Industries and Mediterranean Deforestation in Antiquity. *Journal of Field Archaeology* 10:445–452.

Study: Ancient Empires Affected Global Climate

Monte Morin

EDITOR'S INTRODUCTION

The common assumption that human beings have been significantly degrading worldwide climate for a relatively brief period of recent history—limited to, perhaps, the time after the industrial revolution—appears to be incorrect based on the evidence cited in this article. An examination of cores taken in Greenland's permanent glacial ice, in which datable bits of what amounts to fossilized atmosphere trapped as bubbles, shows a significant jump in the amount of methane in the period between AD 1 and AD 300. This corresponds with the end of the Roman Empire in Europe and end of the Han Dynasty in China. Both of those cultures used wood and other plant material to cook food, to heat their homes, and as fuel in their metallurgical industries. The burning of so much wood, in turn, released substantial amounts of methane into the Earth's atmosphere, changing its chemical makeup and, thus, resulting in climate change, albeit smaller by far than what we face in the modern world but, nevertheless, change.

POINTS TO PONDER

1. How might ancient cultures have affected worldwide climate?
2. What is meant by the term "pyrogenic emissions"?
3. Other than the period AD 1 to AD 300, what other time periods in the Greenland ice core showed jumps in atmospheric methane? How are those explained by the authors of the study?
4. What lessons can we learn from the evidence of ancient methane increase in the Greenland ice core?

Centuries before the Industrial Revolution or the recognition of global warming, the ancient Roman and Chinese empires were already producing powerful greenhouse gases through their daily toil, according to a new study.

The burning of plant matter to cook food, clear cropland and process metals released millions of tons of methane gas into the atmosphere each year during several periods of pre-industrial history, the study published Thursday in the journal Nature states.

Although the quantity of methane produced back then pales in comparison with the emissions released today—the total amount now is about 70 times greater—the findings suggest that humankind's footprint on the climate is larger than previously realized. Until now, scientists assumed that human activity began increasing greenhouse gas levels only after 1750, with the start of the Industrial Revolution.

"The quantities are much smaller because there were fewer people on Earth," said study leader Celia Sapart, an atmospheric chemist at Utrecht University in the Netherlands. "But the amount of methane emitted per person was significant."

Sapart's conclusions were based on an analysis of ice core samples from Greenland. The layered ice columns, which date back 2,000 years, contain tiny air bubbles from different periods and offer scientists a view of the atmosphere's changing chemistry.

The first period of methane production captured in the ice cores—roughly from A.D. 1 to 300—encompassed the tail ends of the Roman empire and the Han dynasty, when charcoal was the preferred form of fuel. The second period of elevated methane emissions occurred during what's known as the Medieval Climate Anomaly, from roughly 800 to 1200, and a third was found during the Little Ice Age between 1300 and 1600.

Methane is one of a handful of gases that contribute to global warming.

"The results show that between 100 B.C. and A.D. 1600, human activity may have been responsible for roughly 20 to 30 percent of the total pyrogenic methane emissions" the authors wrote. Pyrogenic emissions are released by combustion.

The research appeared to be the result of careful and difficult examination of carbon isotopes and could affect global warming estimates for the pre-industrial period, said Ed Dlugokencky, a methane expert at the National Oceanic and Atmospheric Administration's Earth System Research Laboratory.

"The study gives further evidence for a contribution to the global methane burden from anthropogenic (human-related) sources," said Dlugokencky, who was not involved in the study.

4,000 Years Ago, Climate Change Caused Massive Civilization Collapse

Charles Choi

EDITOR'S INTRODUCTION

Just about everybody has at least heard about the ancient civilization of Egypt. The ancient Maya of Mesoamerica garner a tremendous amount of attention in popular media, only partially because of the nonsense surrounding their alleged prediction of the end of the world on December 21, 2012, but also because of their remarkable architecture, art, and mathematical abilities. But far less attention has been paid to, and far fewer are familiar with the amazing ancient civilization that evolved along the Indus River in what today is Pakistan. Dominated by the two major cities, Harappa and Mohenjo Daro, by 4,500 years ago, the Indus Valley civilization became the dominant socio-political force in south Asia for more than 500 years. And after 4,000 years ago that power ebbed coincident with a drying of the region and a subsequent decrease in the amount of water flowing through the rivers that were used to irrigate the agricultural fields that supplied food to the Indus cities. Ironically, an initial decrease in powerful monsoons allowed for the development of civilization in the first place as the great floods caused by those storms declined in severity. However, the continuing decline of the monsoons restricted the amount of water in the rivers, leading to a decline in arable land and, it seems, the collapse of that same civilization.

POINTS TO PONDER

1. What was ironic about the decline in the monsoons of south Asia as shown by paleoclimatological data?
2. How did researchers determine that the ancient monsoons of south Asia declined in severity?
3. What happened to the Indus civilization people? What was their strategy for coping with climate change?
4. What lessons can we learn from the impacts of climate change on agriculture?

The mysterious fall of the largest of the world's earliest urban civilizations nearly 4,000 years ago in what is now India, Pakistan, Nepal and Bangladesh now appears to have a key culprit—ancient climate change, researchers say.

Ancient Egypt and Mesopotamia may be the best known of the first great urban cultures, but the largest was the Indus or Harappan civilization. This culture once extended over more than 386,000 square miles (1 million square kilometers) across the plains of the Indus River from the Arabian Seas to the Ganges, and at its peak may have accounted for 10 percent of the world population. The civilization developed about 5,200 years ago, and slowly disintegrated between 3,900 and 3,000 years ago—populations largely abandoned cities, migrating toward the east.

"Antiquity knew about Egypt and Mesopotamia, but the Indus civilization, which was bigger than these two, was completely forgotten until the 1920s," said researcher Liviu Giosan, a geologist at Woods Hole Oceanographic Institution in Massachusetts. "There are still many things we don't know about them."

Nearly a century ago, researchers began discovering numerous remains of Harappan settlements along the Indus River and its tributaries, as well as in a vast desert region at the border of India and Pakistan. Evidence was uncovered for sophisticated cities, sea links with Mesopotamia, internal trade routes, arts and crafts, and as-yet undeciphered writing.

"They had cities ordered into grids, with exquisite plumbing, which was not encountered again until the Romans," Giosan told LiveScience. "They seem to have been a more democratic society than Mesopotamia and Egypt—no large structures were built for important personalitiess like kings or pharaohs."

Like their contemporaries in Egypt and Mesopotamia, the Harappans, who were named after one of their largest cities, lived next to rivers.

"Until now, speculations abounded about the links between this mysterious ancient culture and its life-giving mighty rivers," Giosan said.

Now Giosan and his colleagues have reconstructed the landscape of the plain and rivers where this long-forgotten civilizations developed. Their findings now shed light on the enigmatic fate of this culture.

"Our research provides one of the clearest examples of climate change leading to the collapse of an entire civilizations," Giosan said.

The researchers first analyzed satellite data of the landscape influenced by the Indus and neighboring rivers. From 2003 to 2008, the researchers then collected samples of sediment from the coast of the Arabian Sea into the fertile irrigated valleys of Punjab and the northern Thar Desert to determine the origins and ages of those sediments and develop a timeline of landscape changes.

"It was challenging working in the desert—temperatures were over 110 degrees Fahrenheit all day long (43 degrees C)," Giosan recalled.

After collecting data on geological history, "we could reexamine what we know about settlements, what crops people were planting and when, and how both agriculture and settlement patterns changed," said researcher Dorian Fuller, an archaeologist with University College London. "This brought new insights into the process of eastward population shift, the change towards many more small farming communities, and the decline of cities during late Harappan times."

Some had suggested that the Harappan heartland received its waters from a large glacier-fed Himalayan river, thought by some to be the Sarasvati, a sacred river of Hindu mythology. However, the researchers found that only rivers fed by monsoon rains flowed through the region.

Previous studies suggest the Ghaggar, an intermittent river that flows only during strong monsoons, may best approximate the location of the Sarasvati. Archaeological evidence suggested the river, which dissipates into the desert along the dried course of Hakra valley, was home to intensive settlement during Harappan times.

"We think we settled a long controversy about the mythic Sarasvati River," Giosan said.

Initially, the monsoon-drenched rivers the researchers identified were prone to devastating floods. Over time, monsoons weakened, enabling agriculture and civilization to flourish along flood-fed riverbanks for nearly 2,000 years.

"The insolation—the solar energy received by the Earth from the sun—varies in cycles, which can impact monsoons," Giosan said. "In the last 10,000 years, the Northern Hemisphere had the highest insolation from 7,000 to 5,000 years ago, and since then insolation there decreased. All climate on Earth is driven by the sun, and so the monsoons were affected by the lower insolation, decreasing in force. This meant less rain got into continental regions affected by monsoons over time."

Eventually, these monsoon-based rivers held too little water and dried, making them unfavorable for civilization.

"The Harappans were an enterprising people taking advantage of a window of opportunity—a kind of "Goldilocks civilization," Giosan said.

Eventually, over the course of centuries, Harappans apparently fled along an escape route to the east toward the Ganges basin, where monsoon rains remained reliable.

"We can envision that this eastern shift involved a change to more localized forms of economy—smaller communities supported by local rain-fed farming and dwindling streams," Fuller said. "This may have produced smaller surpluses, and would not have supported large cities, but would have been reliable."

This change would have spelled disaster for the cities of the Indus, which were built on the large surpluses seen during the earlier, wetter era. The dispersal of the population to the east would have meant there was no longer a concentrated workforce to support urbanism.

"Cities collapsed, but smaller agricultural communities were sustainable and flourished," Fuller said. "Many of the urban arts, such as writing, faded away, but agriculture continued and actually diversified."

These findings could help guide future archaeological explorations of the Indus civilizations. Researchers can now better guess which settlements might have been more significant, based on their relationships with rivers, Giosan said.

It remains uncertain how monsoons will react to modern climate changes. "If we take the devastating floods that caused the largest humanitarian disaster in Pakistan's history as a sign of increased monsoon activity, than this doesn't bode well for the region," Giosan said. "The region has the largest irrigation scheme in the world, and all those dams and channels would become obsolete in the face of the large floods an increased monsoon would bring."

The scientists detailed their findings online May 28 in the journal Proceedings of the National Academy of Sciences.

Climate and the Collapse
of Maya Civilization

Larry Peterson and Gerald H. Haug

EDITOR'S INTRODUCTION

Though the world didn't end on December 12, 2012, the Maya world appears to have gone through if not a complete collapse, at least a major reconfiguration and contraction between about AD 750 and 900. The major population centers in the south in Guatemala, Honduras, Belize, and in Chiapas in Mexico saw the end of pyramid building and Maya population centers largely were abandoned. The Maya didn't disappear at this time; population and power shifted to the north, into the Yucatan Peninsula in Mexico. As shown in other examples in this section, researchers have noted a fascinating correlation between this "collapse" and geographical shift and a change in climate that dates to the same time period. In the article penned by Larry Peterson and Gerald H. Haug, the authors report on their paleoclimatological research of submarine sediments located in a deep basin off the coast of northern South America. The sediments provide what the authors call a "first-millennium rain gauge," which indicates a complex series of drying events in the region that they suggest reflect long and severe droughts that would have had a major impact on agriculture in Maya territory.

POINTS TO PONDER

1. How did the authors conclude that a series of droughts occurred in the Maya world after AD 700?
2. What was the Maya response to these drying periods? Where did they go?
3. In the drought model, how would we explain the growth of Maya population centers to the northern Yucatan after AD 950?
4. What lessons are provided by the Maya response to climate change?

Larry Peterson and Gerald Haug, "Climate and the Collapse of Maya Civilization," *American Scientist*, vol. 93, no. 4, pp. 322-329.

A SERIES OF MULTI-YEAR DROUGHTS HELPED TO DOOM AN ANCIENT CULTURE

With their magnificent architecture and sophisticated knowledge of astronomy and mathematics, the Maya boasted one of the great cultures of the ancient world. Although they had not discovered the wheel and were without metal tools, the Maya constructed massive pyramids, temples and monuments of hewn stone both in large cities and in smaller ceremonial centers throughout the lowlands of the Yucatán Peninsula, which covers parts of what are now southern Mexico and Guatemala and essentially all of Belize. From celestial observatories, such as the one at Chichén Itzá, they tracked the progress of Venus and developed a calendar based on a solar year of 365 days. They created their own system of mathematics, using a base number of 20 with a concept of zero. And they developed a hieroglyphic scheme for writing, one that used hundreds of elaborate signs.

During its Classic period (250–950 A.D.), Maya civilization reached a zenith. At its peak, around 750 A.D., the population may have topped 13 million. Then, between about 750 and 950 A.D., their society imploded. The Maya abandoned what had been densely populated urban centers, leaving their impressive stone edifices to fall into ruin. The demise of Maya civilization (which archaeologists call "the terminal Classic collapse") has been one of the great anthropological mysteries of modern times. What could have happened?

Scholars have advanced a variety of theories over the years, pinning the fault on everything from internal warfare to foreign intrusion, from widespread outbreaks of disease to a dangerous dependence on monocropping, from environmental degradation to climate change. Some combination of these and other factors may well be where the truth lies. However, in recent years, evidence has mounted that unusual shifts in atmospheric patterns took place near the end of the Classic Maya period, lending credence to the notion that climate, and specifically drought, indeed played a hand in the decline of this ancient civilization.

Rainforest Crunch

Given the common image of lost Maya cities buried beneath tangles of jungle vegetation, it may come as a surprise to discover that the Yucatán is, in fact, a seasonal desert. The lush landscape depends heavily on summer rains for nourishment, rains that vary considerably across the peninsula. Annual precipitation ranges from as little as 500 millimeters along the northern coast to as high as 4,000 millimeters in parts of the south. As much as 90 percent of this moisture falls between June and September, and a pronounced winter dry season runs from January to May.

This wet-dry contrast results from the seasonal migration of moisture associated with the intertropical convergence zone, an atmospheric feature that is sometimes known as the "meteorological equator." In this zone, the easterly trade winds of the northern and southern tropics converge, forcing air to rise and bringing on cloudiness and abundant rainfall. During the winter months, the intertropical convergence zone shifts far to the south, and dry conditions prevail over both the Yucatán Peninsula and northern South America. Then, with the coming of summer, this zone migrates north again, bringing life-giving rain to the Yucatán and southern Caribbean region.

The Maya had to deal with this seasonal contrast and, in particular, had to cope with a long dry season each year. This feature of their environment had special significance, because surface waters tend to dissolve the limestone bedrock of the Yucatán, forming caves and underground rivers but leaving little opportunity for water to flow over land. So the Maya could not simply locate their settlements along major watercourses. Even important regional centers—such as Tikal, Caracol and Calakmul—developed in places that were without permanent rivers or lakes. The lack of surface water for four or five months of the year in such areas spurred the construction of large-scale water-collection systems.

Many cities were designed to catch rainfall and channel it into quarries, excavations and natural depressions that had been specially prepared to retain the captured water without letting it seep into the ground. Tikal, for example, had numerous reservoirs, which together were capable of holding enough water to meet the drinking needs of roughly 10,000 people for about 18 months. The Maya also built reservoirs on the tops of hills, using gravity to distribute the water through canals into complex irrigation systems. Despite the sophistication of their hydrological engineering, the Maya ultimately depended on the seasonal rains to replenish their water supplies, natural groundwater being inaccessible over a considerable portion of their realm.

In his fascinating book, *The Great Maya Droughts*, independent archaeologist Richardson B. Gill persuasively argues that a lack of water was a major factor in the terminal Classic collapse. Gill pulls together an enormous amount of information on modern weather and climate, draws on the record of historical droughts and famines, and heaps on evidence from archaeology and from geological studies of ancient climates. To demonstrate the importance of the porous limestone bedrock, for example, he quotes Diego de Landa, Bishop of Yucatán, who in 1566 wrote: "Nature worked so differently in this country in the matter of rivers and springs, which in all the rest of the world run on top of the land, that here in this country all run and flow through secret passages under it."

Gill builds an impressive case. When his work was first published (five years ago), the most compelling evidence for drought came from sediment cores that David A. Hodell, Jason H. Curtis, Mark Brenner and other geologists at the University of Florida had collected from a number of Yucatán lakes. Their measurements of these ancient deposits indicate that the driest interval of the last 7,000 years fell between 800 and 1000 A.D.—coincident with the collapse of Classic Maya civilization. Later work by these same investigators found evidence for a recurrent pattern of drought, which seems also to explain other, less dramatic breaks in Maya cultural evolution.

The Venezuelan Connection

Our own contribution to the understanding of climatic conditions during the time of the terminal Classic collapse comes from a distant location, one not inhabited by the Maya at all. Offshore of the northern coast of Venezuela sits a remarkable depression in the continental shelf known as the Cariaco Basin. Reaching depths of about a kilometer but surrounded by the shallow shelf and banks, the Cariaco Basin acts as a natural sediment trap. What is more, the shallow lip of the basin prevents its deeper waters from mixing readily with the open ocean to the north. As a result, deep Cariaco waters are devoid of dissolved oxygen (and have been since near the end of the last glacial period, some 14,500 years ago). The lack of oxygen means that the muddy floor of the basin cannot support bottom-dwelling marine organisms, which in other places churn up the sediment in their search for food. This lack of a deep-sea fauna preserves the integrity of the sediments, which here are made up of paired light and dark layers, each less than a millimeter thick.

The origin of these layers is easy enough to understand: During Northern Hemisphere winter and spring, the intertropical convergence zone sits at its southernmost position near the equator, which means that little rain falls over the Cariaco Basin. At this time of year, strong trade winds blow along the northern coast of Venezuela, causing cool, nutrient-rich waters to rise, which in turn allows plankton living near the surface to proliferate. When these organisms die, their shelly remains fall to the bottom, where they form a light-colored layer. During the summer, as the northern hemisphere warms, the intertropical convergence zone moves steadily northward until it takes up a position near the northern coast of South America. The trade winds diminish, and the rainy season begins, increasing the flow of local rivers, which then deliver a considerable load of suspended sediment to the sea. These land-derived materials eventually settle out of the water, leaving on the ocean floor a dark-colored layer of mineral grains on top of the earlier accumulation of light-colored microfossil shells.

Although burrowing organisms mix up such seasonal deposits elsewhere, the anoxic Cariaco Basin preserves these distinct light-and-dark couplets. This dramatic alternation in composition provides a built-in clock that geologists can use to determine with yearly resolution just when the sediments were laid down. And fortunately, at least for people interested in the history of Maya civilization, both the Yucatán and northern Venezuela experience the same general pattern of seasonal rainfall, with both areas today near the northern limit of the intertropical convergence zone. Hence marine sediments from the Cariaco Basin hold considerable information about the shifts in climate that the Maya experienced.

Our efforts to read that archive began in 1996, when the scientific drillship *JOIDES Resolution*, operated by an international research collaboration called the Ocean Drilling Program, sailed to the center of the Cariaco Basin. Once there, technicians obtained a 170-meter-long sequence of sediment cores expressly for the purpose of probing tropical climate change. The study of those sediments, which had accumulated at an enormous rate and had remained completely undisturbed since the time of deposition, offered us and other geologists a rare, high-resolution glimpse into the distant past. An important aspect of our work on these sediments has been to use the concentration of mineral grains eroded from land to gauge the amount of rain that fell on adjacent parts of the South American continent.

One could, of course, gain such an understanding by examining these sediments directly under a microscope, but characterizing vast numbers of sediment couplets in this way would have been extraordinarily tedious. So we sought out a more efficient approach. Of the several methods we explored, the most useful proved to be the measurement of titanium and iron, elements that are abundant in most continental rocks but not in the shelly remains of marine organisms. High levels of titanium and iron thus indicate that large amounts of silt and clay were washed off the adjacent land and swept into the basin. That is, finding lots of titanium and iron at a particular level in these sediments means that rainfall in this region—and by inference over the Yucatán—must have been high at the time of deposition. Low titanium and iron, by contrast, means that rain was sparse.

A First-millennium Rain Gauge

The measurement of elemental concentrations in sediments by traditional methods is time consuming and has the further drawback that it destroys the material under study. But recently geologists have overcome these problems with a technique called x-ray fluorescence, which involves illuminating a sample with x rays and measuring the amount of light given off as a function of wavelength. Suitable analysis of this light spectrum (which can be fully automated) reveals the concentration of various elements in the sample. This approach allows for the rapid assessment of elemental abundances in sediment cores that have been split down the middle, producing records that are far more detailed than what could be expected from extracting and measuring individual samples.

We initially made measurements of x-ray fluorescence using a core scanner housed at Bremen University in Germany, where the Ocean Drilling Program maintains a repository of cores. We determined the titanium and iron concentration at 2-millimeter spacings over a sediment section of interest, one that had already been dated using radiocarbon, but after finding nearly identical variations in these two elements, we chose to track only titanium.

Within this interval, and at this measurement resolution, the most obvious feature is the generally low titanium level in layers deposited between about 500 and 200 years ago, a period that corresponds to what some climatologists call the Little Ice Age. These results presumably reflect dry conditions and indicate that the intertropical convergence zone and its associated rainfall must not have reached as far north as they do now. We also found several other broad intervals of low titanium, including one in sediments deposited between about 800 and 1000 A.D., which corresponds to the period of severe drought that Hodell and his colleagues had inferred from their Yucatán lake cores.

Hodell's work had led to the impression that an extended "megadrought" plagued the Maya homeland for a century or two, with devastating consequences for the indigenous population. But this interpretation troubled some Mayanists. They pointed out archaeological evidence for considerable variability in the timing and regional pattern of collapse. A "one drought fits all" model seems too simplistic, given that the collapse apparently happened at different places at different times, while affecting some population centers hardly at all.

Although the Cariaco Basin is quite distant from the Yucatán, its unique sediments offered the possibility of obtaining an immensely detailed chronology of ancient climate swings, and we wanted to push the record as far as it would go so as to provide further insight into the climate during the Maya collapse. Unfortunately, we had reached the maximum analytical resolution of the Bremen core scanner. But with the help of Detlef Günther and Beat Aeschlimann at the Swiss Federal Institute of Technology in Zurich, we did much better using a special "micro" x-ray fluorescence system they had set up in their lab. This instrument was designed for small samples, not long stretches of deep-sea sediment, but it could accommodate short slabs of material cut from our cores. This device allowed us to make elemental analyses with a 50-micrometer measurement spacing, which in the Cariaco cores corresponds to about two months of time—an incredibly fine resolution for marine sediments, which more typically encompass hundreds to thousands of years of geologic history in a single sample.

Using Günther and Aeschlimann's wonderful instrument, we measured two slabs of sediment that together cover the time interval from about 200 to 1000 A.D., focusing on those layers deposited during the terminal Classic collapse. This interval revealed a series of four distinct titanium minima—likely multi-year droughts, which took place during a period that was already drier than normal. When exactly did these intense dry spells settle over the Maya heartland? Although the counting of sediment couplets gives precise information on the duration of these droughts (which range from three to nine years) and the spacing between them (around 40 to 50 years), the absolute dating of these events remains a little vague. Radiocarbon measurements for the core we used in combination with counting couplets would indicate that the four droughts struck around 760, 810, 860 and 910 A.D., but quoting such precise dates is somewhat misleading, given that the radiocarbon technique has an uncertainty of about ±30 years for samples of this age.

All in the Timing

Scholars generally agree that the terminal Classic collapse occurred first in the southern and central Yucatán lowlands and that many areas of the northern lowlands underwent their own decline a century or more later. This pattern of abandonment is opposite to what one might expect based on the modern pattern of rainfall, which diminishes markedly from south to north. Some Mayanists have pointed to this incongruity as evidence against drought having played a significant role. However, an additional factor that must be considered is the availability and access to natural water sources, which could have sustained the population during extended periods of drought.

During the peak of Maya civilization, as now, an important source of fresh water for human activities was from the natural underground aquifer. This aquifer is generally more accessible in the northern end of the peninsula, where the Maya were able to reach the water table at various sinkholes (places where the roof of an underground cavern had collapsed) or by digging wells. However, as one moves to the south, the landscape rises in elevation, and the depth to  the water table increases, making direct access to groundwater unfeasible, at least for the Classic Maya with the technology of their time. Thus the more southern settlements, which were totally dependent on rainfall and reservoirs for their water needs, were more likely to be susceptible to the effects of prolonged drought than were cities with direct access to subsurface sources. This critical difference helps explain why drought could have caused greater problems in the normally wetter south.

Although there is general agreement that the abandonment of major population centers began first in the south and then spread to the north, Gill proposed a more controversial tripartite pattern of collapse. Based on an analysis of the last recorded dates carved into stone monuments known as stelae at major Maya sites. Gill argued that there were, in fact, three phases of drought-related collapse between about 760 and 910 A.D., with a distinct regional progression.

The first phase, according to Gill, occurred between 760 and 810. The second phase was largely over by about 860. The third and final phase terminated around 910. Noting a similarity between the end dates of these three phases and the timing of especially severe cold spells in Europe (as evidenced in Swedish tree-ring records), Gill speculated that the abandonments occurred rather abruptly at the end of each phase, that they were primarily the result of droughts and that these droughts were linked to the cold conditions at higher latitudes.

Gill's model of three phases of collapse, and especially the archaeological basis for their proposed timing, has been the subject of much debate. There is considerable disagreement, for example, over the interpretation of the last dated inscriptions on stelae as accurate records of city abandonment. Furthermore, Gill considered only the largest Maya sites in his original analysis. So there is certainly some room for doubt. Nevertheless, the drought events we inferred from the Cariaco Basin record match Gill's three phases of abandonment remarkably well.

The onset of Gill's first phase at about 760 A.D. is clearly marked in the Cariaco record by an abrupt decrease in inferred rainfall. Over the subsequent 40 years or so, there appears to have been a slight long-term drying trend. This period then culminated in roughly a decade or more of severe drought, which, within the limits of our chronology, agrees well with the end of Gill's first phase. Societal collapse at this time was limited to the western lowlands, a region with little accessible groundwater and where the inhabitants depended almost entirely on rainfall to satisfy their needs.

The end of Gill's second phase of collapse is also marked in the Cariaco Basin record by a distinct interval of low titanium concentrations, suggesting an unusually severe drought that lasted for three or four years. City abandonment during this phase of collapse was largely restricted to the southeastern portion of the lowlands, a region where freshwater lagoons may have provided a source of water up to that point.

According to Gill, the third and final phase of collapse occurred at about 910 A.D., affecting population centers in the central and northern lowlands. And low titanium values in the Cariaco Basin sediments indicate yet another coincident period of drought, one that lasted for five or six years.

Although the match between Gill's drought model and our findings is quite good, we accept that no single cause is likely to explain a phenomenon as complex as the Maya decline. In his recent book *Collapse: How Societies Choose to Fail or Succeed*, Jared Diamond argues that a confluence of factors may have combined to doom the Maya. These include an expanding population that was operating at or near the limits of available resources, environmental degradation in the form of deforestation and hillside erosion, increased internal warfare and a leadership focused on short-term concerns. (Sound familiar?) Nevertheless, Diamond posits that climate change, in the form of droughts, may have helped bring things to a head, triggering a series of events that destabilized Maya society.

Some archaeologists have pointed out that the control of water reserves provided a centralized source of political authority for the ruling Maya elites. Periods of drought might then have undermined the institution of Maya rulership when existing technologies and rituals failed to provide sufficient water. Large population centers dependent on this control were abandoned and people moved sequentially eastward and then northward during the successive droughts to find more stable sources of water. However, unlike what transpired during previous intervals of too little rainfall, which the Maya must certainly have weathered before, the landscape during the final stages of collapse was at carrying capacity (because of the growth of Maya population during wetter times), and migration to areas less affected by drought was no longer possible. In short, they ran out of options.

Climate in Human History

The ability to combine geological archives with traditional archaeological and historical information provides a powerful means to examine the societal response to climate shifts of the distant past. Although the socioeconomic impacts of recent El Niño events or of the infamous Dust Bowl drought of the 1930s are easy enough to study, climatologists still know relatively little about the consequences of older and longer-period changes in climate. In recent years, however, high-resolution records from ice cores, tree rings, corals and certain deep-sea and lake sediments have begun to provide an increasingly precise record of climate change for the past few millennia.

The coincidence of drought and collapse within the Maya civilization is just one example. In the American Southwest, tree-ring evidence for a prolonged drying of climate between about 1275 and 1300 has long been thought to play a role in the disappearance of the cliff-dwelling Anasazi people. And there are indications that similar changes in climate may have been responsible for other major events in human history as well. The collapse of the Akkadian Empire in Mesopotamia about 4,200 years ago, the decline of the Mochica culture in coastal Peru about 1,500 years ago and the end of the Tiwanaku culture on the Bolivian-Peruvian altiplano some 1,000 years ago have all now been linked to persistent long-term drought in those regions. Before the geological evidence for these ancient droughts became available, each of these cultural collapses, like that of the Maya, had been interpreted solely in terms of human factors—warfare, overpopulation, resource depletion.

The rise and fall of the Classic Maya provides a textbook example of human social evolution. It is therefore significant to discover that the history of the Maya was so closely tied to environmental constraints. If Maya civilization could collapse under the weight of natural climate events, it is of more than academic interest to ponder how modern society will fare in the face of an uncertain climate in the years ahead. An understanding of how ancient cultures responded to climatic changes in the past may thus provide important lessons for humanity in the future.

BIBLIOGRAPHY

Carr, R. F., and J. E. Hazard. 1961. *Tikal Report No. 11: Map of the Ruins of Tikal, El Peten, Guatemala.* Philadelphia: University Museum, University of Pennsylvania.

deMenocal, P. B. 2001. Cultural responses to climate change during the Late Holocene. *Science* 292:667–673.

Diamond, J. 2005. *Collapse: How Societies Choose to Fail or Succeed.* New York: Viking.

Gill, R. B. 2000. *The Great Maya Droughts: Water, Life, and Death.* Albuquerque: University of New Mexico Press.

Haug, G. H., D. Günther, L. C. Peterson, D. M. Sigman, K. A. Hughen and B. Aeschlimann. 2003. Climate and the collapse of Maya civilization.*Science* 299:1731–1735.

Hodell, D. A., J. H. Curtis and M. Brenner. 1995. Possible role of climate in the collapse of Classic Maya civilization. *Nature* 375:391–394.

Section 2

ARCHAEOLOGY AS ADVOCACY: SERVING COMMUNITIES THROUGH ARCHAEOLOGY

The articles in this section include narrative reports of the archaeological research conducted at sites that represent the villages, workplaces, and cemeteries of people otherwise marginalized or forgotten by history including African captives; Native Americans; Native Hawaiians; poor, rural white folks; and people of mixed ancestry. In each case, the descendants of the people who left behind archaeological manifestations of their lives—and deaths—were involved in the work that helped illuminate the lives of their ancestors. In a very real and fundamental sense, those descendants benefited directly from the archaeological study of the communities of their ancestors. One of the articles I present here was written expressly for this book by one of those descendants.

Most archaeologists serve at least two constituencies. The first of these, of course, is the community of other professional archaeologists. Archaeological researchers and teachers need to be up to date in the latest discoveries, techniques, and theories in their field. Colleagues regularly report on these in professional journals. For example, most professional American archaeologists who conduct research in North America belong to the Society for American Archaeology, whose major publication is the periodical *American Antiquity*. In Great Britain, the journal *Antiquity* and in Latin America, the journal *Latin American Antiquity* serve a similar function (yes, there is a pattern here reflected by the use of the term "antiquity" in all of these titles). In the United States, archaeologists who focus on sites dating to the period beginning with European colonial settlement of the Western Hemisphere subscribe to the journal *Historical Archaeology*, the periodical published by the professional organization, the Society for Historical Archaeology. There are plenty of other extremely informative journals devoted to professional archaeologists: *World Archaeology, the Journal of Field Archaeology*, and a host of local or regional journals.

Essentially, the pages of these professional journals are filled with detailed, usually highly technical, and often quite theoretically focused articles written by archaeologists expressly for other archaeologists, geologists, or historians. They cannot be characterized as light reading, but anyone who works in the field of archaeology is obliged to keep abreast of recent developments—and researchers are similarly obliged to report their work in these publications. Whether or not the work relates to one's own particular scholarly or research focus, if it is about the human past, the community of archaeologists is interested and desires—and needs—to know more. These professional journals, along with professional conferences, represent important ways in which archaeologists share their work with each other.

This brings us to the second and, I think, equally important constituency that professional archaeologists serve: the archaeologically curious public. Archaeology attracts a great deal of attention and media coverage. Many people are drawn to the human past and are curious about the work done by archaeologists. Though some archaeologists eschew popular publishing, opting to write only for their colleagues in archaeology, many archaeologists take quite seriously the view that without a public interested in the human past and willing to pay for the research that illuminates that past, there would be no archaeology. As a result, along with writing for their own professional journals, many archaeologists also write less-technical summaries of their work or present speeches about their research for the general reading and listening public.

For example, the glossy magazines *Archaeology* and *American Archaeology* are wholly devoted to disseminating archaeological information to this public constituency. Also, it is almost impossible to find an issue of the popular science magazines *Discover, Natural History,* or *National Geographic* that do not have a substantial article about archaeology, always with spectacular photographs of magnificent ruins, beautiful ancient art objects, and the impressive natural surroundings of ancient sites. All of these publications serve the admirable purpose of keeping an interested public informed about the research and results of modern archaeology.

Along with professional archaeologists and the general non-archaeologist public, there also is another, a bit more specific constituency served by archaeologists. This group—actually, these groups—represents a sub-set of the broader, archaeologically aware public. My friend and colleague, archaeologist Warren Perry, refers to the archaeology he conducts as a kind of "community service," referring specifically to communities of non-archaeologists who feel a special tie or bond to a particular province of the archaeological record. In most cases, this special attachment is recognized by people who are members of the directly descendant communities of those who produced the archaeological record in question. In other words, not surprisingly, many people, whether they are generally interested in the past or not, have a particular curiosity about and reverence for the archaeological remains left behind by their own direct ancestors. The intellectual as well as emotional relationship that exists, for example, between Native Americans and the sites of their ancestors in the western hemisphere, between African Americans and the sites of their ancestors in North America, between contemporary Indigenous Australians and the archaeological record of native Australia, between modern Jews and the archaeology of the ancient Hebrews in Israel; these all represent a unique connection, a cultural and biological tie that transcends time. In some cases, the archaeologists themselves are a part of these communities, researching the ancestors of their own people, but this is not a prerequisite. In fact, most prehistoric archaeologists in North America are not Indian, most historical archaeologists researching the lives of slaves and slave descendants are not African American, and most Australian archaeologists are not Aboriginal Australians.

Regardless of their own specific backgrounds and personal histories, however, most archaeologists recognize that descendant communities have invaluable and unique insights concerning the ancient people we all study—after all, they are members of the same cultural continuum. Importantly, most archaeologists also recognize that, though the work we do serves the broad purpose of informing a world community interested in the past of all people, there is a special, perhaps unique obligation to the living descendants of the people who produced the particular archaeological remains we so painstakingly recover and that we so carefully analyze.

The articles presented in this section of the reader reflect the concept of archaeologists serving this public constituency: the community of descendants of those who left the archaeological record being studied.

Digging in the Documents, Digging in the Dirt

Ken Feder

EDITOR'S INTRODUCTION

The story of the Lighthouse community of Barkhamsted, Connecticut, has all the elements of legend. A young, wealthy white woman living in mid-eighteenth-century Connecticut escapes an overbearing and controlling father, abandons her comfortable and safe life, and runs away with a virtual stranger who happens also to be a Narragansett Indian. They marry, disappear into the wilderness of northwest Connecticut, and begin having children in their forest hideaway. As their family grows—ultimately, to eight children—their settlement became a magnet for outcasts including other Native Americans, as well as people of African and European descent. In essence, the Lighthouse became a multi-cultural and multi-ethnic community, long before these concepts and terms came into widespread use. The people who ultimately made up the Lighthouse community were not the type on whom traditional history concentrates its attention. They weren't wealthy or famous. They didn't lead armies into battle. They didn't sign the Declaration of Independence. They were, in fact, poor and powerless. And archaeology is helping to illuminate their fascinating and significant story

POINTS TO PONDER

1. Who were the people of the Lighthouse? How did they come to live on the side of a mountain in Northwest Connecticut?
2. How does archaeology contribute to our understanding of the lives of people who lived at the economic, social, and political margins in seventeenth-, eighteenth-, and nineteenth-century America?
3. What does the archaeological record tell us about the degree of isolation experienced by the inhabitants of the Lighthouse community?
4. What lesson does the Lighthouse project teach about the ability of archaeology to fill in the story of American history?

Kenneth L. Feder, "Digging in the Documents, Digging in the Dirt," *Connecticut History*, vol. 46, no. 2, pp. 184-187, 191, 195-204. Copyright © 2007 by Association for the Study of Connecticut History. Reprinted with permission.

ENCOUNTERING THE LIGHTHOUSE

I t was the summer of 1990 and we had just finished four weeks in the field at the archaeological site created by the inhabitants of the legendary "Lighthouse" community. Located some sixty miles from the Long Island Sound coast, this settlement, though so named, was not a lighthouse at all. It was, instead, an eighteenth and nineteenth century village in the western hills of the Farmington River valley, populated by a fascinating mixture of Native Americans, people of European descent, and freed or escaped African-American slaves[1]

I was working in the vault of the Barkhamsted Town Hall where local historical records—tax lists, deed transferals, and vital records—are housed. Documentary research made a critical contribution to our archaeological investigation and I was, in a very real sense, "digging" in the documents. There is something quite remarkable, even humbling, about holding an artifact recently unearthed or perusing an ancient document just encountered. These things resonate with the life of a past people and create, even in the most jaded, a feeling of connection that transcends the barrier of time. A human being who lived hundreds or even thousands of years ago—a human being in many ways like you or me—made and used a tool, wrote a letter, or left an official record. The tool was lost, the letter hidden away, the document filed and forgotten. Now that person is gone and all that is left to mark his or her existence is the tool that you now hold in your hand, the fragment of the letter, or the official record of birth, marriage, or death. The object rescued from the earth, the letter recovered from oblivion, or the documentary record examined after decades or centuries of neglect all reverberate with the life of some long gone individual.

It was apparent in that first season of fieldwork that with each discovery related to the Lighthouse village, we were making just that sort of connection. Nothing prepared me, however, for what I was to encounter in the Barkhamsted Town Hall vault when our first field season was over.

I was there examining the town's vital records, all handwritten, the pages yellowed, brittle, and frayed, marked by ink and water stains. The records were arranged in a series of columns. These columns organized the information considered significant by the town clerks of nineteenth century Connecticut: date of birth, baby's name, sex of the child, names of parents, ages of the parents, color of the child, and place of parents' residence. I spent several hours poring over these records, looking for any clues regarding the inhabitants of the Lighthouse community.

That is how I found her. A baby girl was born in Barkhamsted on May 14, 1858. No name was recorded for the baby, but Solomon Webster was listed as the father. His wife, the baby's mother, was given as Mary. In another document, Solomon's father, Montgumery Webster, was listed. His "color" was specified as "Mohegan," an Indian tribal name from southern and eastern Connecticut. Solomon's mother, Sibel, was listed as being "Creole." It turns out that Sol's wife, Mary, was a direct descendant of the original settlers of the Lighthouse village, a white woman named Molly Barber, and James Chaugham, her Narragansett Indian husband.

Under the column heading "Color," most of the babies on the page bore the designation "White," reflecting the racial makeup of nineteenth century Barkhamsted. On other pages in the Barkhamsted records, a very few babies bore the label "Negro" and there were several categorized as "Creole," or mixed. Sol and Mary's child bore none of the common designators for color. In fact, its racial label was unique in the entire volume of Barkhamsted's vital records; Sol and Mary's baby's color was listed as "Nearly White". It would seem that town clerks in nineteenth century Connecticut were already grappling with the vexing and inevitably flexible nature of racial designation.

As remarkable as I found the color designation for baby Webster, the column for parental residence was just as interesting. The town of Barkhamsted is one of 169 incorporated Connecticut towns. Within many of these towns are smaller entities with names but little or no political significance today beyond having a separate zip code and, perhaps, a post office. Within the nineteenth century boundaries of the town of Barkhamsted, for example, were the villages of Pleasant Valley and Hitchcocksville (now called Riverton). In the parental residence column in Barkhamsted's vital records, most parents were listed as residing in Barkhamsted. A few were listed as living in Pleasant Valley, a few listed Hitchcocksville. Just as the baby bore a unique listing for its race, however, Sol and Mary Webster had a unique designation for their place of residence. It was given as "Barkhamsted Light House." This was the first government document I had seen that listed the "Lighthouse" as a named, officially designated, and recognized community.

The Primary Record of the Lighthouse People

Remarkably, there are quite a few primary records related to the Lighthouse inhabitants. We can begin with James Chaugham. The legend states that James was from Block Island. And, interestingly, a version of the Chaugham name shows up on that island—there is even a body of water there called "Chagum Pond." Beyond this, the name appears twice in the legal records of Block Island. First, in a court account dated October 9, 1711, a local resident, John Dodge, "brought up an Indian Man by warant [sic] to the Cunstable [sic] … for stealing a canoe and running away." The Indian, apparently already an indentured servant, was punished by being fined fifty shillings and by being assessed a six month extension of his contracted servitude. The Indian man's name was recorded as Samuel Chagum.

Later in the Block Island records, there is the last will and testament of a Mr. Samuel Sands. Dated December 11, 1713, Mr. Sands' will provides instructions for his funeral and disposes of his real and personal property. Sands was married and he and his wife Elizabeth had five daughters. To his unmarried daughters, Ann and Mary, he left some money, some doubtless treasured personal effects, and instructed that each be allowed to live on the family farm on Block Island until they were married. Daughter Mary, moreover, was given by her father "an Indian boy named James the son of Priscilla" and the money necessary to raise the boy until he attained the age of seven years.

This information is intriguing indeed. In our search for the roots of James Chaugham, we have found an Indian boy named "James" of the right age on the right island, and the Chaugham family name appears during the same period for an Indian on the island. Is the young Indian boy bequeathed to Mary Sands by her dying father to raise until his seventh birthday, in fact, the very James Chaugham who married Molly Barber? The limited data currently available do not contradict that interpretation, but there simply is not enough information to assess this possibility with any degree of certainty.

What about Molly? The legend states that Molly was from Wethersfield, Connecticut. That town's vital records have been intensively examined and published and those records have been very closely scrutinized in our research. If there had been a Molly Barber (or Barker or Baker) in Wethersfield in the 1710s, 1720s, 1730s, or 1740s, she should have been in those vital records. But there is no Molly Barber, in fact there are no "Barbers" at all in Wethersfield at the appropriate time. In all likelihood this means that, despite the assertion of the legend, Molly could not have been from a well-established family in Wethersfield.

The indisputable paper trail left by the Lighthouse people and preserved in the primary documentary record, begins in 1770, thirty years after the legend tells us the settlement was established in Barkhamsted. In the land records, not of Barkhamsted, but of the adjacent town of New Hartford, Connecticut, it is recorded that, on December 11, 1770, Noadiah Hooker sold a small parcel of land, to a gentleman by the name of "James Chaughom" for £5, ten shillings. Less than a year later, also in New Hartford, there is a report of the sale of another parcel, this time forty acres, by a "Cornelius Indian" of Farmington, Connecticut, to "James Chaughom, an Indian" for £15. In May of 1775, it was further recorded that "James Chaugham" purchased from Asher Hinmon another twenty acres in New Hartford. This land adjoined that already purchased by James and cost him £8. So, by 1775, an Indian man by the name of James Chaughom owned more than sixty acres of land in the town of New Hartford, Connecticut. Clearly, in these land records we have found James, patriarch of the Lighthouse village.[16]

The family name first appears in the Barkhamsted land records on March 3, 1779 when Abraham Kellog of New Hartford sells to James Chogam, for £21, seventy acres that "lyeth at a place called Ragged Mountain." Soon thereafter, in 1782, another sale is recorded, this time of forty-nine acres, by Samuel Hall Williams of Branford, Connecticut, to "Samuel Choggum" for £9, "being and lying most of it on Ragged Mountain, so-called." Ragged Mountain, you will recall, was the location of the Lighthouse village as indicated by various secondary and tertiary historical sources.[17] Also remember that, according to those same sources, Samuel Choggum is one of James and Molly's two sons.

Though Molly's origin remains a mystery, her end does not. According to church records, "Mrs. Choggum" passed away on February 6, 1818, at her son-in-law William Wilson's house at the age of 104 years. We even know the value of her estate when she died: all she owned in personal property was an iron kettle whose value was assessed at $1.25, a small kettle worth $.50, and an old chest of drawers whose estimated value also was $.50. Her probate also lists fourteen acres appraised at $10 per acre—for a real estate total of $140 and a final total value of her estate of $142.25.[18]

Excavation at the Lighthouse Site

As important and valuable as all of these official documents, historical records, speeches, and poetic musings have been to our investigation of the Lighthouse people, there is still something missing from this story, what historical archaeologist James Deetz characterizes as "the texture" of the lives of a past people.[19] We revealed elements of that "texture" during two seasons of archaeological fieldwork at the Lighthouse village site in 1990 and 1991.

We began our investigation at the historically recorded location of the village with a thorough walkover of the flat terrace at the base of Ragged Mountain, during which our the crew located a number of important items: 1) the remains of ten structures, largely foundations and cellar holes, 2) a stone quarry from which residents extracted and shaped the stones that became the structural elements of their house foundations, 3) several charcoal furnaces, 4) a large grinding stone made from a glacial boulder, and 5) a cluster of more than fifty upright stones, apparent grave makers, surrounded by the faint remains of a narrow trench containing remnants of a stockade fence.

Following our intensive walkover, we excavated fifteen one-meter-square excavation units and fourteen two-meter-square units scattered across the spatial extent of the site as defined by the presence of the foundations and cellar holes identified in the pedestrian survey. From these excavations we amassed an artifact assemblage consisting of over 12,000 items including ceramic

Figure 1: One of the Lighthouse community stone-lined cellar holes. The stones show clear evidence of quarrying and have been neatly cut at right angles. (Photograph, K. Feder)

Figure 2: Stone quarry located immediately adjacent to the cellar hole shown in the figure 1. White arrows point to quarry marks where the stone was drilled to separate two large pieces of rock which were never used in construction at the site. The scale is one-meter rod; the scaled arrow (divided in centimeter units) points north. (Photograph, K. Feder)

pieces, nails, shards of window, bottle and lamp glass, gun flints and gun parts, and buttons (Table 1).

The Lighthouse legend presents the story of a Connecticut community at least initially purposely isolated from the outside world. The material record supports the isolated nature of the village and very few artifacts recovered in our excavations date to the early years of the village's existence. The Lighthouse artifact assemblage, however, also reflects the evolution of the village from an isolated outpost to a recognized community in northwestern Connecticut, economically connected to its immediate neighbors and, ultimately, hooked into a world economic system. With regular stage coach traffic past the Lighthouse village in the late eighteenth century and the development of communities like Riverton and Pleasant Valley, Euro-American items became increasingly accessible to people living in the village. The stratigraphic sequence revealed through our excavations shows this clearly, with a distinct increase in Euro-American objects from the original settlement sometime in the mid-eighteenth century—with very few artifacts dated to this period—until the early nineteenth century when material culture, even including dishes made in Staffordshire, England, are found at the site.

The button assemblage similarly reflects the growth in importance of Euro-American material culture at the site in the nineteenth century. Using researcher Stanley South's and Ivor Noel Hume's button chronologies, we were able to determine broadly the dates of 88 out of the 179 buttons

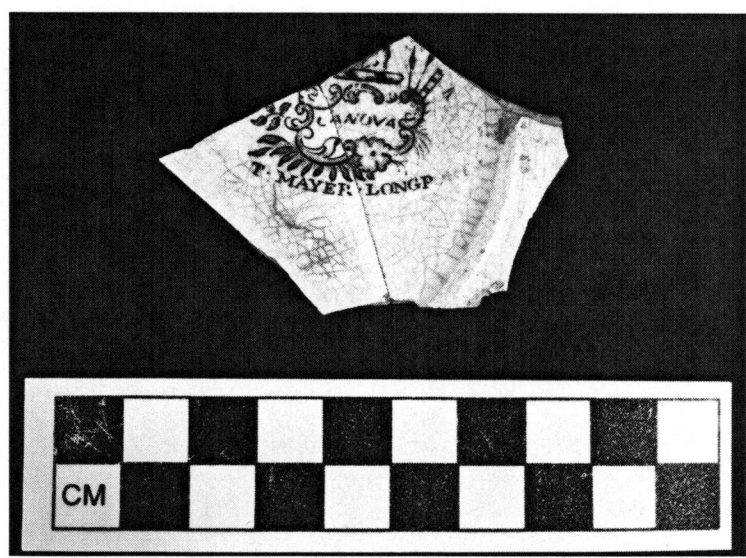

Figure 3: Conjoined fragments of a dish found at the Lighthouse. The manufacturer was Thomas Mayer whose pottery was located in Longport, Staffordshire, England. The pattern printed on this dish was called "Canova," and has a Greek revival style. Though living in an isolated hamlet, by the early decades of the nineteenth century, the people at the Lighthouse had access to the products of a world economic system. (Photograph, K. Feder)

recovered in our excavations.[20] Of the 88 dateable buttons, the manufacture of only 4 (4.5%) can be confidently dated to the eighteenth century, with one additional button possibly dating to this period. The other 83 (94%) of the dateable buttons reflected styles and technologies traceable to the nineteenth century and 48 of those (55% of the 88 dateable buttons) were manufactured almost certainly after 1837.

Something absent from the documents concerning the "texture" of the lives of the Lighthouse people is any reference to their diet. Something as mundane—and as vital—as foodways went unrecorded both by official record keepers as well as by chroniclers of the legend. Our archaeological research, fortunately, fills in some of this gap. More than 1100 animal bone fragments were recovered in our excavations, about 75% of which exhibited evidence of burning, almost certainly resulting from cooking. The vast majority of these bones have been badly fragmented during food preparation as well as by the biologically active and acidic New England forest soils in which they were deposited. As a result, though we know that the Lighthouse people included meat in their diet, most of the bone remains are unidentifiable as to species. Still, 3% of the recovered bones could be identified; most are from white-tail deer and the rest are from small mammals and fish. A handful of cow bones round out the faunal assemblage. The recovery of gun flints and firearm parts suggest that such weapons were used in subsistence pursuits. Clearly, the inhabitants of the Lighthouse subsisted on a combination of local game and domesticated animals.

It is interesting that the material culture of the Lighthouse people was largely European-American in its content. Archaeologist Kevin McBride has noted a similar quality in the eighteenth and nineteenth century archaeological sites of the Pequot in southeastern Connecticut.[21] There too, the material culture as reflected in the inventory of objects that local Native Americans used and in the catalogue of archaeological specimens that results, is largely European. According to McBride, it was in the character of their social lives, rather than in their hardware, that their own cultures were maintained. In Pequot village sites, as in the village site of the descendants of James and Molly, this is reflected in how European material culture is used and how it is expressed. The stone walls commonly used by colonists to divide the holdings of private property are lacking on the Pequot Reservation as well as on Ragged Mountain. Both on the Pequot reservation as well as at the Lighthouse, the residents, apparently, did not feel the need to demarcate individual homesteads and, instead, clustered the houses of their community. At the same time, the small and irregular configuration of the footprints of the domestic structures—no standard, colonial sixteen-foot square foundation units are found on Ragged Mountain—may reflect a non-European material and likely socio-economic element of the lives of Lighthouse residents.[22]

CONCLUSION

In historian William Wallace Lee's Barkhamsted centennial celebration address he pokes fun at those who every so often revisit the Lighthouse legend:

> Every few years some city chap, with a pen behind his ear, comes out among these plain country folk, puts on airs, shows off large, and in return gets badly sold...and forthwith is launched a new version of the Lighthouse story and doubtless this process will be repeated for years to come.[23]

Table 1

ARTIFACT	COUNT	PERCENT OF TOTAL
Ceramics	4733	38.46
Pipes	398	3.23
Coins	5	0.04
Bricks	191	1.55
Glass:		
Window glass	737	5.99
Bottle glass	876	7.12
Lamp glass	745	6.05
Glass beads	4	0.03
Unidentifiable/Burned	461	3.75
Gun related	45	0.37
Stone tools	71	0.58
Buttons	179	1.45
Metal fragments	1396	11.34
Nails	2439	19.82
Cutlery	22	0.18
Slate pencils	3	0.02
Total	12305	100.00

Guilty as charged. I must admit that, at least in a general sense, we fulfill Lee's prophecy in our research. I think, however, Lee would applaud our goals of illuminating the forgotten lives of an all but forgotten group of people and of reminding us that once, these people, sharing in common only the fact that they had nowhere else to go, created a community on the banks of the Farmington River in northwestern Connecticut.

NOTES

1   Kenneth L. Feder, "The Lighthouse: History and Archaeology of An Outcast Village, *Northeast Anthropology* 46 (1993): 39–59; Kenneth L. Feder, *A Village of Outcasts: Historical Archaeology and Documentary Research at the Lighthouse Site* (Mountain View: Mayfield Publishing, 1994); Kenneth L. Feder, "Material Culture at the Lighthouse Village: The legend and the Evidence, in L, Weinstein, ed., *Enduring Traditions: The Native Peoples of New England* (Westport: Bergin and Garvey), 57–77.

2   G.E. White, *Folk Tales of Connecticut* (Meriden: The Journal Press, 1977).

3   Lewis S. Mills, T*he Legend of Barkhamsted Lighthouse* (Hartford: L.S. Mills, 1952).

4   Ibid, 15.

5   Ibid, 16.

6   Ibid, 41-2.

7   Ibid, 55.

8   Ibid, 71.

9   "The Barkhamsted Lighthouse," *Mountain Country Herald*, September 30, 1854; W.W. Lee, *Barkhamsted, Connecticut and its Centennial*, 1879 (Meriden: W.W. Lee, 1881); "The Old Lighthouse," *Connecticut Courant*, January 29, 1900.

10 "The Barkhamsted Lighthouse," *Mountain County Herald*.

11 Ibid.

12 Ibid.

13 Ibid.

14 Lee, *Barkhamsted, Connecticut and its Centennial*, 39.

15 Eyewitness account of J.E. Mason

16 Noadiah Hooker to James Chaughom, December 11, 1770, New Hartford Land Records, vol. 2, 113; Cornelius Indian to James Chaughom, Sptember 1771, New Hartford Land Records, vol. 3, 219; Asher Hinmon to James Chaugham, May 1775, New Hartford Land Record, vol. 3, 221.

17 Abraham Kellog to James Chogam, March 3, 1779, Barkhamsted Land Record, vol. 1, 205–6; Samuel Hall Williams to James Choggum, November 5, 1782, Barkhamsted Land Records, vol. 1, 101.

18 Chogum Probate Estate Papers, Simsbury Probate District, Document715, Barkhamsted, CT.

19 James Deetz, In Small Things Forgotten: The Archaeology of Early American Life (Garden City: Anchor Books, 1977).

20 Stanley South, "Analysis of buttons from Brunswick Town and For Fisher," *Florida Anthropologist* 17(2) (1964): 113–133; Ivor Noel Hume, *A Guide to Artifacts of Colonial America* (New York: Vintage Books, 1996.

21 Personal Communication, Kevin McBride to Kenneth L. Feder.

22 Deetz, *In Small Things* Forgotten; Henry H. Glassie, *Folk Housing in Middle Virginia* (Knoxville: University of Tennesee Press, 1975).

23 Lee, *Barkhamsted, Connecticut and its Centennial*, 41.

24 Mills, T*he Legend of Barkhamsted Lighthouse*, 97.

How Archaeology Exposes the Nature of African Captivity

Janet Woodruff, Gerald F. Sawyer, and Warren R. Perry

EDITOR'S INTRODUCTION

We don't usually think of southern New England as a slave state. In fact, many of us in Connecticut are proud of our state's role in the abolition movement and as a hub on the Underground Railroad, helping African captives make their way to freedom in Canada. Nevertheless, as shown in this article, there were plenty of slaves in Connecticut and there were certainly what we can accurately call "plantations" here whose economic base depended on slavery. While we don't read much in the history books about Connecticut's economic reliance on slavery, archaeology is revealing its significance. At least as important is the role of archaeology in revealing what amounts to a hidden history of resistance to slavery on the part of African captives. Practicing elements of their traditional religions, these Africans secreted sacred objects and the work done by Woodruff, Sawyer, and Perry has revealed them. Though they may not have known it at the time, Connecticut's African captives practicing their religion as a form of resistance to captivity were also sending a message through. Archaeology has revealed that message.

POINTS TO PONDER

1. Why not simply rely on the historical record to illuminate the lives of the African captives of Connecticut?
2. How has the archaeology of the New Salem plantation forced historians to rethink the role of slavery in southern New England?
3. Why conduct the archaeology of slavery? Why not just rely on eighteenth- and nineteenth-century written accounts about slaves and slavery?
4. What are the lessons of the archaeology of New Salem Plantation on which the authors of this article report?

Janet Woodruff, Gerald Sawyer, and Warren Perry, "How Archaeology Exposes the Nature of African Captivity," *Connecticut History*, vol. 46, no. 2, pp. 155-164, 179-183. Copyright © 2007 by Association for the Study of Connecticut History. Reprinted with permission.

Until fairly recently, the early history of Africans in Connecticut has largely been ignored. Over the past few decades, however, there has been a surge of interest in this once-forgotten, but important aspect of our state's past. Still, historians and archeologists have just begun to scratch the surface concerning the presence of the many people of African birth or ancestry who lived and worked in Connecticut throughout the eighteenth and nineteenth centuries.[1] One of the reasons for the paucity of such histories, especially reliable histories, is that documentary records provide little insight into the conditions under which African people lived during this time.

The very nature of the white hegemonic society, with Blacks holding marginalized roles, whether as captive or free, left little room for accurate, unbiased accounts. Indeed, most works from the period that mention Black people, captive or free, were written by white people, overwhelmingly male, and middle to upper-class. Only a handful of first-person accounts of life under enslavement in Connecticut are known to exist.[2] Some of these narratives, notably that of Broteer Venture Smith of East Haddam, were edited and paraphrased to such an extent that the tale may not bear much resemblance to the conditions of life for the purported author of a given memoir.

These biased and oftentimes misleading accounts can be countered through the recovery and examination of material items centuries after those who left them are long gone. Archaeological evidence preserves without regard to race, class, gender or educational level. Its preservation depends only on the chemical conditions of the material itself and the matrix in which it was deposited. Archaeological evidence, therefore, is essentially free of social boundaries.

Although their methodologies overlap in many ways, historians and historical archaeologists approach the study of the past through different avenues.[3] Archaeologists base their analyses predominately on the material that people leave behind in the course of their day-to-day lives. The documentary evidence upon which historians base their studies provides a framework and a context for the material evidence, the "ground truth" with which archaeologists reconstruct the lives of those people whose stories were told mostly in the third person.

Material and documentary evidence must be interpreted through the eyes of those who generated it. Many historians and archaeologists alike are often unaware of the regional and generational differences in African descendant culture; neither do they consider the broad range of cultural origins of eighteenth and nineteenth-century Africans in the Americas.[4] In African Diaspora archaeology, archaeologists must examine the cultural material remains "through African eyes:" that is, with an understanding of the multivalent uses of artifacts that appear to be European in origin and in use. Archaeologists Warren Perry and Robert Paynter define multivalency as existing "when an object or set of objects takes on strikingly different meanings for different social groups, with dominating groups often totally ignorant of the meaning system of subordinated groups."[5] Without considering this issue of multivalency it is often difficult to distinguish between an African, Native, and African-Native (often pejoratively referred to as *Black Indian*) artifactual deposition, which further obscures the identification of an African presence.[6]

Historical archaeologists do not claim that their discipline takes a dispassionate or disinterested view of the cultures that they reconstruct.[7] Quite the opposite: the archaeological examination of the lives of marginalized, disenfranchised people like captive Africans in Connecticut is a passion for those few who study it. It is virtually impossible to uncover the hidden stories of the African people of early Connecticut without becoming deeply involved in the drama that surrounded their lives, their resistance, and the fervor with which they struggled to maintain their cultures, rights, and freedom. Their stories of courage and strength have often been obliterated by the construction of a "whitewashed" history and a very deliberate suppression of the cultures they struggled to maintain.

For the past several years, with the support of Central Connecticut State University's Department of Anthropology, we have focused on the rediscovery of eighteenth and nineteenth century sites with an historical African presence. More recently, the Department of Anthropology and the Center for Africans Studies at CCSU have partnered together to create the Archaeology Laboratory for African & African Diaspora Studies (ALAADS), a facility dedicated to researching and exposing the suppressed evidence of the character of African captivity in Connecticut.

It has been long claimed, in contrast to southern or Caribbean-style plantation captivity, that enslavement in Connecticut was small-scale in nature and largely domestic or artisanal.[8] More recently, however, through both documentary and material evidence, a different picture has been drawn of the African presence in early Connecticut. The reality is that Connecticut was deeply involved in the infamous Atlantic Trade, also misleadingly called the Triangle Trade, which involved the trafficking of consumer goods from Europe to Africa, where they were traded for captive people; the Caribbean, where Africans were forced into labor on sugar plantations or traded north to the mainland United States, along with molasses and sugar to be distilled into rum; and rum and other goods, raw and finished, to be traded back to Europe. Rather than following this fixed path, the trade routes crisscrossed between all of points of the cycle, but the movement of commodities followed a general pattern of interdependence on raw materials, finished goods, and the labor with which to convert the former into the latter.[9]

NEW SALEM PLANTATION

The rediscovery of New Salem Plantation in southeastern Connecticut belies the myth of small-scale and benevolent African enslavement in New England. In the late 1990s, an avocational historian named Abraham Abdul Haqq contacted Dr. Warren Perry with some startling revelations. Haqq had uncovered documentaiy evidence to indicate that virtually the entire town of Salem, Connecticut, where he lived, was built on the site of an eighteenth-century provisioning plantation encompassing about 13,000 acres and worked by over a hundred captive African laborers.[10] This plantation was a global-scale enterprise involved in commercial farming, providing the sugar-growing islands of the Caribbean with beef, wheat, corn, and barrel staves in exchange for sugar, molasses for distilling rum, and Africans for labor in the fields.[11] The New Salem Plantation existed as part of a system of international agribusinesses in southeastern New England; other plantations have been identified in Lebanon and Brooklyn, Connecticut, and throughout Rhode Island, which was also infamous for its trafficking in captive people between Africa and the Americas.[12]

Colonel Samuel Browne of Salem, Massachusetts purchased the New Salem property from Lieutenant James Harris between 1718 and 1729. Browne (1669–1731), who was one of the wealthiest maritime merchants of Salem, Massachusetts, made much of his fortune by running African captives up the coast from the Caribbean. In about 1729, Browne moved sixty captive families to the new plantation in order to work the previously uncultivated fields. John Mumford, Junior, of Rhode Island, was hired to manage the property.[13]

The Browne family passed down the property through three generations, ending with William Browne, grandson of Colonel Samuel Browne, who, in the middle of the eighteenth century, inherited the land, buildings, and other property, including captive Africans. A Loyalist during the Revolution, Browne fled to England and his belongings, which included at least nine captive Africans as well as the plantation land, were seized by the government of Connecticut and sold off to numerous other property owners in Lyme and Colchester.

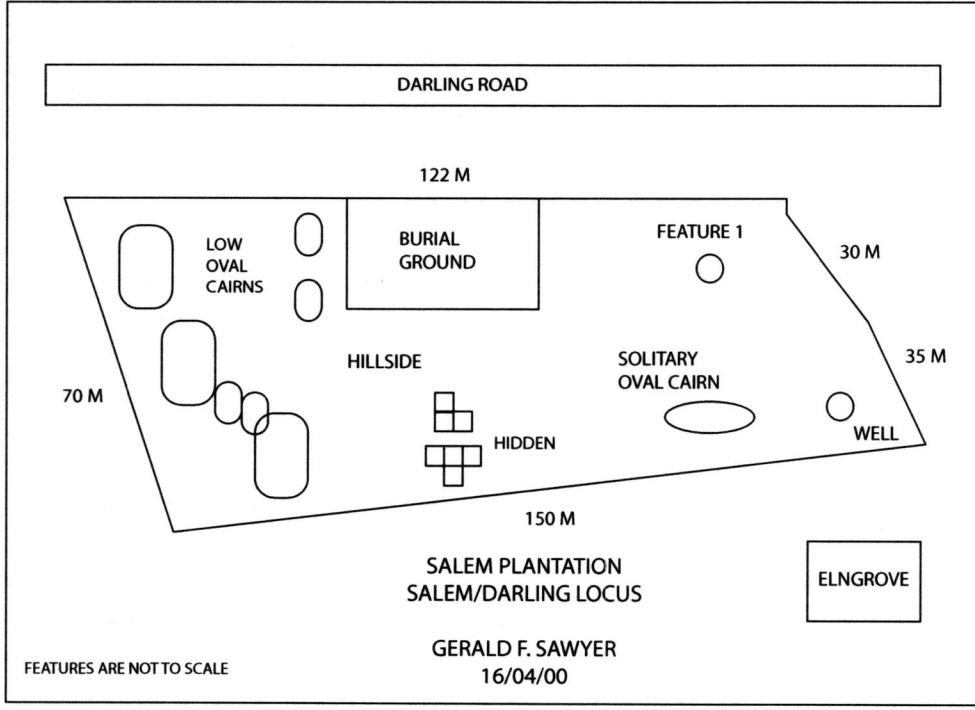

Firgure 6.1. Plan of the hillside cemetary where captive Africans from the New Salem Plantation were buried. Map Gerald F. Sawyer

The graveyard in which these Africans were buried became the site of an archaeological survey and exploration starting in the summer of 1999. The area was cleared of its heavy undergrowth and mapped, and excavation units were laid out. The cemetery was also examined with a direct-current ground resistivity unit, which measured the soil density to ascertain the presence of unmarked grave shafts. The units in the graveyard were excavated to a depth of twenty centimeters (approximately eight inches) to determine whether headstones may have fallen and become covered with soil. The shallow excavation also yielded evidence that the ostensibly Christian-style graves may have been commemorated with African traditional practices as well. Numerous large pieces of clear and white quartz crystal were found around the headstones, at a depth of ten to fifteen centimeters (approximately four to six inches). Crystals are a frequent component of assemblages relating to African spiritual practices, and their presence on graves, particularly, speaks to the continuance of these traditions.[14]

Other intriguing features of the burial ground are the numerous stone cairns located (with one exception) around the grave area. Stone cairns are common in the New England woodlands, as the artifacts of either field-clearing or the construction of stone fences. Yet two types of cairns found at the Salem site are not typical of the region. The Salem cairns bear remarkable similarity to those found in Ghana, West Africa, and in Jamaica, where they are used to mark burials.[15] One cairn type consists of two large stones positioned a few feet apart, with the interstice filled with numerous smaller stones. In Africa and the Caribbean, such cairns often hold burials under the small stones. The other type of cairn is ovate, very low to the ground, and generally about 280 centimeters by 140 centimeters (110 inches by 55 inches), again similar to burial cairns elsewhere in the African Diaspora.

Archaeologist Roger Moeller asserts that stone cairns in New England have never been associated with burials.[16] Considering multivalent cultural practices, however, may reveal that the cairns at Salem are more than merely a pile of stones. Members of the Paugausetts, on observing the cairns in the Salem burial ground, noted that they bear remarkable resemblance to their ancient burial methods. In particular, the burial cairn of the late war chief, Moon Face Bear (who died in 1996) is quite similar to one of the cairns at Salem. Moreover, there is no substantial issue regarding the presence or absence of burials directly beneath the Salem cairns. Kofi Agorsah argues that Ghanaian burial cairns are sometimes offset from the actual burial to deter grave robbers, and that cairns may be used to delineate a field of burials rather than individual graves.[17] The Salem cairns may very well support this latter point, especially when considering the inclusion of Christianity among captive Africans. Some of the Salem cairns are at the corners of the Christian-style burial area; others are in a small field at the base of a hill below the burial ground. Additionally, resistivity readings taken on the hillside indicated anomalies, suggesting possible grave shafts in the area. These oval cairns are also associated with the cardinal points of the compass. In each of these instances, the cairn's long axis is aligned either with true north-south or true east-west.[18] This suggests that they may have been deliberately aligned, using celestial observation for direction to the cardinal points.

Another oval cairn is located far from the others, in the wetlands at the lowest elevation of the site. This is the only low oval cairn that is separated from the others and is not aligned with the cardinal points. Its significance is unknown, but it is possible that it marks the burial of someone who was in some way exceptional, either because s/he was different in some way and/or held a particular standing in the African community: for example, a healer, a respected elder, or a religious leader; conversely, it may be the grave of someone who was feared or shunned.[19] The area near this solitary cairn contained another archaeological feature that warranted closer scrutiny. In the marshy area, excavators uncovered a midden area strewn with materials dating from the late nineteenth through the early twentieth century. The area was carefully examined and the overlying material collected. Beneath the surface layer of relatively recent debris, the underlying ground revealed the remains of an exceedingly modest structure, which appears to have burned and fallen, forming the base for the hundred-year-old dumping area.

Further examination of the ground area revealed that the structure had been supported on four large corner stones and had had a small stone hearth in the center of the dirt floor. The corner stones formed a square approximately twelve feet on a side. This measurement was particularly revealing, as the ten to twelve-foot dimension was not common in European-built houses, which tended to be scaled on multiples of sixteen feet. The smaller dimension is more typical of African built houses, both on the continent and in the Americas.[20] The presence of a hearth and the numerous domestic objects recovered, such as dinnerware that substantially predate the midden deposits, imply that for at least some of its useful life, the structure was probably a dwelling. Its location on swampy ground and near the burial area further indicates that it was most likely associated with persons of marginal social status; if the nearby solitary cairn is indeed a burial, it may be the grave of the person who lived in this very humble home.

In the ensuing years the investigation expanded to the periphery of the former plantation, looking at how land was used in the plantation era, from roughly 1718 to 1776, and for clues, to the conditions of life for the captive and freed Africans who worked on the land and in the houses of the Browne family and the Mumford family, as well as the overseers who managed the plantation's day-to-day operations.

One of the sites on the periphery of the New Salem Plantation was a small settlement known as Cockle Hill. In the late eighteenth century this area was occupied mostly by African Americans. Later it became home to a well-to-do white family named Treadway. In the summer of 2002, CCSU conducted an excavation on this property and unearthed some intriguing materials beneath a porch foundation at the corner of the house. The assemblage consisted of a sizeable quartz crystal placed so that the points faced downward, a cache of nails, an iron wheel hub, and a horseshoe. These disparate materials were stacked tightly in a vertical grouping, indicating that they had been deliberately placed together. Materials resembling these have been identified in other sites as evidence of the continuation of African-derived spiritual practices.

Their presence in a Connecticut site supports the wider argument that people of African descent continued their own cultural practices, despite the potential and often real threat of violence or death for engaging in customs that were considered dangerous or rebellious by their captors. The practices also denote the strength of African people to resist the dominance of a white, European, Christian culture and a determination to transmit that culture to their children.

Each of the elements found beneath the porch relate directly to recognized African spiritual concepts: the positioning beneath the earth represents the direction in which the assemblage is focused (downward, to the world of spirits); the quartz, being reflective, represents water, the boundary between the physical and spirit worlds; the wheel hub represents motion and is both made of iron and in the form of a circle, significant in West and West Central African religions; the horseshoe has long been used as a protective device in Africa as well as Europe, and is also made of iron; nails have been used to awaken spirits and call on their assistance. This will be discussed in more detail later in this article.[21]

CONCLUSION

Some of the recovered spiritual materials discussed herein were found without what is generally perceived as "archaeology:" that is, excavating with shovels and trowels through layers of soil. Yet archaeology includes much more than excavation: its essential goal is the re-creation of people's lives by analyzing the materials that they made and/or used. As archaeologists, we search not merely for "treasures" from the past, however treasure may be defined: we are searching for insights into the lives of the people who made, used and, yes, treasured the objects that we recover. Most of the marginalized people of Connecticut's past could not preserve their stories in their own words, in the documentary record. Thus the study of their tools and treasures is our direct line into learning how they lived, using this evidence to demonstrate the interplay of dominance and resistance in relationships based on perceived racial and class differences. African Diaspora archaeology must be conducted with an awareness of the material expressions of African cultures and their suppression, as well as the often subtle multivalent adaptations that ensured the continuation of these cultures.

African Diaspora archaeology in Connecticut is a relatively new field of study, and most of the stories of the thousands of African and African American people who lived here remain undiscovered. The overlap between history and historical archaeology offers the opportunity to greatly enrich our understanding of the past, with history providing a framework and context for artifactual material, and archaeology supporting or challenging the documentary record. Historians have made great strides in rediscovering the hidden African American presence in Connecticut. As archaeologists, we work to fill in the missing details of their day-to-day lives. Collaboration between these two disciplines offers the greatest opportunity for learning about the once-hidden history of Africans in Connecticut.

NOTES

1   See *Connecticut History* 44, No. 2 (Fall 2005); "Complicity: How Connecticut Chained Itself to Slavery" *Hartford Couran Northeast* special issue, September 29, 2002; see also, Dr. Katherinc Harris's research on Connecticut's Black Governors, conducted for the Connecticut Historical Commission, for examples of innovative scholarship regarding the African presence in Connecticut. Additionally, the Connecticut Heritage Gateway offers resources on materials relating to captivity in Connecticut through its website: http://www.ctheritage.org.

2   Another notable first-person account is the autobiography of James Mars, who was born into a captive family in Connecticut and later became a church deacon. In the introduction, Mr. Mars states that," ... many of the people now on the stage of life do not know that slavery ever lived in Connecticut," despite the fact that African captivity was legal in Connecticut until 1848, less than a generation before Mars wrote his book. See James Mars, *Life of James Mars* (1868). More recent additions of Mars' story can be found in Arna Bontemps, ed., *Five Black Lives* (Middletown: Wesleyan University Press, 1971; see also, David O. White, "The Real Life of James Mars," *Connecticut History* 43, No. 1 (Spring 2004): 28-46.

3   Thomas C. Patterson, "Archaeologists and Historians Confront Civilization: Relativism and Post- structuralism in the Late 20th Century." Unpublished manuscript; Peter R. Schmidt and Thomas C. Patterson, "Introduction: From Constructing to Making Alternative Histories," in *Making Alternative Histories: the Practice of Archaeology and History in Non-Western Settings* (Santa Fe; School of American Research Press, 1995), 1–24.

4   Beth Ann Bower, "Material Culture in Boston: The Black Experience," in Randall H. McGuire and Robert Paynter, eds., *The Archaeology of Inequality* (Farmingdale: Baywood, 1991). 55–63; Theresa A. Singleton, "The Archaeology of Slavery in North America," *Annual Review of Anthropology* 24 (October 1995):119–40; Warren R. Perry, Jean Howson, and Barbara Bianco, eds., *New York African Burial Ground Archaeology Final Report, Volume I* (Howard University, Washington D.C. for the United States General Services Administration, Northeastern and Caribbean Region, 2006); hereafter referred to as Perry et al.

5   Warren R. Perry and Robert Paynter, "Epilogue: Artifacts, Ethnicity and the Archaeology of African Americans," in Theresa Singleton, ed., *I Too Am America: Archaeological Studies of African-American Life* (Charlottesville: University Press of Virginia, 1999), 299–310.

6   Leland Ferguson, *Uncommon Ground: Archaeology and Early African America, 1650–1800* (Washington, DC: Smithsonian Institution Press, 1992).

7   Perry et al.

8   Lorenzo J. Greene, *The Negro in Colonial New England* (New York: Columbia University Press, 1942; Winthrop D. Jordan, 'The Influence of the West Indies on the Origins of New England Slavery," *William and Mary Quarterly,* 3rd Ser., 18, No. 2 (April 1961): 243–250; William Piersen, *Black Yankees* (Amherst: University of Massachusetts Press, 1988).

9   Jay Coughtry, *The Notorious Triangle: Rhode Island and the African Slave Trade, 1700–1807* (Philadelphia: Temple University Press, 1981).

10 The town of Salem was incorporated in 1819 and named after the former plantation, but in the eighteenth century when it was a single parcel of land owned by the Browne family, it was officially part of the towns of Lyme (the southern portion of the plantation) and Colchester (the northern portion).

11 Alfred M. Bingham, "Squatter Settlements of Freed Slaves in New England," *Connecticut Historical Society Bulletin,* 41, No. 3 (July 1976): 65–80.

12 Gerald F. Sawyer, A Preliminary Site Report on an Archaeological Investigation of an 18th Century Plantation in Salem, Connecticut (Unpublished site report, 2002); Joanne Pope Melish, *Disowning Slavery: Gradual Emancipation and "Race" in New England, 1780-1860* (Ithaca: Cornell University Press, 1998).

13 Bingham, "Squatter Settlements of Freed Slaves in New England."

14 Mark P. Leone and Gladys-Marie Fry, "Conjuring in the Big House Kitchen: An Interpretation of African American Belief Systems Based on the Uses of Archaeology and Folklore Sources," *Journal of American Folklore* 112 (445) (1999): 372–403; Jerome S. Handler, "Problematic Glass Artifacts from Newton Plantation Slave Cemetery, Barbados," *African American Archaeology: Newsletter of the African American Archaeology Network,* 20 (Late Winter 1998): I, 5–6; Christopher C. Fennell, "Group Identity, Individual Creativity, and Symbolic Generation in a BaKongo Diaspora," *International Journal of Historical Archaeology,* 7, No. 1 (March 2003): 1, 20.

15 E. Kofi Agorsah, "African Burial Systems and the African Diaspora," (New York African Burial Ground Project Report, 1998).

16 Roger Moeller, "Stone Walls, Stone Lines, and Supposed Indian Graves," *Bulletin of the Archaeological Society of Connecticut,* No. 50 (1987).

17 Agorsah, "African Burial Systems and the African Diaspora."

18 The magnetic anomaly for this area is fifteen degrees off of true north, and the cairns are each approximately fifteen degrees off either magnetic north-south or east-west.

19 Jerome S. Handler, "A Prone Burial from a Plantation Slave Cemetery in Barbados, West Indies," *Historical Archaeology,* 30 (3): 76–88.

20 James Deetz, *In Small Things Forgotten: An Archaeology of Early American Life* (New York: Anchor Books, 1996), 155, 196; Ferguson, *Uncommon Ground,* 73, 81.

21 Newbell Niles Puckett, *Folk Beliefs of the Southern Negro* (Kessinger Publishing, 2003, [reprint of 1926 original]), 107, 111–112, 140, 142, 158–159, 207–208, 210, 218, 231, 234, 240, 256, 267–268, 270–271, 274, 283, 285–286, 293, 291, 295, 315–316, 337, 370, 376–377, 388, 408, 468, 476–478, 483; Robert Farris Thompson, *Flash of the Spirit: African & Afro-American Art & Philosophy* (New York: Random House/Vintage Books, 1984), 52–57; Robert Farris Thompson and Joseph Cornet, *Four Moments of the Sun: Kongo Art in Two Worlds* (Washington: National Gallery of Art, 1981), 17, 38–39; Fennell, "Group Identity, Individual Creativity, and Symbolic Generation in a BaKongo Diaspora," 21–22, 23; Kenneth L. Brown, "Interwoven Traditions: Archaeology of the Conjurer's Cabins and the African American Cemetery at the Jordan and Frogman: Manor Plantations," in *Places of Cultural Memory: African Reflections on the American Landscape* (Published Proceedings of National Park Service Conference, May

9–12, 2001, Atlanta, Georgia), 102, 108. Available online at http://www.cr.nps.gov/crdi/conferences/AFR_99-114_KBrown.pdf

22 Venture Smith, *A Narrative of the Life and Adventures of Venture, a Native of Africa, but Resident above Sixty Years in the United States of America* (New-London: Printed by C. Holt, at the Bee- Office 1798; a new addition was published by Kessinger Publishing in 2004). An electronic version at of the Narrative is available at http://docsouth.unc.edu/neh/venture/venture.html.— The Narrative is clear about the origins of his names: Broteer was the name given by his father, a prince, to his eldest son and heir. Venture was the name given by a ship's steward to someone he considered a piece of merchandise. Smith was the name of one of his captors. There is a profound difference between the attitudes with which the names were conferred, and as a matter of respect, ALAADS' archaeologists use the name Broteer.

23 A *Narrative of the Life and Adventures of Venture.*

24 Thompson and Cornet, *Four Moments of the Sun,* 34–35; Scott MacEachern, 'Two Thousand Years of West African History," in Ann Brower Stahl, ed., *African Archaeology* (Malden: Blackwell Publishing, 2005).

25 Thompson, *Flash of the Spirit;* John Michael Vlach, *The Afro-American Tradition in Decorative Arts* (Athens: Brown Thrasher Books/The University of Georgia Press. 1990); Grey Gundaker, *Signs of Diaspora/Diaspora of Signs: Literacies, Creolization, and Vernacular Practice in African America* (New York: Oxford Press, 1998).

26 Vlach, *The Afro-American Tradition in Decorative Arts;* Handler, "Problematic Glass Artifacts from Newton Plantation Slave Cemetery, Barbados" African-American Archaeology: Newsletter of the African-American Archaeology Network 20 (Late Winter): 1, 5–6; Gundaker, *Signs of Diaspora/Diaspora of Signs.*

27 Brown, "Interwoven Traditions; Fennell, "Group Identity, Individual Creativity, and Symbolic Generation in a BaKongo Diaspora"; Leone and Frye, "Conjuring in the Big House Kitchen."

28 The seeking of spirit-world interventions, usually called conjuration or rootwork, is referred to in the past tense to reflect the archaeological recovery of material. It is not to be inferred that these are "dead" practices; African-derived spiritualities have formed the basis of numerous syncretic religions worldwide and are presently practiced internationally in their non-sycretic forms as well.

29 Thompson, *Flash of the* Spirit, 106, 108–116; Fennell, "Group Identity, Individual Creativity, and Symbolic Generation in a BaKongo Diaspora"; Leland Ferguson, "The Cross is a Magic Sign:" Marks on 18th Century Bowls from South Carolina," in Theresa Singleton, ed., *I Too Am America: Archaeological Studies of African-American Life,* 116–131; Timothy Ruppel, Jessica Neuwirth, Mark P. Leone, and Gladys-Marie Fry, "Hidden in View: African spiritual spaces in North American Landscapes," *Antiquity* 77 (2003):321–335.

30 See Gundaker, *Signs of Diaspora/Diaspora of Signs,* for a comprehensive discussion of the symbolism and literacies in African-derived spiritual practices.

31 Joshua Hempstead, *The Diary of Joshua Hempstead, 1711–1758* (CD-ROM version copyrighted by Asymetrix Corporation/The Oldham Publishing Service, 1999). Hempstead "bought" Adam in 1727, and for the rest of the account, logs Adam's activities almost daily. Hempstead frequently refers to himself as "helping Adam" with tasks, exemplifying the reliance that he placed on the captive worker.

32 Brian Hoggard, a researcher who studies concealed materials and written "charms" in medieval and post-medieval England, has corroborated that in his experience these materials are inevitably found in poor households or in servants' areas of wealthy households. He attributes this to the differential in economic status, which restricted access to mainstream healing and solace in the Christian churches of England. (Personal communication with author.)

33 Joel Lang, "The Plantation Next Door: How Salem Slaves, Wethersfield Onions, and West Indies Sugar Made Connecticut Rich," in "Complicity," *Hartford Courant Northeast* special issue, September 29, 2002, 7; "Putnam Elms: The Homestead of Daniel Putnam 1782–1953, compiled from documents and copies of documents belonging to the Colonel Daniel Putnam Association and in the custody of its historian, Ann Putnam Browne." http://putnamelms.org/Pamflet.htm.

34 Leland Ferguson, "The Cross is a Magic Sign:" Marks on 18th Century Bowls from South Carolina, in Theresa Singleton, ed., *I Too Am America,* 116–131.

35 Dawn Hutchins Bobryk, Director, Phelps Tavern Museum & Homestead, (Personal communication with author.)

36 Gundaker, *Signs of Diaspora/Diaspora of Signs.*

37 Leone and Frye, "Conjuring in the Big House Kitchen"; Brown, "Interwoven Traditions"; Ferguson, "The Cross is a Magic Sign."

38 Newbell Niles Puckett, *Folk Beliefs of the Southern Negro* (Kessinger Publishing, 2003; originally published, 1926); Gundaker, *Signs of Diaspora/Diaspora of Signs.*

39 Ralph Merrifield, *The Archaeology of Ritual and Magic* (New York: New Amsterdam Books, 1988); Brian Hoggard, Apotropaios, http://www.apotropaios.co.uk/, (Personal communication with author.)

40 Complicity page 18.

41 Daniel Cruson, *Newtown's Slaves: A Case Study in Early Connecticut Rural Black History* (Newtown: Newtown Historical Society, 1994), 48–54.

42 One of the best-known examples of this bonding along class lines occurred during the 1741 "conspiracy" in New York City, in which working-class Irish and Africans, both marginalized groups, banded together in an uprising against the white power structure. For the transcription of the trials of the "conspirators," see Daniel Horsmanden, *The New York Conspiracy* (Boston: Beacon Press, 1971); Thomas J. Davis, "These Enemies of Their Own Household: A Note on the Troublesome Slave Population in Eighteenth-Century New York City," *Journal of the Afro-American Historical and Genealogical Society* (1984): 133–147; and Thomas J. Davis, *Rumor of Revolt: The "Great Negro Plot" in Colonial New York* (New York: The Free Press, 1985).

My Ancestors

The Lighthouse People

Coni Allen Dubois

EDITOR'S INTRODUCTION

The theme of this section is "serving communities." This article, written by one of the living descendants of the Lighthouse community, exemplifies that on the scale of the individual. I first heard from Coni Dubois several years ago. Our trajectories converged as I researched the archaeology of the Lighthouse community as an archaeologist and Coni, as a member of a family, researched the story of her family. In Coni's search for her own roots and her own story, she discovered the story of the Lighthouse and that included information about the research being done by an academic archaeologist in Connecticut: me. Since our initial contact we have worked collaboratively on the story of her family. I dig in the dirt, Coni digs in the documents. The archaeological excavations I have directed at the site have allowed Coni to imagine the hardscrabble life lived by her ancestors. Her genealogical work has allowed us to give names and tell the personal stories of the flesh-and-blood people who were the residents of the Lighthouse. Coni tells what the ability to reveal the story of her family means to her.

POINTS TO PONDER

1. How does the archaeological research at the Lighthouse exemplify the ability of archaeology to serve the needs of living communities?
2. To whom does Coni trace back her ancestry in the Lighthouse family?
3. What has archaeology provided Coni that her genealogical research has not?
4. What are the lessons gleaned from Coni's experience?

More than twenty years ago my father, Rex Allen, made what seemed at the time to be a simple request: find our Native American roots. My father knew he was of Native American descent but he had no idea as to what tribe we were affiliated with or where, ultimately, our ancestors had come from. So I began researching our family tree and genealogy. I painstakingly worked my way back in our family history generation by generation. Each document I encountered provided a new clue until my genealogical research led me to a possible ancestor from what was sometimes referred to in historical documents as the Barkhamsted Lighthouse Tribe.

I started researching the Barkhamsted, Connecticut, area and that's when the excitement really began for me. I contacted the Barkhamsted Historical Society at their headquarters located at Squires Tavern, an eighteenth-century building that had served as a tavern and inn along the Farmington River turnpike, a stagecoach road that connected to the much larger Albany Turnpike that led from Albany to Boston. My contacts at the Barkhamsted Historical Society told me that Ken Feder of Central Connecticut State University was the archaeologist working at the Barkhamsted Lighthouse site and had conducted several digs there. They helped me get in touch with him.

Just after I sent an email to Ken, I did an online search of his name and saw that he had published a book called *A Village of Outcasts* about the Lighthouse people. Initially I was distraught because I couldn't find a copy to order anywhere! Ken Feder contacted me immediately and we exchanged files. I told him of my dilemma of not being able to find a copy of his book. A few days later in the mail I received his signed book. In it he wrote this for me:

9/17/09 Coni—Happy 42nd!
Thanks for sharing your research
It's an honor getting to know someone in James's & Molly's "Ever Widening Circle"
Kenny Feder

His book was full of documentation and records of my ancestors, proof of my Native American lineage. To hold in my hands actual archeological evidence of my family's life on Ragged Mountain in Connecticut was overwhelming.

My father's request has changed my life. What started as a hobby has become my life's mission. Ken Feder and his archaeological research truly fueled the fire of my desire to find out more about my ancestors. He has shared his archaeological work and research with me and now I am sharing my genealogical research with him. Jointly, the work has opened many new leads and provided clues allowing me to illuminate the "ever-widening circle" of my family. Archaeology has helped immeasurably in my quest, revealing the true history of my ancestors. I cannot thank Ken Feder and his team enough for all the hard work they did.

Coni Dubois
www.conidubois.wordpress.com

Figure 7.1. Coni Dubois at the Lighthouse community cemetery.

Rescue, Research, and Reburial

Walton Family Cemetery, Griswold, Connecticut

Nicholas F. Bellantoni, Paul S. Sledzik, and David A. Poirier

EDITOR'S INTRODUCTION

The Waltons was a popular, folksy television show in the 1970s and 1980s about an extended family of poor, appealing, wisdom-spouting country people living in rural Virginia in the period 1933–1946. It turns out that Connecticut had its own Waltons who also were simply country folk who, unlike the fictional Waltons, apparently suffered from a bout of vampirism. Well, not actually, but they believed that were being afflicted by vampirism in what actually was an epidemic of tuberculosis. The Walton family cemetery had been lost for decades, was found again only accidentally, and then excavated by archaeologists. When the skeletons of the Waltons were found, it was clear, in one instance in particular, that the grave had been violated soon after the interment had taken place, and the bones reconfigured in what was an attempt to keep the deceased from exiting his grave, walking the earth, and attacking the living in a search for fresh blood. This was years before Buffy the Vampire Slayer or the Twilight books and movies. The researchers here have produced an amazing piece of detective work that includes history, archaeology, and paleopathology. They also served the community of Walton descendants who now know their ancestors better than they ever could have and who also know that their graves are once again safe and sound.

POINTS TO PONDER

1. On what basis did some people in southern New England in the nineteenth century believe that vampires walked the earth?
2. What evidence was found at the Walton family cemetery that indicated ceremonies were being performed on the dead after their initial burial?
3. Who were the Walton Family vampires? What is the scientific explanation for what was happening to members of the Walton family?
4. What lessons can be learned from the investigation of the Walton family cemetery?

DISCOVERY

The Connecticut State Police and the Office of the State Chief Medical Examiner were notified in the late fall of 1990 that two human crania had been discovered by three preteen-age boys playing in a privately operated sand-and-gravel mine in Griswold, Connecticut. Sliding down the slope of the gravel pit, the boys dislodged two skulls, which proceeded to tumble down the embankment with them. The chief medical examiner notified the state archaeologist as mandated by state statutes whenever "historic" human remains are uncovered that are not part of a modern criminal investigation. Local officials assumed that the remains might be Native American because legends note an early historic "battleground" in the area. However, laboratory analysis indicated a European biological affiliation for the two crania.

On-site inspection of the exposed side wall of the gravel quarry revealed six darkened soil stains extending 3 to 4 feet in depth from a disturbed ground surface. These distinctions in the soil profile were immediately interpreted as grave shafts; it became readily apparent that the gravel operation had encountered the first row of a historic cemetery. By law, the developer was only required to conduct title searches for the property dating back 40 years. No mention of a cemetery was discovered. However, he did have access to the *Hale Index* and suspected a historic cemetery on his property, but not in the area to be mined. The Office of State Archaeology was satisfied that the owner had no prior knowledge that the cemetery was located in his quarry site until human remains were accidentally exposed.

Emergency efforts were immediately undertaken by the Office of State Archaeology, the University of Connecticut, and the State Historic Preservation Office to rescue and recover human remains endangered by erosion. Unfortunately, the instability of the sand-and-gravel quarry (Plate 8.1) precluded *in situ* preservation and necessitated total archaeological excavation of the remaining burials. Twenty-seven individuals were eventually excavated from the cemetery, including 5 adult males, 8 adult females, and 14 children ranging from infants through adolescents (Tables 8.1 and 8.2). The property owner voluntarily assisted the rescue excavations in a number of ways including suspending his gravel removal activities, donating financial aid and labor from his work force, and constructing a temporary structure heated by propane to permit fieldwork through the winter season.

ARCHAEOLOGICAL RESCUE

Fieldwork at the Walton Family Cemetery began immediately upon our initial inspection of the site. A request for volunteer assistance resulted in students from the University of Connecticut and amateur archaeologists from the Albert Morgan Archaeological Society responding and participating in the rescue excavations. The Public Archaeology Survey Team, Inc., established a grid system

Table 8.1 Overview of the Walton Cemetery Skeletal Remains, Including Sex, Age, Stature, and Pathological Condition

BURIAL #	SEX	AGE	STATURE	PATHOLOGY
1	F	55–59	159.07	Vertebral and joint OA, Schmorl's nodes
2	M	60+	173.94	Joint OA
3	F	30–35	161.21	None
4	M	50–55	180.40	Vertebral and joint OA, healed fractures, periostitis, tuberculosis
4A	F	45–54	177.60	Vertebral and joint OA, temporomandibular joint OA
5	S	10–11	N/A	None
6	S	1–1.5	N/A	None
7	S	6–7	N/A	None
8	M	20–35	174.55	None
9	F	20–29	170.87	None
10	S	0.5–0.75	N/A	None
11	F	35–44	156.75	None
12		NO BURIAL REMAINS			
13	S	8–9	N/A	None
14	F	50–65	N/A	Edentulous
15	M	60+	N/A	Vertebral and joint OA
16	S	1–1.5	N/A	None
17	S	1.5–2,5	N/A	None
18	F	60–75	N/A	Osteopenia, unhealed femoral neck fracture, vertebral OA
19	S	2–3	N/A	None
20	M	30–34	180.71	Heavy dental calculus
21	S	11–12	N/A	None
22	F	22–26	167.46	None
23	S	12–14	N/A	None
24	S	1–2	N/A	None
25	S	7–8	N/A	None
26	S	6–7	N/A	None
27	S	6–7	N/A	None

Note: Sex estimates are given for males, females, subadults; age numbers are in years; stature is recorded in centimeters; N/A means data not applicable; and OA abbreviates osteoarthritis.

as excavations began along the gravel cliff. The owner cooperated by stock-piling soils against the gravel bank in an effort to reduce erosional loss.

Archaeological field methods included the location and mapping of soil feature stains indicative of burial shafts that existed back from the vertical edge of the gravel bank. In previous years, the knoll had been prepared for the sand-and-gravel operation in phases that included deforestation and the stripping of topsoil to a depth of 2 feet. This resulted in the mechanical removal of fieldstones and other cemetery markers. Nonetheless, elimination of the topsoil permitted efficient use of

Table 8.2 Walton Cemetery Demographic Patterns

AGE	MALES	FEMALES	SUBADULTS	TOTAL	BURIAL NUMBER
<1 yr			1	1	10
1–4 yrs			5	5	6, 16, 17, 19, 24
5–9 yrs			5	5	7,13,25,26,27
10–14 yrs			3	3	5,21,23
15–19 yrs					
20–29 yrs	1	2			8,9,22
30–39 yrs	1	2		3	3,11,20
40–49 yrs		1		1	4A
50+ yrs	3	3		6	1,2,4,14,15,18
Total	5 (18%)	8 (30%)	14 (52%)	27	

shovel-scraping with flat-edged blades to locate grave shafts in the upper level of the B horizon. In addition, soil cores were systematically sampled across the knoll as a back-up approach to locating burial features by shovel-scraping.

Field methods also included mapping, illustrative and photographic recording at various stages of the excavation, and the systematic removal of each skeletal element within the burials. Excavation stages began within the soil stains, which eventually exposed a thin, dark brown, linear stain representing the sideboards of the wooden coffin. A series of rusted hardware coffin nails, usually with preserved wood attached, were located along the top and bottom of the sideboards. These two rows of coffin nails provided information on depth and coffin-making technology. Once coffin dimensions were recorded, excavation continued inside the vertical sideboards until human remains were encountered.

Upon exposure of the skeletal remains, the following descriptive information was recorded: orientation of the skeleton, positioning of the arms and legs, state of preservation, preliminary estimates of age and sex, artifacts associated with the burial, and inventories of each skeletal element recovered. In addition, whenever possible, samples of hair, wood, and soil were taken. Skeletal elements were placed in acid-free tissue and bubble wrap for transportation to the Archaeology Laboratory at the University of Connecticut. Once the skeletal remains were removed, excavations continued beneath the coffins and along the sideboards to recover any additional bone and/or hardware present.

The most persistent field problem was the rate of soil erosion off the gravel bank. In the first two weeks, the outermost edge of the embankment collapsed in over 7 feet in some areas, threatening the second row of the cemetery. Ironically, erosional rates were enhanced by the combined weights of the archaeologists working on the cliff edge. Although various stabilization efforts were employed, significant soil loss was not uncommon and required constant monitoring during field excavations.

WALTON FAMILY CEMETERY

The rescue excavations at the Walton Family Cemetery resulted in the recovery of 27 individuals in 28 graves. Burial 12 yielded a pattern of coffin nails but no organic preservation of wood or bone within it. The burials were placed in somewhat poorly defined rows, which were in a north-south alignment. Each burial was oriented east-west, with the head of the individual to the west, a standard mortuary practice for colonial period Christian burials. Three exceptions are Burials 10, 14, and 15, which have a southwest-northeast orientation. The configuration of the cemetery suggests clusters of burials as opposed to an orderly arrangement of rows. The 2 rows nearest the gravel bank exposure toward the west are discernible. However, toward the east, clusters of burials occur in the north and south portions of the cemetery. For example, the northern cluster is composed of 7 graves in close proximity that are the remains of small children and may represent a disease epidemic within the family or community.

All deceased family members were placed in wooden coffins, of which 12 were hexagonal and 11 were rectangular in shape, while 5 coffin shapes could not be discerned due to erosional collapse prior to rescue excavations. Nine of the 12 hexagonal and all of the unknown coffin shapes are associated with adult individuals, while all of the 11 rectangular coffins are associated with subadults. When preservation permitted, wood samples were taken from top, side, and bottom coffin boards and analyzed by Lucinda McWeeney (1992) for species identification. Identifications from 17 burials showed that white pine (*Pinus strobus*) was used predominately (11 coffins), while red and white oak were used to a lesser extent (6 coffins). In addition, McWeeney (1992) identified paint stains on the lids of two coffins: black paint associated with Burial 5, and red paint with Burial 4.

Coffin hardware, analyzed by Ross Harper (1992), was limited and consisted primarily of hand-wrought nails. While every coffin yielded a series of hand-wrought nails, only Burials 4, 4A, 5, and 18 had coffin screws and brass tacks as part of the coffin hardware material. In addition, Burials 4, 5 and 18 have copper dowel hinges on the lids of the coffin. According to Rumford (1965:78), hinged and divided coffin lids begin to appear in the early nineteenth century. The lid of the coffin was divided in order to expose the head area to view the face of the deceased. Burials yielding no hinges are interpreted as having plain one-piece lids. Burial 15 produced a series of three nails located longitudinally along the axial skeleton and may suggest a gable-lidded coffin (Noel Hume 1982). However, for the most part, the cemetery consists of rather plain, undecorated hexagonal coffins for adults and rectangular coffins for children. We found no evidence of decorative butterfly hinges,

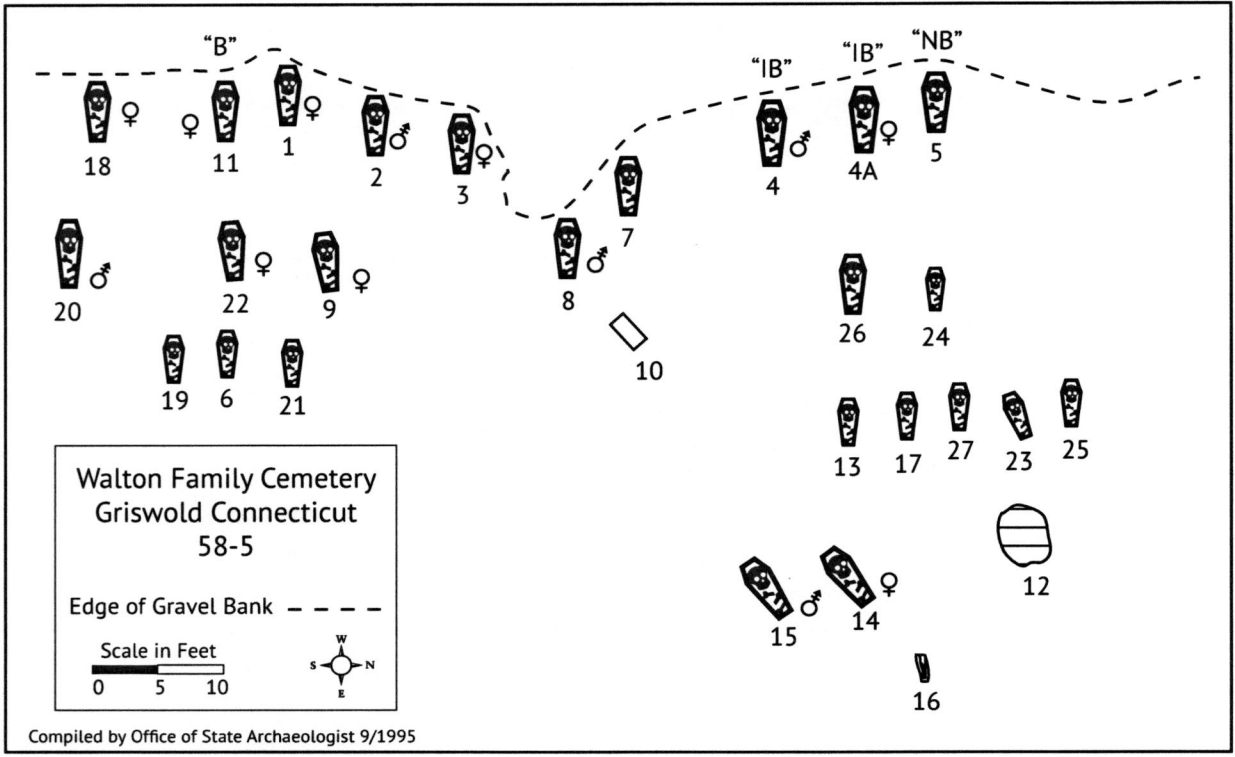

Figure 8.1. Map of burials excavated from Walton Family Cemetery.

handles, glass viewing plates, or lining tacks. No machine cut nails were recovered, suggesting that all the burials predate the 1830s.

Two burials (Nos. 4 and 5) were placed in stone and unmortared brick crypts. The hexagonal coffin in Burial 5, consisting of a two-piece lid with brass tacks arranged in the initials and number "NB 13," was located within several courses of unmortared bricks built on single brick width and covered by slabs of fieldstones. "NB" are the initials of the deceased and "13" is the age of death. Sex could not be determined for this adolescent individual. The coffin in Burial 4 is similar; however, the crypt consists of stone slabs set vertically and horizontally along the sides and top, enclosing the coffin. A few bricks do appear along the sideboards of the coffin as structural supports. Brass tacks form the initials and number "JB 55." The corpse is an adult male. The appearance of crypts are more likely interpreted as changes in mortuary practices in the nineteenth century as well as socioeconomic factors.

No evidence of clothing, including boots, buttons, or buckles, was recovered from the burials. The only material culture associated with the skeletal remains was the presence of two-piece, copper-headed, brass and silver straight pins. Recovered from 11 burials, these pins were aligned to one side of the body and used to hold a burial shroud in place. Burial 14 yielded a small shard of a slipware bowl rim. However, this ceramic appears to have been introduced into the grave from backfilling the burial shaft rather than as a funerary object.

Burial depth from the original ground level was impossible to calculate due to the extensive activities of the sand and gravel mining. However, the graves of the children were encountered at the surface of the stripped knoll or within a foot of excavation. Adult burials were always recovered from deeper levels. We estimate that the children were buried around 3 feet in depth while adult graves were dug to an average of 5 to 6 feet.

OSTEOLOGICAL RESEARCH

Preliminary analysis of the skeletal remains from the Walton Family Cemetery was conducted at the University of Connecticut as each burial was processed in the laboratory upon field recovery. Extensive analysis was conducted by Paul S. Sledzik and Allison Webb Wilcox at the National Museum of Health and Medicine, Armed Forces Institute of Pathology, in Washington, D.C. Table 8.1 presents an overview of age, sex, and stature estimates and pathological conditions in the Walton Cemetery skeletal remains.

Demographic Discussion

The striking demographic statistic in the mortality distribution is the number of children represented in the cemetery (Table 8.2). Fifty percent of the burials are preteenagers. Six individuals, almost one-fourth of the cemetery population, are infants under the age of 2 years. As the Walton Family Cemetery most likely represents a biological lineage, that is, a breeding population, the disproportionate number of children may reflect the hardships of survival in colonial New England. Seasons of low nutrition, unsanitary conditions, and overcrowded rural farmsteads may account for the spread of communicable diseases among New England farming families. Children were especially vulnerable to outbreaks of measles, colds, yellow fever, tuberculosis, smallpox, and other pathologies (Clark et al. 1987). Town of Norwich Death Records indicate a measles epidemic in 1759 and a smallpox epidemic in 1790. Either of these events could be represented in this cemetery population. Due to a child's limited resistance to these pathogens and subsequent expeditious death, the evidence for these diseases were not manifest on the osteological remains.

Striking also is the high percentage of (23%) of individuals over 50 years of age. Age distribution frequencies are bimodal: children and older adults. Combined, these age groups represent almost 75% of the total cemetery population. The disproportionately low number of young and middle-aged adults is probably a result of developed immunities and stronger resistance to disease. The demographic pattern appears to reflect what we would expect in a historic cemetery population.

BIOARCHAEOLOGICAL INTERPRETATIONS

In historical bioarchaeologial research, investigators use historical information to interpret osteological and archaeological evidence. Such information allows researchers to test the reliability of historical documents and interpretations and can lead to insights into unique cultural practices (Owsley 1990; Bell, this volume). The Walton Family Cemetery offered us insight into a distinctively New England folk practice.

Burial 4 contained the skeletal remains of "JB 55," a 50-to 55-year-old male interred in a stone-lined crypt, When the grave was opened, the skull-and-femora were found in a "skull-and-crossbones" orientation on top of the ribs and vertebrae, which were also found in disarray (Plate 8.2). Taphonomically, the physical arrangement of the skeletal remains in the grave indicates that no soft tissue was present at the time of rearrangement, which may have been 5 to 10 years after death. No other burial had been so desecrated at the cemetery. The coffin style and crypt suggest an early nineteenth-century temporal placement for the burial. Historic research to date has been unsuccessful in determining the *B* family surname. Griswold town and Congregational Church records show a series of families beginning with the letter *B* interacting with the Waltons and the community (e.g., Brown, Bishop, Bennett, Burnham, Bissell, Burton). Unfortunately, we have been unable to identify the appropriate family and their relationship to the Waltons. It appears that the B family may have utilized the burial ground after the Waltons' departure from Griswold. Although historical research into the family and colonial community had begun with the field rescue of the cemetery, this desecrated burial raised a new concern.

Historical research continued searching for a plausible explanation to what was observed in the archaeological context. An intriguing piece of evidence was found in an historic newspaper account:

> In the May 20, 1854, issue of the *Norwich [Connecticut] Courier,* there is the account of an incident that occurred at Jewett [City], a city in that vicinity. About eight years previously, Horace Ray of Griswold had died of consumption. Afterwards, two of his children—grown up sons—died of the same disease, the last one dying about 1852. Not long before the date of the newspaper the same fatal disease had seized another son, whereupon it was determined to exhume the bodies of the two brothers and burn them, because the dead were supposed to feed upon the living; and so long as the dead body in the grave remained undecomposed, either wholly or in part, the surviving members of the family must continue to furnish substance on which the dead body could feed. Acting under the influence of this strange superstition, the family and friends of the deceased

proceeded to the burial ground on June 8, 1854, dug up the bodies of the deceased brothers, and burned them on the spot. (Wright 1973)

This account places a New England vampire folk belief in the Griswold area two miles from the Walton Cemetery just a few years after the time span of the projected death of "JB."

The term "vampire" conjures up images of Dracula, Bram Stoker's fictional character. The reality behind the fiction and the popular cultural manifestations of the vampire are rooted in historic European and American folklore. In this folklore, the vampire was a dead person or spirit who acted in various ways to "drain" the life from the living. To stop these actions, the bodies of supposed vampires were exhumed to look for indications of "life," such as a bloated chest, long fingernails, and blood draining from the mouth. These changes are now known to be the result of postmortem decomposition (Barber 1988; Mann et al. 1990). Deaths resulting from disease epidemics were also blamed on vampires. To stop the epidemic, vampires were sought out and "killed" by various methods (Perkowski 1989).

In nineteenth-century New England, residents of rural areas of Rhode Island, Connecticut, Massachusetts, and Vermont held a belief similar to the European vampire folklore (Stetson 1898; Sledzik and Bellantoni 1994). These New Englanders believed that a deceased tuberculosis victim could return from the dead as a vampire, causing surviving relatives to "waste away." The actions of the vampire were stopped by exhuming the body of the consumptive and disrupting the corpse in various ways. Numerous historic accounts of this activity indicate that the belief was not uncommon in nineteenth-century New England (See Sledzik and Bellantoni 1994, Table 1).

This interpretation of contagion is consistent with the etiology of tuberculosis. The historic accounts incorporate tuberculosis and examination of the body of the vampire for putative signs of life. Following the death of a family member from tuberculosis (also known as consumption), other family members who became infected began to show signs of tuberculosis infection. The "wasting away" of these family members was attributed to the deceased consumptive, who was returning from the dead to drain the lives of the surviving relatives. To kill the vampire, the corpse was exhumed, and if found undecomposed, the heart was removed and burned. In other circumstances, the corpse was turned face down, burned, or disrupted in other ways.

Based on the historical accounts, actual evidence of the New England vampire folklore should be found in New England cemeteries. The Walton Cemetery contains three pieces of evidence supporting the folklore: (1) the postmortem rearrangement of skeletal elements in Burial 4; (2) paleo pathological evidence of tuberculosis in this burial; and (3) the historical account of the vampire folk belief from mid-nineteenth-century Griswold, Connecticut, discussed above. We hypothesize that, in the absence of a heart to be burned, the apotropaic remedy was to place the bones in a "skull-and-crossbones" arrangement. In support of this hypothesis, we note that decapitation was a common European method of dispatching a dead vampire, and that the Celts and Neolithic

Egyptians were known to separate the head from the body, supposedly to prevent the dead from doing harm (Barber 1988).

Among the numerous pathological conditions observed in the skeleton of Burial 4 was evidence of tuberculosis in the second, third, and fourth left ribs. The whitish-gray, pitted lesions were observed on the visceral rib surface near the rib head adjacent to the pleura. The lesions, respectively 30 mm, 35 mm, and 25 mm in length, comprise an area of approximately 30 cm mediolaterally and 45 cm superiorly-inferiorly when considered in anatomical position. The lesions are similar to those described by Kelley and Micozzi (1984) and Roberts, Lucy, and Manchester (1994) as being associated with primary pulmonary tuberculosis.

The New England vampire folklore is also consistent with modern knowledge of the transmission of tuberculosis. Many of the historic vampire accounts indicate that family members living in close association became infected with the disease before or soon after the death of the "vampire." Tuberculosis is notorious for being transmitted between individuals of different generations living under crowded conditions, a situation common in rural nineteenth-century New England farming communities (Hawke 1988). Seasonal periods of low nutrition and the unsanitary conditions of eighteenth- and nineteenth-century farming compounds increased the opportunity for the transmission of tuberculosis between family members (Clark et al. 1987; Kelley and Eisenberg 1987). Although there is no evidence of tuberculosis in the remaining Walton cemetery skeletons, an 1801 narrative of Griswold history indicates that during the 25 years preceding the account "consumptions have proved to be mortal to a number" (Phillips 1929).

FAMILY RENEWAL AND REBURIAL

"In the fall of 1992, a reburial ceremony was conducted for the eighteenth-and nineteenth-century Walton family members who had been archaeologically rescued from their historic resting place. Since archival evidence demonstrated that the Walton family had belonged to the First Congregational Church in the Town of Griswold, current church members graciously hosted a reception for Walton relatives who attended from as far away as Nevada. At the invitation of the First Congregational Church, the state archaeologist shared a preliminary analysis of the historic and archaeological data with family, friends, and church members. The Rev. Michael Beynon performed a traditional Puritan recomittal ceremony at the nearby town-owned Hopeville Cemetery. The reburial in this historic cemetery was arranged by the town's First Selectman. Skeletal remains were arranged according to the archaeological excavation records such that the integrity of rows, body orientation, and relative positions were re-established.

The Walton Cemetery project triggered a number of very sensitive and emotional concerns from a diverse constituency. The property owner, town and state officials, archaeologists, community residents, family members, and religious representatives participated and shared in the decision-making process regarding the respectful removal and subsequent reburial of the Walton family remains. Connecticut statutes provided the administrative guidelines, while the archaeological community offered the sensitivity, diplomacy, and professionalism required for dealing with both the endangered osteological population and their surviving descendants and other interested parties.

ACKNOWLEDGMENTS

The authors wish to acknowledge the assistance of individuals who worked on this project in the field and conducting historic research: Lisa Ostop, Julie Hartman, Robert Gradie III, Jeffrey Bendremer, Kevin McBride, Joseph Cunningham, David George, Peggy Wishart, Marina DeLuca, Christopher Wikman, Thomas Nichols, Paul Costa, Peter Evans, Tess Rondo, Daniel Adler, Jill Kaufman, Nancy Wilson, Marc Banks, Anita Sherman, Laura Histillo, Alan Bicknell, David Cooke, June Cooke, Richard LaRose, Andrea Rand, Robert Cless, Jean O'Meara, Marina Mozzi, Tom Kennedy and Rob Kleft. A special thanks to David Geer and his family for the cooperation, support, and labor they provided in the course of the field-work and reburial; and to Alison Webb Wilcox and Kendra Shih for assistance in the osteological analysis. Rev. Michael Beynon performed the reburial ceremony as well as contributed to our understanding of early Congregational mortuary practices. Our appreciation to Dr. H. Wayne Carver, Chief State Medical Examiner, and John W. Shannahan, Connecticut Historical Commission, for the support they and their staff provided. Lucinda McWeeney conducted analysis of wood samples and Ross Harper identified coffin hardware. Michael Bell, Rhode Island Folklorist, shared his research into the New England vampire belief. A very special appreciation is extended to Jeanne Church-Abrams and Frances Allen Dunne, descendants of Nathaniel Walton, who provided us with family histories, genealogies, and hair samples.

REFERENCES

Angel, J. Lawrence. 1976. "Colonial to Modern Skeletal Change in the U.S.A." *American Journal of Physical Anthropology* 45:723–736.

Barber, Paul. 1988. *Vampires, Burial, and Death: Folklore and Reality.* New Haven, Conn.: Yale University Press.

Clark, George A., Marc A. Kelley, J. M. Grane, and M. Cassandra Hill. 1987. "The Evolution of Mycobacterial Disease in Human Populations." *Current Anthropology* 28:45–51.

Harper, Ross. 1992. "Material Culture Identifications: Walton Family Cemetery." Manuscript on file with Office of State Archaeology, University of Connecticut, Storrs.

Hawke, David F. 1988. *Everyday Life in Early America.* New York: Harper and Row.

Kelley, Marc A., and Leslie E. Eisenberg. 1987. "Blastomycosis and Tuberculosis in Early American Indians: A Biocultural View." *Midcontinental Journal of Archeology* 12:89–116.

Kelley, Marc A., and Marc S. Micozzi. 1984. "Rib Lesions and Chronic Pulmonary Tuberculosis." *American Journal of Physical Anthropology* 65:381–86.

Mann, Robert W., William M. Bass, and Lee Meadows. 1990. "Time since Death and Decomposition of the Human Body: Variables and Observations in Case and Experimental Field Studies." *Journal of Forensic Sciences* 35:103–111.

McWeeney, Lucinda. 1992. "Walton Family Burial Ground." Report Prepared for the Connecticut Office of State Archaeology. Manuscript on file with Office of State Archaeology, University of Connecticut, Storrs.

Noel Hume, Ivor. 1982. *Martin's Hundred: The Discovery of a Lost Colonial Virginia Settlement.* New York: Dell.

Owsley, Douglas W. 1990. "The Skeletal Biology of North American Historical Populations." In *A Life in Science: Papers in Honor of J. Lawrence Angel,* edited by Jane E. Buikstra, 171-90. Kampsville, Ill.: Center for American Archeology.

Perkowski, Jan L. 1989. *The Darkling: A Treatise on Slavic Vampirism.* Columbus, Ohio: Slavica Publishers.

Pfeiffer, Susan, J. Christopher Dudar, and Susan Austin. 1992. "Prospect Hill: Skeletal Remains from a 19th Century Methodist Cemetery, Newmarket, Ontario." *Northeast Historical Archaeology* 21: 29–48.

Phillips, Daniel L. 1918. *Griswold Connecticut Cemeteries: History and Inscriptions 1724-1918.* Unpublished manuscript. Slater Library, Griswold, Connecticut.

_____. 1929. *A History, Being a History of the Town of Griswold, Connecticut, from the Earliest Times to the Entrance of Our Country into the World War in 1917.* New Haven, Conn.: Tuttle, Morehouse and Taylor Co.

Roberts, Charlotte, David Lucy, and Keith Manchester. 1994. "Inflammatory Lesions of the Ribs: An Analysis of the Terry Collection." *American journal of Physical Anthropology* 95:169–82.

Rumford, Beatrix T. 1965. *The Role of Death as Reflected in the Art and Folkways of the Northeast in the Eighteenth and Nineteenth Centuries.* Master's thesis, State University of New York, Oneonta, New York.

Saunders, Shelley. 1991. "Sex Determination, Stature, and Size and Shape Variation of the Limb Bones." In *Snake Hill: An Investigation of a Military Cemetery from the War of 1812,* edited by Susan Pfeiffer and Ronald E. Williamson, 176-97. Toronto: Dundurn Press.

Sledzik, Paul S., and Nicholas F. Bellantoni. 1994. "Bioarchaelogical and Biocultu-Tal Evidence for the New England Vampire Folk Belief." *American journal of Physical Anthropology* 94:269–74.

Sledzik, Paul S., and Peer H. Moore-Jansen. 1991. "Dental Disease in Nineteenth Century Military Skeletal Samples." In *Advances in Dental Anthropology,* edited by Marc A. Kelley and Clark S. Larsen, 215-24. New York: Wiley-Liss.

Steegman, A. Theodore. 1986, "Skeletal Stature Compared to Archival Stature in Mid-18th Century America: Ft. William Henry." *American journal of Physical Anthropology* 71:431–35.

Steegman, A. Theodore. 1991. "Stature in an Early Mid-19th Century Poorhouse Population: Highland Park, Rochester, New York." *American Journal of Physical Anthropology* 85:261–68.

Stetson, George. 1898. "The Animistic Vampire in New England." *American Anthropologist* 9:1–13.

Weslowsky, Al B. 1989. "The Osteology of the Uxbridge Paupers." In *Archaeological Excavations at the Uxbridge Almshouse Burial Ground in Uxbridge, Mass.,* edited by Ricardo J. Elia and Al B. Weslowsky, 303–336. Office of Public Archaeology Report of Investigations, No. 76. Boston University.

Wright, Dudley. 1973. *The Book of Vampires.* New York: Causeway Books.

African Burial Ground Final Report

Warren R. Perry, Jean Howson, and Barbara A. Bianco

EDITOR'S INTRODUCTION

I will admit to being shocked when I read the statistic presented in this piece: New York City had the second-highest proportion of people of African descent of any city in North America during the colonial period. Even more shocking to us northerners who feel so superior to southerners when it comes to the institution of slavery—they had slaves, we didn't—in fact, many of those Africans living in New York during that time, indeed, were slaves. The African Burial Ground project on the lower end of Manhattan (conducted in the shadow of the now-destroyed World Trade Center) reflected the realities of history: there were slaves in the North, those slaves were treated brutally with many of them essentially worked to death, but in death, and in the burial ceremonies and treatment that the living afforded the deceased, the archaeological record shows the maintenance of their African cultures. The African captives of New York City cannot speak to us across the centuries in books or journals, but they can tell us their stories of servitude and resistance and freedom through the lens of the archaeologist.

POINTS TO PONDER

1. How do the researchers of the African Burial Ground explain the apparent uniformity of the graves they excavated?
2. What evidence of heavy labors and a harsh life has been detected from the more than 400 skeletons recovered at the African Burial Ground?
3. What evidence of "African-ness" has been interpreted in the graves at the African Burial Ground?
4. What lessons do you come away with from this article? What does this research teach us about the North's complicity in slavery, the treatment of human beings who were viewed as something less than human, and of the human ability to resist oppression?

Warren R. Perry, Jean Howson, and Barbara A. Bianco, "Summary and Conclusions," *African Burial Ground Final Report: Chapter 15,* pp. 444-455. Copyright © 2006 by Warren R. Perry, Jean Howson, and Barbara A. Bianco. Reprinted with permission.

The African Burial Ground, located in lower Manhattan, New York City and County, proved to be the largest excavated African cemetery from colonial America, and contained the largest sample of human skeletal remains ever studied from any African Diaspora cemetery, anywhere. The total number of graves identified in the excavated portion of the cemetery was 424, and the total number of individuals for whom skeletal remains could be inventoried numbered 419.

The area investigated archaeologically during 1991–1992 represents but a fraction—less than 4%—of the cemetery's estimated original extent. Although the maximum footprint of the New York African Burial Ground is not known, the total area designated a National Historic Landmark in 1993 is approximately seven acres, nearly 305,000 square feet. In contrast, the portion of the archaeological site where burials were excavated encompassed about 9,500 square feet. The site was located on Block 154, bounded on the north by Duane Street, on the south by Reade Street, on the west by Broadway, and on the east by Elk Street. Block 154 is now home to the 290 Broadway Federal Office Building and to a small, publicly accessible part of the cemetery where unexcavated graves are protected. The publicly accessible area is where the re-interment of the excavated remains was held in October 2003. This area memorializes all of the men, women, and children laid to rest at the African Burial Ground.

For much of the colonial period, New York City had a higher proportion of Africans in its population than any other urban center except Charleston, South Carolina. Nearly all African city residents lived under enslavement until after the Revolutionary War. Most would likely have been interred in the African Burial Ground, which was in use until 1795. While no documentation about the cemetery's opening has come to light, the African Burial Ground may have originated as early as the middle of the 17th century and no later than the beginning of the 18th century; it may have contained 15,000 or more graves.

The occupants of the graves that were excavated archaeologically constitute a large sample but cannot be assumed to be statistically representative of the entire cemetery population. Further archaeological excavation that could provide information about the majority of the individuals once interred in the entire African Burial Ground is not likely to be undertaken. Additions to the thin documentary record on the African Burial Ground may someday come to light, but for now, the skeletal and non-skeletal remains from the excavated site provide a unique window on Manhattan's African community during the colonial and early federal periods.

Here we summarize the key archaeological findings presented in this report. We revisit the research agenda and the archaeological methods used to address it. We then review the findings and their implications and identify topics for future study.

ANCESTORS, DESCENDANTS, AND THE RESEARCH AGENDA

Howard University's New York African Burial Ground Project is a bioarchaeological investigation conducted by multidisciplinary teams of archaeologists, bioanthropologists, and historians with expertise on Africa and the African Diaspora. Inaugurated in 1993 under a contract with the U.S. General Services Administration, the Project's investigation of the cemetery is an outcome of public intervention.

Archaeologists, bioanthropologists, and historians are accountable to their peers and professional associations but also to their "ethical" clients—the people whose lives we study and the descendant communities our studies impact. Members of the descendant community and their allies were steadfastly committed to ensuring that the skeletal remains uncovered at the site were treated respectfully and re-interred with dignity, that African-American scholars were appointed to direct the scientific study, and that the realities of enslavement in colonial Manhattan be brought to wide public attention.[1] Howard University's New York African Burial Ground Project owes much to the vigilance of African-Americans and others who wanted to learn the truth about their urban predecessors and to recover a history that has been hidden for centuries. Their intervention was a crucial and deciding factor in how the Project's research agenda was designed and implemented.

Four overarching topics of concern to the descendent community were identified during public hearings. These topics included the cultural and geographical origins of the men, women, and children whose remains were uncovered at the cemetery; the quality of their lives under captivity; the ways they resisted enslavement; and the transformation from African to African-American—in other words, the ways they made new identities and formed new communities.

The language of this report as well as its scope and substance addresses the concerns of the descendent community. The African-American descendant community is multi-dimensional and ideologically heterogeneous. Even so, all felt that the term "slave" was insulting and outdated, and expressed a strong preference for the use of "captive Africans" to describe the individuals laid to rest at the African Burial Ground. The term "captive African" differs substantially from the word "slave." "Captive" used as an adjective rather than a noun avoids denoting the condition under which people lived as if it were their entire identity. As a mark of respect for the African-American community, whose members have the greatest right to speak for the black population of New Amsterdam/New York, the researchers under Howard University's auspices refer to the ancestors with a phrase their descendants have chosen.

---

1   The New York African Burial Ground Project has an Office of Public Education and Interpretation that informs and involves the public in the scientific research. Based in New York City, the office is supported and operated under the auspices of the U.S. General Services Administration. It was headed until September 2005 by Dr. Sherrill Wilson.

LOCATION AND DATING OF THE EXCAVATED SITE

Standard archaeological methods were used to turn the material record into information that might speak to the research agenda. Our first methodological task as historical archaeologists was to sort out the spatial and temporal dimensions of the excavated site. This involved systematizing the excavation and laboratory records, reconstructing the stratigraphic position of each grave, and charting the development of the cemetery during and after its use as a burial ground.

The historic African Burial Ground was situated at the edge of the Collect Pond, on the once-northerly outskirts of New Amsterdam/New York.[2] Farms owned by Africans and Europeans were established in the area in the 1640s. The cemetery may date back to that time. Though graves in the excavated portion may span much of the cemetery's period of use, it is not possible to determine whether the earliest generations of captive Africans who labored in colonial Manhattan were interred within the excavated site.

The excavated site, which was in the northern part of the historic African Burial Ground, overlapped a former fence line that once separated the Van Borsum patent from the Calk Hook Farm; these two parcels of land were granted to Dutchmen during the second half of the 17th century. By the mid 18th century, the Van Borsum patent had come to be known as the "Negroes Burial Ground."

The excavated site, and the cemetery as a whole, was dramatically impacted by several phases of development, civic and private, industrial and residential. The excavated site included a portion of the cemetery that was very densely used and a portion that was relatively thinly used (south and north of the fence line, respectively). It is possible the cemetery grew in area during its early period, and then contracted during the second half of the 18th century as various kinds of development encroached. After 1730, factories such as the Crolius and Remmey pottery; institutions such as a military barracks, an almshouse and a jail; and residential construction including houses, fences, and outbuildings encroached upon the cemetery. With this encroachment, the density of interments and the superimposition of graves within the remaining ground would have increased.

After 1795, intensive, full-scale development covered the area, damaging or destroying some of the graves while bypassing others. Mechanical stripping of the site down to grave shaft outlines or, worse, the tops of coffins themselves resulted in further loss of the original ground surface during the construction of the 290 Broadway Federal Office Building in 1991. This may have obliterated irreplaceable material evidence of early African American burial practices.

Relative and absolute dating of the graves was complicated by the paucity of material culture found in direct association with the skeletal remains and from within the grave shafts. We therefore

---

2 The location near water may have held spiritual significance for some of the African people who used the burial ground. In some coastal West African and West Central African communities, cemeteries were associated with bodies of water where spirits reside (Ferguson 1992, 1999; Medford 2004:150–152, 196; Samford 1994; Thompson 1983:135–38; Thompson and Cornet 198:197–98).

used a combination of factors to establish relative temporal groups. Burials were assigned to one of four groups based on physical features (fence lines and concentrated areas of pottery waste), artifact dating, burial stratigraphy and spatial patterning, and coffin shape.

The Early Group (n = 51) includes adults with four-sided coffins that tapered toward the foot and the children associated with the adults. Many of the graves underlay, and some were truncated by, ensuing burials. Early Group burials seem to pre-date the heavy dumping of kiln waste from nearby potteries, which were in operation by 1730.

Most burials (n = 259) lacked strong evidence for earlier or later assignment, and thus were placed in a Middle Group (n = 199) or Late-Middle Group (n = 60). Stratigraphic relationships, and occasionally artifacts from grave shafts or coffins, were the primary criteria for inclusion in the Late-Middle Group. Since temporal assignments are based on relative factors, the list of burials in the middle groups cannot be considered definitive or absolute. This holds especially for children. The higher proportion of children in the Middle Group probably indicates that some of these children's graves should be assigned to the Late-Middle Group or even to the Late Group. But there is no way to sort out which ones.

Assignment to the Late Group (n=114) was based on location north of the former boundary fence (which apparently stood until the British occupation of the city during the Revolutionary War) and/or the presence of artifacts with *termini post quem* of similar or later dates; in a few cases, stratigraphic relationships to other burials was a determining factor. The removal of the fence is used to date the Late Group.

BURIAL PRACTICES WITHIN THE EXCAVATED SITE

Our second methodological task was to examine patterns in burial practice for the site as a whole as well as within and across each temporal group. What was typical and what was unusual in how African New Yorkers interred their community's dead? Seven aspects of burial practice were examined: coffin use, grave orientation, body position, individual versus co-interment, burial attire, the presence of adornment and other possessions or goods, and grave markers. In addition, we also looked at the cemetery's internal geography. Were the graves of men, women, and children arranged in configurations or distributed evenhandedly? Was there any patterning along gender or generational lines?

Four of these variables showed remarkable homogeneity regardless of the deceased's age, sex, or temporal group assignment. These include coffin use (91.6%), body orientation with the head to the west (97.8%), extended supine body position (100%), and individual burial. Only two coffins contained more than one individual, and relatively few grave shafts were shared.

We think shrouding of the dead may also have been typical. Small, copper-alloy straight pins with wire-wound heads were among the most numerous artifacts recovered in direct association with the deceased—only coffin remains outnumbered pins. Straight pins were observed in and/or recovered from half of the burials. In the absence of cloth or any evidence for street clothes, winding sheets or shrouds without durable fasteners may reasonably be inferred.

The case for grave markers as a typical burial practice is unclear. Grave markers were observed in the southwest corner of the excavated site, an area where the original ground surface was still intact. Grave markers took the form of smooth stone cobbles (arranged on the ground in lines and in one case an arc, so as to demarcate a grave or possibly groups of graves) and of rectangular stone slabs (placed vertically at the heads of the graves). Since such markers were found in the one area where their preservation was possible, we think it is likely that markers were used elsewhere at the cemetery. It is likely that a vertical wood post attached to the headboard of a coffin marked a grave in the northern part of the site; presumably, the post extended above the ground.

Relatively few individuals appear to have been buried in street clothing (indicated by the types and locations of buttons and cuff links directly associated with the skeletal remains). Personal adornment and other goods were also unusual. Among the items recovered were glass beads (nine of which were likely manufactured in western Africa); finger rings and metal jewelry; and coins, shells, pipes, and unique objects such as a small ceramic ball with an embossed metal band. It is also possible that floral tributes had been placed in a few of the graves.

Most burials were placed within a foot or two of neighboring graves but the internal geography of the excavated site was not uniform. In addition to shared grave shafts, there were several locations where burials appeared either to have been clustered together or placed in possible rows.

The shared or possible shared grave shafts (n = 26) held two (but sometimes three) individuals, typically infants or young children (n = 11) or an infant or a child with an adult (n = 12 or 13). In some cases, the individuals in shared or possible shared grave shafts appear to have been interred at the same time; in other cases there may have been an interval after which a second burial was placed in a grave shaft already in use.

Burial clusters encompassed individuals from different age groups (infants and young children interred near adults) as well as child burials and, occasionally, pairs of adults. Possible rows of graves (aligned roughly north-to-south) were easiest to discern in the northern part of the site, although some of these apparent rows may have extended all the way to the site's southern edge.

In the northern part of the site, where graves were not as crowded as elsewhere, burial practices as well as the demographic profile were somewhat distinct. There was a preponderance of men, and almost all of the coffin-less burials were here. Clothing fasteners were more frequent, as were goods such as coins, knives, and pipes. We think that burial practices in this area reflect both a shorter period of use and a response to the demographic displacement and social privation that accompanied the Revolutionary War. There was a large influx of fugitive Africans during the British occupation, followed by a mass exodus after the British troops decamped. With the exception of the northern part of the site, the graves of men, women, and children were distributed more or less evenly across the excavated space.

Differences in burial practices for men and women were not observed. While men were more likely than women to have been buried without coffins, we attribute this to the increased presence of men during the Revolutionary War. Buttons were more typically associated with men, but since working women's clothing from that era seldom fastened with buttons, it is not possible to state that men were more likely to be buried in street clothes. Pollen representing possible floral tributes was identified with more men than women but the sample is too small to generalize from. The two south-headed burials for which sex could be determined held women; the east-headed burials held either men or children.

Burial practices for adults and children differed in some ways. All children had coffins, (except for one infant who was buried in the arms of a woman), even in the northern part of the site where numerous adults had none. The shapes of children's coffins appear to have varied throughout the site's entire time span; in contrast, adult coffins were more uniform once the shoulder-shaped variety was adopted (from the Middle Group on). One possible explanation is that children's coffins were more likely to be made by families rather than purchased. Pins are present in all age groups but they were observed in a higher percentage of children's graves than adults' graves. Many adults had pins on the cranium only, which was much less common proportionally for children. Some infants had pins along their entire bodies, and a purely functional explanation is unlikely. It is possible pins had a special role in the ritual preparation of the bodies of youngsters.

Buttons were not found with children, but, as was the case with women, some pins may have fastened children's clothes. Adornment was just as likely to be found on children as on women (beads and rings) and men (decorative buttons and cuff links). Glass beads, a silver pendent, and a glass and metal filigree ornament were recovered with young children and infants. Unlike adults, children could not have obtained adornments on their own; children's adornments were gifts from adults, whether bestowed in life or at death.

INDIVIDUALS AND COMMUNITIES

Variation in burial practice at a public cemetery in use for a century or more is not unexpected, particularly in a cemetery serving an urban community that continually absorbed newcomers from a wide range of cultures and places. Yet the scope of variation at the African Burial Ground was narrow. Viewed from the excavated site, a typical or "proper" burial in African New Amsterdam/New York entailed a coffin large enough to hold a supine, extended body that was probably covered with a shroud and placed head-to-west in a grave of its own.

We had assumed that a "proper" burial would have multiple configurations because no documentary evidence about municipal or outsider oversight of the cemetery came to light. Municipal codes enacted during the 1720s and 1730s specified the time and size of black funerals but carried no stipulations about coffin use, grave orientation, burial attire, or the positioning of the corpse. No evidence that white New Yorkers played a role at the gravesides in the African Burial Ground has been found.

It seems, however, that black New Yorkers may have arrived at a provisional consensus about how to deal with death early on.[3] The consistency in the archaeological record suggests that a model of a proper burial was in place by the time the graves in the excavated portion of the cemetery had been interred. Conformity can be seen in the context of the individual's relationship to family and to the larger community. Funerals were communal and public expressions of loss, transformation, and restoration, and the cemetery provided3 a space where such rituals could help to forge a developing African American identity.

It is clear, though, that the concept of a proper burial was elastic enough to accommodate the expression of individuality. Consider, for example, four distinctive interments in the excavated portion of the African Burial Ground. Each of the individuals (in Burials 340, 22, 101, and 147, one from each of our temporal groups), had a coffin, was probably shrouded, had been laid with the head to the west, and was in a grave of his or her own. Each also had skeletal indicators of work, illness, or nutritional stress that remind us of their likely common lot as captive laborers in an 18th-century city.[4] Each, however, was buried with distinctive items.

Burial 340, an Early Group grave of a woman between thirty-nine and sixty-four years old, was buried with an African-style strand of beads around her waist. Her molecular genetic affinities point to West Africa, and her incisors were modified, suggesting African nativity—but skeletal evidence suggests a later life of hard labor and possible nutritional stress. Though skeletal preservation was generally poor, the bones showed several pathologies, including scarring on the femurs where the muscles attached and hypertrophy (the enlargement of an area of bone probably caused by repeated stress) on the scapulae and ulnae (shoulders and lower arms). Moderate osteoarthritis affected the hip and the vertebrae of the neck and lower back, and there was possible evidence of anemia in the cranial bone.[4]

This woman's distinctive African-style adornment seems to bespeak her commitment to her cultural ancestry.[5] Women's waist beads, associated as they are with femininity, sexuality, and female friendship, are recognizable as a form of adornment that had a wide geographical spread in western and central Africa.

---

3 The author thanks Grey Gundaker for articulating the idea of a "provisional consensus" with reference to burial practices.

4 The Howard University Skeletal Biology Team provided information on skeletal pathologies and on genetic and chemical analyses.

5 Although there appears to have been a substantial break in the continuity of waist bead wearing in the African Diaspora, waist beads have in recent years become fashionable among some African-descended women in the United States as a way of reclaiming and proclaiming their African identities. A similar practice may be the African-American "nation sack," a bundle or bag of varied materials worn on a string around a woman's waist. A nation sack is intended to protect the wearer rather than to ornament her. It worn beneath the clothing and is seen only occasionally by close female kin, never by men.

Burial 22, a Middle Group grave of a child between two-and-a-half and four-and-a-half years old, was found with a shell (clam, of a species native to New York waters) located above the left collarbone. Perhaps the shell was placed in the coffin by mourners for its association with water, to mark the ritual transformation of the child's status via an analogy between crossing through water and crossing from life to death. The use of shells in this manner is known from Africa and the African Diaspora. The child in Burial 22 was probably born in New York, and strontium isotope levels measured in the teeth support this assumption, falling within the narrow range of the other young children in the sample tested. During his or her short life, the child suffered from an infection or an injury that left scars on the bones of the lower and upper limbs.

The shouldered coffin that held the child straddled two underlying adult burials, one of a woman (Burial 46) and the other of a probable man (Burial 29). The child and the adults were part of a cluster of graves bordered by a row of white cobblestones, apparently water-smoothed rocks. This style of grave marking has been observed throughout the African Diaspora over a broad temporal span. The relationship of the child to others in the community probably guided the placement of the grave within this cluster.

Burial 101, of a man in his early thirties, was assigned to the Late-Middle Group. Lead levels in his teeth were consistent with African birth, while strontium isotope levels overlapped the ranges of both American and African birth. Preservation of the skeleton was excellent, and several pathologies were observed, including bone scarring due to inflammation from bacterial infection or injury on the cranium and legs. The muscle attachments at the man's elbows were enlarged from stress, mild to severe arthritis affected his joints, layers of his teeth indicated that he experienced nutritional stress in childhood, and cavities were severe (he probably had abscesses and perhaps infections of the surrounding bone). The tibiae were malformed in a way called "saber shin," suggesting he had yaws.

This man's coffin lid was decorated with a heart-shaped design formed of tinned or silvered iron tacks with an interior pattern formed of smaller tacks.[6] Heart-shaped decorations may not have evoked the same meanings for Africans as for Europeans. The coffin design may have called to mind the Sankofa symbol that originated with the Akan people of Ghana and the Ivory Coast; the symbol refers to of the need to remember one's ancestors.[7] If the mourners who interred the man

---

6   Iron tacks may have been chosen for this coffin based on the symbolic importance of iron in some African cultures (Puckett 1926:218, Thompson 1983:52–61) and in African-American conjuration (Puckett 1926:208, 230, 237, 252, 277, 478).

7   James Denbow offers another interpretation of the Sankofa/heart shape. His study of heart-shaped designs on tombstones dating to the early 20th century in the Loango coast of West Central Africa found that the "heart" was perceived as the location of "the soul of the inner body, called *mwela* [...] manifested physically by the breath" (Denbow 1999:412). Thus, Denbow saw the heart shape as representing the soul of the deceased. Perhaps the symbol was recognized (though differently) by both West and West-Central Africans. As Fennell (2003:23–24) noted, symbols become widespread through cultural contact, and cultures assign nuances of encoded meaning to them. However, Denbow also cites earlier sources that considered the soul to be contained in the head, and represented heads as "cruciform and helioform" (Denbow

in Burial 101 viewed the heart-shaped decoration as a Sankofa symbol, then the design on the coffin lid would provide evidence of the portability of expressive culture and its importance to cultural survival. The multivalence of a familiar sign provided the opportunity to incorporate an African symbol into a funeral observance.

Figure 1: One Version of the West African Sankofa symbol. Source: Macdonald (2001).

Burial 147, one of the Late Group graves, held the remains of one of the oldest individuals in the excavated sample, a man between fifty-five and sixty-five years old when he died. His arm and leg bones had scarring from infection or injury, and the sites of muscle attachments were enlarged from repeated stress. Moderate to severe osteoarthritis affected all of the major joint complexes and the spine. Porous bones of the cranium and eye orbits suggested nutritional stress in childhood, possibly anemia, and childhood nutritional deficiencies were also recorded in his teeth (hypoplasias).

The man was buried with a cluster of small copper-alloy wire rings between his upper right arm and chest. Pins that were aligned precisely along his right upper arm indicated that cloth may have been attached in that location, possibly enclosing the rings—perhaps an armband or underarm pouch. The rings may have been part of a conjuring bundle of some kind, which would have been concealed on his person in life. This elderly man may have had powers that were offered to or sought out by others in the community. His conjuring apparatus went with him to the grave, perhaps pointing to a close association of the items themselves with the practitioner. The location of the burial, in the northern part of the cemetery, suggests that he died during or after the Revolution, and it is possible he was one of the many refugees who came to the city during the war.

ANCESTORS, CULTURAL ROOTS, AND THE TRANSFORMATION OF AFRICAN TO AFRICAN AMERICAN IDENTITIES

Characteristic of today's African American sensibility is the apparently straightforward query, "Who are your people?" This question asks both "Where did you come from?" and "How do we relate to one another?" The abhorrent circumstances under which people were separated from their families and homelands complicates the search for origins and cultural roots of African-descendant people throughout the Diaspora. The multidisciplinary African Burial Ground Project has developed new

---

1999:413). The "heart" as a two-lobed, pointed-base figure does not necessarily represent the concept as it would have been expressed in the 18th century Loango region.

lines of data, and a host of questions, about the origins of early African New Yorkers, through historical research, preliminary genetic and craniometric data, and archaeological analysis.

As noted, the project's History Report (Medford 2004) highlights the scope of the trade in captives and the range of societies from which the burial ground population derived. The Skeletal Biology Report (Blakey and Rankin-Hill 2004) has examined the physical remains of the ancestors for indications of their places of origin. Their research found a range of probable birthplaces, from the continent of Africa to the Caribbean to New York. The archaeology has been less specific in its investigation of roots. But what we do observe in a number of instances is that even if today we cannot read specific places in Africa from the material record, we can read that people were declaring to one another that their people were African.

Although none of the objects associated with distinctive burials precisely answers the question of origins, the mobilization of material culture is a thread that appears to run through the temporal groups. It would not be surprising if materials and associations that held particular significance in Africa continued to be important to African people in New York. The deceased may have been people newly captured from Africa (possibly in Burials 340 and 101), a child born into captivity in New York (Burial 22), or second- or third-generation African-Americans whose forbears maintained and transmitted African cultural practices despite, or as a respite from, the brutality of their lives in North America (the elderly man in Burial 147). The material from these graves clearly points out that at least some of the African people of 18th-century New York remembered and honored their ancestral traditions.

FUTURE RESEARCH

The archaeological excavation of the New York African Burial Ground has opened a window on how Africans under slavery cared for their dead in a key center of colonial America's urban north. It makes sense, then, to design research agendas around the findings the burial ground's archaeological record has brought to light. Future research might focus more deeply on how African New Yorkers used the burial ground for community purposes of their own. Several lines of investigation show promise of providing a fuller grasp of the cemetery as a setting for reshaping social ties within and across generations:

1. The connections among individuals interred in close proximity, be it within the same grave shaft or within a burial cluster. Genetic analysis of the remains might reveal kinship or home-place ties between the individuals in these graves. Such information, if coupled with data on nutrition,

disease, and physical trauma, might yield a more fine-grained picture of the biocultural experiences that marked kin, compatriots, or friends whose graves were clustered together.[8]

2. Rural-to-urban migration during the Revolutionary War and its immediate aftermath. During the 1700s, the promise of freedom pulled Africans from near and far to New York City, but the movement of blacks into Manhattan accelerated during the British occupation. A systematic look at documentation relevant to Africans on the move after 1776, along with a close examination of the bioskeletal signatures of Late Group burials, might furnish insights into the social/regional roots of the burial patterns and material culture in the northern part of the cemetery.

3. The social and material production of a "proper" burial in the independent black churches that provided burial facilities after the African Burial Ground had closed. How was the "proper" burial of the 17th/18th century reconfigured in the liturgies and in the burial yards and vaults of the city's 19th century black churches? Were the accouterments, logistics, and divisions of labor that comprised a "proper" burial altered during periods of heightened social suffering, such as the yellow fever or cholera years? Using the African Burial Ground as a baseline might offer a more sophisticated grasp of how a rite of passage is remade when the organizing structures in the world around it have changed.

We suggest a new look at one of the key stories of early African American history in New York, the founding of the A.M.E. Zion and St. Philip's Churches. It should make a difference if one imagines, as we do, that the African Burial Ground provided an institutional basis as well as founding personnel for the churches. The African Methodist and Episcopal churches might have had a century and a half worth of African and then African-American religious philosophy and ritual practice upon which to build.

More generally, the information obtained from the African Burial Ground archaeological investigation adds significantly to an ever-growing database on the historic material culture of the African Diaspora. It is hoped that the findings reported here will be useful to a large research community. For example, changing ritual practices of African descendant people and the symbolic dimensions of their material culture should continue to be interrogated through African eyes. Symbols, especially those used by oppressed populations, are not necessarily accessible to outsiders; the multivalent aspect of symbolic practices enables divergent meanings to be cloaked. Historical archaeologists, with input from historians, anthropologists, and folklorists, continually explore new ways to recognize and interpret symbols used by African-Americans. Fresh examination of objects and their associations should continue to be fruitful, and it is hoped that items recovered at the African Burial Ground will become part of this broader project.

---

8 We assume that African people buried at the cemetery formed families—quite simply, the birth of children would have begun families, and however strained the logistics of maintaining ties, family relationships would have built exponentially.

The archaeological data from the New York African Burial Ground should continue to be analyzed within a worldwide context. This site did not exist in a historical, geographic, or cultural vacuum. As important as the African Burial Ground is, the excavated site offers but a glimpse of African life in a cosmopolitan center of colonial American. The burial ground adds to a growing multidimensional perspective Africans during the 17th and 18th centuries, but it bears closer comparison to other sites in Africa, North and South America, and the Caribbean.

The African Burial Ground will not be forgotten again. This is due as much to the keen interest of African descendants in their community's material past as to the insights and data compiled here. The research offers new avenues for teaching and learning about the people of the African Diaspora and for hearing their long-stifled voices. We hope this report, along with the Skeletal Biology Report and the History Report, will inspire and educate both academics and the public. We also hope to engage students, colleagues, and the public in a broader examination of the African-American past and to create inclusive histories that transform our views of the past, the present, and the future. Creating inclusive histories involves breaking down boundaries between the academy and African-American descendant communities so that we all can learn from oral history, apply African-American perspectives on material culture, and create memorials that honor the long history of the African Diaspora.

EPILOGUE

Warren R. Perry

The African Burial Ground has become a symbol of the strength, spirit, and agency of African descendant people in New York over nearly four centuries of exploitation and inequality. The site has attracted tens of thousands of visitors and is the focus of deeply felt reverence by many people in the United States, Africa and throughout the African Diaspora.

The Rites of Ancestral Return culminated in New York City on Friday, October 3 and Saturday, October 4, 2003. Four individual coffins, representing the men, women, boys, and girls among the ancestors, were brought in a procession up Broadway to the African Burial Ground Memorial Site. The event was both a funeral and a celebration, and the ceremonies were exhilarating as well as profoundly solemn. An overnight vigil marked the ancestors' last hours away from their rightful resting place.

Dr. Michael Blakey and the Institute for Historical Biology at the College of William and Mary, which he now heads, invited African Burial Ground Project staff and researchers to attend a Friday night reception in the Presidential Suite at the Millennium Hilton Hotel. Following this event, several members of the Howard University research teams returned to the site to pay final respects to the ancestors before the next day's re-interment ceremonies.

It was nearing midnight when we arrived at the memorial site. It had been a long and emotionally charged day, but each of us felt drawn to spend a last few personal moments with the ancestors, remembering them not as the subjects of scientific research but as living people who had endured lives of pain and struggle, love and sadness, strength and meaning.

Most of the day's attendees had left by this time. Among those who remained were several members of the descendant community who had spoken out and advocated for the ancestors since the early 1990s, among them Queen Mother Delois Blakely, Queen Mother Jordan, and the Chief Alagba Egunfemi Adegbolola. The night had gone chill and the spotlights had gone out, but the descendants that remained seemed to draw light and heat and sustenance from the presence of the once-forgotten ones who were returning to their rightful place.

We offered our farewell to the ancestors and turned to leave, passing by the memorial site and the platform on which many of the descendants still clustered. As we walked up Elk Street, a young man ran up from behind. Mother Blakely had sent him to ask for elders for the naming ceremony. "Would we come back to participate?" the young man asked.

Our first impulse was to offer a polite excuse and continue on. It was cold, we were tired, and the morning's observances were but a few hours away. But the voices of the ancestors resounded in our heads:

Were we not cold?
Were we not tired?
Did we not wish for home and rest?

We could not refuse this summons, on the eve of their reburial, and we returned to the site, where Dr. Michael Blakey, as the project's Scientific Director, was to be named in the African tradition. We spoke in low voices, which could not have been overheard: "I am cold," and at that moment a blanket was offered; "I am tired," and a chair appeared almost from thin air. We felt as though the ancestors had acknowledged our sincerity in returning to the vigil and favored us with respite from our discomforts.

It has been a tremendous privilege to work for the African Burial Ground Project. "Privilege," in this case, is not to be confused with "ease." In many ways it has been one of the most difficult projects we will ever conduct. It was also one of the most spiritually rewarding. We have been blessed to be offered the opportunity to share a fraction of the ancestors' experiences: the hard work, the setbacks, the pain of loss. We also have been blessed by the strength and sense of purpose that comes from building a cadre of committed workers. Much as the ancestors built new social networks, cultures, and identities for themselves, the people who have worked and fought for the African Burial Ground have shared deep bonds. The ancestors inspired us to keep moving forward through our tribulations and to keep in mind that our commitment was to honor their courage, strength, and dignity.

American Refugees

Marion Blackburn

EDITOR'S INTRODUCTION

I've been hearing about the Underground Railroad since grade school. This clandestine escape path out of the servitude in the South to the North and ultimately freedom in Canada brings up images of terrified African natives being slowly shepherded north by caring white abolitionists. The image is evocative, indeed, and it really did happen. I did not know, however, that many African natives resisted and escaped slavery in the South essentially on the basis of their own will and skills and ended up not in the North but in the South, in a vast and largely inhospitable place called the Dismal Swamp, located in Virginia and North Carolina. There, these escaped African captives found a place whose reputation was so bad, even the economic incentive to bring them back to captivity was not enough, allowing hundreds, even thousands, to carve out a life in freedom not that far from where they had escaped and where many of their brothers and sisters continued to languish in slavery. These people found habitable high ground in the swamp and carved out communities, not of escaped slaves, but of free people. They left behind quiet traces of their survival in the swamp in the form of house remains, smoking pipe fragments, broken ceramics, and rusted tools. In recovering these traces, the long-term archaeological project directed by Dan Sayers and his students is revealing the nature of the lives of these people who resisted captivity, escaped servitude, and emerged as free people.

POINTS TO PONDER

1. Why were escaped African captives relatively safe in the region called the Great Dismal Swamp?
2. How are the communities of the Great Dismal Swamp emblematic of resistance to captivity?
3. What kinds of evidence has archaeology revealed of the lives of the inhabitants of the Great Dismal Swamp?
4. What are the lessons of the Great Dismal Swamp archaeological excavations carried out by Dan Sayers and his students?

Marion Blackburn, "American Refugees," *Archaeology*, vol. 64, no. 5, pp. 49-50, 52, 54, 56, 58. Copyright © 2011 by Archaeological Institute of America. Reprinted with permission.

Thousands of escaped slaves made a new life in one of the world's most unwelcoming places—unwelcoming places—the Great Dismal Swamp, full of sink holes, thorns, snakes, bears and bugs—for a chance at self-determination.

thread my legs into snake guards—canvas chaps with hard plastic shin covers that hook to my jeans. Standing beside a rented van, I see the same scenery all around—thick woods scalloped by broom straw and river cane, I silently lace muck boots, don an expedition hat, heft a backpack, and join a small group of students preparing to hike into the heart of the Great Dismal Swamp. I ask the person standing next to me if the snake guards stay on all day. I get a look that I interpret as, "Are you kidding?" I've doused myself with bug spray, pushed my socks into my boots, and stowed a half-liter of water in my bag, along with crackers and raisins I later realize won't get me through the day's hike.

The Great Dismal Swamp spans about 200 square miles of North Carolina and Virginia, down from 2,000, due in part to an aggressive canal project that divided and drained it by 1805. Despite that development and all that has come since, it lives up to its name—unsettling, isolated, and uncivilized. As we head out, American University graduate student Cynthia Goode invites me to stick close. "I know where the deep holes are," she says.

The place is so inhospitable that when it was surveyed in 1728, Col. William Byrd II, a commissioner charged with setting a boundary between North Carolina and Virginia, wrote, "We found the ground moist and trembling under our feet like a quagmire, insomuch that it was an easy matter to run a ten foot pole up to the head in it, without exerting any uncommon strength to do it," He added, "Never was rum, that cordial of life, found more necessary than it was in this dirty place."

We set off from a clearing within the Great Dismal Swamp National Wildlife Refuge, about 45 minutes from its main entrance in Suffolk, Virginia. We are going to an interior site so remote that it's impossible to find without an experienced guide like American University anthropologist Daniel Sayers. He's spent most of the past eight years in this place, searching one shovelful of dirt at a time for the rare traces of escaped slaves who made homes in this unforgiving place. For these fugitive slaves, known as maroons, facing the Dismal's heat, quicksand, bugs, snakes, and bears was a reasonable price for a chance at freedom and self-determination.

Maroons appear wherever slavery has existed—such as in the Caribbean and South America. The provenance of the term "maroon" is unclear. Some trace it to the Spanish word *cimarrón*, which means "wild" or "runaway slave," but recent scholarship shows it may have derived from a Spanish translation of an ancient Arawak or Taino word meaning "fierce" and "wild." In the American South, maroons often hid in swamps to evade the trained dogs, armed bands of angry whites, and even soldiers who pursued them. The isolation of these communities—the obscurity on which they depended—often means they have been overlooked by historians.

The Great Dismal Swamp was long such a sanctuary. Native Americans found refuge here after Europeans arrived. Soon after, maroons made their way to the same high and dry areas, known as mesic islands, that are found far from the swamp's marshy edges. The islands' unmatched natural defense—surrounded by several boggy miles—allowed complex refugee communities to arise here, with sustainable agriculture, commerce, and cultural arts, Sayers says. The escaped slaves threw off captivity and created a self-reliant subsistence society using available materials. Starting with the expansion of slavery after 1660 and continuing until the mid-1800s, the swamp was a parallel world for escapees, where maroons could live freely in a state Sayers calls "self-emancipation"—a difficult life, but a free one,

"There were hardships," says Sayers. "But working in the brutal cotton fields with overseers, not to mention life after the day's labors—compared to this? You may have to work for five hours to grow food, but there was really a self-reliant ethos."

Sayers and Austin often have only changes in soil color to help them identify habitation sites from the Great Dismal Swamp's refugee community.

While accounts from the time agree that the swamp hid hundreds or even thousands of escaped slaves, they lack clear information about their daily life and social structures. Here's where the Great Dismal Swamp Landscape Study, as the overall project is known, will help.

A narrow footbridge, across a nineteenth-century canal, tinkles with the gentle sound of bells to scare off bears. We cross the bridge, following a route that lies underwater for much of the year. Soon we are up to our knees in muck. We encounter insects, thorny vines, brush, and brambles so thick that even after weeks of use this field season, the path still needs to be cleared by machete. After about 2,000 feet, the trail dries and the land gradually rises. We are close to one of the raised, interior islands, with up to 20 acres of clearings and wooded areas.

Sayers, a tall man with long hair and a rugged, handsome face, has explored the Dismal since 2003, alone or with small teams of students and archaeologists, searching for traces left by the maroons. These days, he's fully at home here, describing landmarks and distances as if talking about his backyard. He's unfazed by the heat and heavy gear, and walks among the excavation squares with a measured, unhurried pace. Because he is the first to excavate in the modern swamp, it has taken time to find sites, soil features, and artifacts. Last year he received a $200,000 "We the People" award from the National Endowment for the Humanities that has allowed him to dig deeper, enlarge his area of study, and conduct soil tests.

Some distance through the woods, we arrive at one of Sayers' earliest study areas, a one-and-a-half acre area he calls the "grotto." Except for the bugs, it's easy to forget I'm in a swamp. The ground is crunchy with dead leaves and free of brush tangles. A deer passes, then bounds away. With a sweep of his arm Sayers points out where, in 2004, he found a semicircle of 83 round postholes. About three inches below the surface, they likely represented a structure erected by Native Americans in the very early historical period (ca. 1600-1650). He also found lead shot, knife-cut bone, and several stone artifacts. "I thought 'Okay, we know this is here, let's expand on it'" he says. "You have all this documentation pointing to the fact that potentially thousands of people went in there prior to 1800, even some outcast or criminalized Europeans."

On the other side of the clearing he indicates the location of a fire pit and at least one cabin, the latter probably dating to the second half of the seventeenth century. It was probably built by refugee slaves, but the grotto, like most of the swamp, was home to a succession of communities over the centuries. Here, Sayers found the partial footprint of another cabin that appears to have been set using round posts. A square posthole, which would have been made after European contact, also appears on the site. Between the posts he found evidence of fill, likely from logs placed between them. During more than a year of extensive work at the grotto, he found evidence of 150 features representing at least five cabins, including one L-shaped section of a structure—a doorway and outer wall. These indicate a thriving maroon community, he believes. Because the site is so remote, it remained largely undisturbed except for wildlife activity. The architectural features, when exposed, appear as dark shapes against the orange clay soil layer beneath a loose covering of leaves, organic debris, and peat. A technique called optically stimulated luminescence dating, which determines when sand was last exposed to natural light, dates the site to sometime between 1600 and 1759. "We know no one else was out here—there's no other explanation for who's building cabins except what the documents are indicating, which is that a lot of people fled here," Sayers says. Indeed, Byrd's 1728 survey team came across an African-American family who claimed to be free (which Byrd doubted). Another writer, J.F.D. Smyth, wrote, "Run-away negroes have resided in these places for twelve, twenty, or thirty years and upwards, subsisting themselves in the swamp upon corn, hogs, and fowls that they raised on some of the spots not perpetually under water, nor subject to be flooded, as forty-nine parts out of fifty are; and on such spots they have erected habitations, and cleared small fields around them."

We walk along a gentle rise in the clearing to this years excavation area, which Sayers calls the "crest." About a dozen students crouch over one-meter squares with trowels, buckets, and brushes. They are removing soil one centimeter at a time and sifting it through a double layer of screens to capture small artifacts. The process is critical for these maroon sites, which typically have few artifacts. No natural rocks are present in the swamp and maroons scoured the area for anything leftover from previous inhabitants.

Cynthia Goode, the doctoral student who guided me in with the team, opens a bag containing her finds from the previous day, taken from a depth of about three centimeters. An irregular lump about the size of a fingernail is a piece of handmade ceramic and a thin piece of light-colored stone is a quartzite flake created during tool-making. There's also a piece of lead shot and an iron nail covered in corrosion. For this site, it's quite a haul, Goode chose American University because of the Dismal Swamp project and hopes to continue it by excavating outside the swamp in now-developed areas, where logging began sometime around 1800 when the canal was built, an act that changed the dynamics of maroon and swamp life forever.

"We're trying to figure out to what extent the maroons may have communicated with these 'edge' groups" she says. The goal is "testing the model of maroon settlement in areas that are outside the swamp, where slaves would have been logging."

In a nearby area called the "north plateau," graduate student Jordan Riccio is working on a telling indentation. It appears that a round post sat here in a hole lined with ancient Native American ceramic pieces, of the Croaker Landing style (1200-800 B.C.). Under normal circumstances, these pieces would be far deeper in the soil; their presence so near the surface indicates they were found and reused by later residents, probably maroons. Nearby, a dark soil patch indicates a trench between what appears to be more round postholes. Sayers has seen such trenches between posts throughout the excavation. It's possible Native Americans and maroons both used trenches to stabilize posts for what were likely wattle-and-daub houses.

Riccio has exposed two ceramic pieces aligned with the posthole. One is larger than a golf ball, a significant size for the site. The day after my visit, they find white clay tobacco pipe pieces here. But over-all, the scarcity and small size of the artifacts attest to the nonmaterialistic nature of the settlements and form a significant pillar of Sayers' theories about maroon culture. An escaped slave would have been aware that there was little chance of avoiding recapture once he or she left the swamp to acquire supplies. Sayers believes the maroons developed a sense of pride and self-containment by resisting the exterior world's values and materialistic culture.

"How that translates on the ground is that we're not going to find many outside-world objects," he says. "The materials I expect to find are those available in the swamp, a lot of organic materials, animal byproducts, plants, or baskets, [though] I haven't found much preserved wood. On the flip side, the indigenous Americans had used these areas for thousands of years, so there was some mining for stuff that was already there." Once they had these items, Sayers says, they used and reused them until almost nothing remained. Even flakes of stone that resulted from sharpening a prehistoric point would be used, as would any man-made object. For example, excavations have uncovered reused pieces of lead shot, gun flint, glass, and chipped stone, as well as a reworked projectile point. This consistent reuse of materials is another distinction of the site.

In the Dismal, traces of settlement are ephemeral. "It could reflect shortness of time of use. These people had such a low-impact footprint, it's just not the kind of feature that historical archaeologists are used to seeing," Sayers says, "I've worked on sites throughout the country and this really is unique. Some might find it boring——here's a collection of stuff and it's all the size of a penny——but the signature makes it fascinating because it's so connected with their community and how they ran things.

"If they found a bottle, and it broke, they are going to use the pieces. You're not going to have a whole bottle thrown into a pit. If they acquire a white clay pipe, and a chip comes off the bowl, they're going to use it. Same if the stem breaks." The scarcity of artifacts means that excavations will remain problematic and interpretation will depend on a larger context, "The Dismal Swamp is acidic and wet," says Warren Perry, anthropologist and director of the Archaeology Laboratory for African and African Diaspora Studies at Central Connecticut State University. Maroons, Perry adds, "are in these places so people don't find them. You're going to have limited artifacts. People aren't going to build big towns, because that will get you caught. In maroon sites in Jamaica, there's a lot more material, but still not a bunch." "We see sites themselves as artifacts," he continues. "The location and the distribution of these sites across the landscapes begin to tell us something."

Sayers believes maroon culture underwent significant changes after the canal projects began, as well as commerce outside it. The Dismal Swamp Canal Company incorporated in 1784, and laborers were hired freedmen as well as slaves commissioned from landowners so that work could begin in 1793. The next 12 years brought changes to the maroon communities, as some people assumed jobs on the canal and moved away. Other canal laborers may have temporarily lived in maroon settlements. Sayers and others believe that from this time forward, contact between maroons and the outside world increased. As more logging for cypress shingles took place in the swamp, maroons may have exchanged work for goods with companies that overlooked their fugitive status. Eventually the communities dwindled, so that after the Civil War, they were mostly deserted. A few hermits, living in the occasional cabin, may have remained.

What they left behind—the nails, glass fragments, and shadow cabin outlines—will lead to a fuller picture of this unique American resistance movement. Specifically, this work might be able to tell us more about how the escaped slaves cooperated with their Native American swamp neighbors, how they fought off armed militias that came searching for them, and how they managed to survive for decades in this mysterious place.

The Great Dismal Swamp Landscape Study will change the way we think about runaway slave culture in the South—and around the world. Traditionally, little work has been done on these maroon swamp communities, but they are pervasive in the region; New Orleans and the swamps of Alabama, Florida, Georgia, and South Carolina have signs of maroon life. Yet they have been largely excluded from study, in part because they are difficult to reach and the artifacts so scarce. Such communities have been much better examined around the world; and their historical significance noted. For instance, in Jamaica in 1740, the British freed maroons and gave them 2,500 acres, as long as they returned future escaped slaves. Revolutionary maroons in Haiti established a nation in 1804, and maroons in Suriname gained sovereign status in the 1800s after attacking nearby plantations.

While the American maroons never succeeded in claiming freedom for themselves in that way, there are commonalities with other refugees around the world, such as establishing a resistance community in thick jungles, tugged terrains, and difficult surroundings. "This project is fitting into that global view," Sayers says, "But in North America, there's not as much discussion of maroons. You talk about runaways, but it's fragmented." For instance, the Underground Railroad was a maroon movement, but is often considered apart from these other maroon efforts. It's both glorified and separated. Sayers asserts that this is because of the involvement of benevolent white people. "We need to start thinking of processes such as the Underground Railroad as part of this global marron-age," he says. Sojourner Truth, Frederick Douglass, and Harriet Tubman should be considered key maroon figures. As a step in connecting them, the Dismal became the first National Wildlife Refuge to be officially designated a link in the "Underground Railroad Network to Freedom" in 2003. A new public exhibit at the refuge is expected to open in fall 2011.

"The Underground Railroad is lauded, while maroons remain nameless fugitives," Sayers says. "In the traditional view, it's the flight that's important, not the lives that maroons led after flight."

According to Perry, Sayers' work will debunk misconceptions about slavery—specifically that resistance was limited or that slaves only escaped with the help of benevolent whites. Instead, he says, refugee communities existed throughout the region. "We have to get away from the idea that they are few and far between," Perry says. "It's much more prevalent than we thought."

While this dig and others to come could eventually give us a better idea of the lives of maroons, much will remain a mystery. Sayers says he's yet to find descendants of these swamp dwellers, who may know the names or stories of some refugees. Their survival depended on their ability to disappear, so our understanding of them may always be partial, hidden by the extraordinary—and welcoming—secrecy of the Dismal.

In Front of the Mirror

Native Americans and Academic Archaeology

Dorothy Lippert

EDITOR'S INTRODUCTION

The relationship between Native Americans and North American archaeologists is often a tense one. The vast majority of academic archaeologists who focus on native sites are not, themselves, native people. As a result, and given the sad history of exploitation suffered by native people, many Native Americans view archaeology as yet another variety of exploitation and archaeologists as a category of people who are exploiters. Archaeologists today have more than a little to make up for over the often thoughtless actions of archaeologists of the past. Nevertheless, archaeology can be a valuable tool for native people in helping to tell the stories of the aboriginal people of North America. Fortunately, some Native Americans have recognized the potential of archaeological research as an important way to supplement and complement their oral histories and some of those people have become archaeologists themselves, illuminating the story of their own ancestors. Dorothy Lippert is one of these scholars and here tells the story of her journey to become an archaeologist of her own people.

POINTS TO PONDER

1. Why do so many Native Americans mistrust archaeologists?
2. How does Dorothy Lippert explain the potential of archaeology to skeptical Native Americans?
3. What does Lippert mean when she refers to a "voice made of bone"?
4. What are the lessons of Dorothy Lippert's journey to become an archaeologist?

The role of Native Americans within the world of academic archaeology is currently undergoing a great deal of change and revitalization. In part due to legally directed consultation, more and more Indians are becoming involved in archaeology. A growing number of us have chosen to pursue the discipline of archaeology as a career, and in this paper I would like to consider some of the many factors that affect us as we work at this vocation.

The pressures involved in becoming an archaeologist are somewhat different for a Native American than they are for nonnatives. In addition to expectations from within the profession, other, more personal stresses can be involved. Some of these are directly related to the history of archaeology in America, while others relate to current political activities. University education about the Native American past may also serve as a barrier to one's desire to study our history in an academic context, as a distressing personal example shows. A key to presenting archaeology as a profession open to Native American input is communication. This is a very simple thing to say, but it is more complex in its execution.

Finally, I would argue that archaeology as a discipline must realistically consider not only the roles of Native Americans within the discipline, but also Indian perspectives on the past. We can bring many views on the ancient people to our work, the most important being an impression of the ancients as ancestors. As Indian archaeologists we feel the heavy burden of telling their stories, not just for reasons of furthering academic knowledge, but also out of respect for our elders and those who were here before us.

HISTORY

The history of interaction between academic archaeologists and native peoples fuels much of the resentment many Indian people feel toward the discipline. Anthropologists from the early years of the discipline sought to study and record as much information as possible about various tribes out of a fear that cultural ways were fast disappearing (Trigger 1989). For many tribes this was indeed the case, and, in fact, there have been instances in which knowledge preserved by anthropologists has become an important source of information for continuing cultural practices (Hubert 1989b). However, in many more cases native peoples found anthropologists to be intrusive and annoying. Much of the information shared with ethnographers was published, and tribes came to resent the fact that local and sometimes sacred knowledge was taken and used improperly. Many Indians were made to feel like interesting specimens rather than people.

Archaeology might have seemed to escape this problem because of a focus on past or extinct cultural groups. However, this formulation of the discipline reflected a divergent concept of the ancient history of the North American continent from that implied by anthropology. Publications in both the popular and scholarly press reflected a bias against existing tribes, seeing Indian peoples as remnants of a once noble past. With the days of glory long gone, contemporary Indian life could hold no keys to understanding the mysteries of the past.

The seeds for the repatriation dispute were planted in this era. The idea had been formed that the ancient past could only be unlocked using scientific reasoning, which belonged to the archaeologists. Native perspectives on what became known as "prehistory" were defined as myth and folklore, neither of which was as powerful as science. Such an understanding of the past cut out the only peoples who are actually related to the ancient North Americans. The need to make this point clear factored into much of the determination Indian activists felt when trying to explain why it is necessary to see the modern tribes as historically, genetically, and emotionally linked to ancient peoples.

Again, with the collecting of skeletal material, Native Americans were made to feel like specimens. This imagery underlies much of the dialogue about repatriation today (Lippert 1992). In part because native peoples and native knowledge were not seen as vital to the discipline of archaeology, few Indians attempted to gain academic credentials and participate in the profession. In addition, other factors, notably economic and social, played into this situation. Then, as today, Native Americans fall below the poverty level in staggering numbers. For many Indians, higher education has never been a viable choice.

In the fall of 1990, Native Americans made up less than 1 percent of the total number of students enrolled in institutions of higher education (Reddy 1993)—a figure comparable to their representation within the general population. However, it is certain that a fraction of these students are not, in fact, related to the original inhabitants of this continent. At the University of Texas at Austin, ethnicity is self-determined, and judging from lists of Indian students obtained by the Native American Student Organization (NASO), it is apparent that the original ancestry of at least 5 percent of the individuals listed was in India!

Further up in the academic strata, the number of Native Americans becomes smaller. In 1988–1989, less than a quarter of 1 percent of students receiving doctorates were Native Americans (84 out of 35,692). This rate moves up to nearly a third of a percent when one considers the social sciences, but it is still somewhat less than admirable. In 1990, out of a total of 2,047 doctorates in the social sciences, American Indians received 6 (Reddy 1993).

ACADEMIA AND NATIVE AMERICANS

Many Native Americans who choose to study anthropology do so out of a desire to explore their ethnic background. It is not always easy to make or maintain this choice within the academic arena. At the University of Texas, I once enrolled in a course (not in the Anthropology Department) that promised to consider the ways in which the image of Indianness has been constructed using texts written by and about Native Americans. However, I found that the professor was so steeped in his own perspectives of the Indian as "Noble Savage" that he was somewhat less than knowledgeable or sympathetic to modern Indian concerns about identity.

Unable to escape the class after the drop deadline, I endured weeks of irritation. He compared the intellect of the painters of southwestern rock art with that of elementary school children because he thought the drawings looked similar to children's artwork. At one point, he seemed to regret that all of the Indians in Texas had either been killed or moved out of the state. Hearing a statement like this could indeed lead a Native American student to seriously question her presence at the university! In fact, according to the 1990 census, Texas ranks eighth in the country for numbers of Native American residents (Reddy 1993). I include this class description not merely to blow off some steam, but to point out that academia is not neutral in its approach to the study of Native American history: sometimes things can get downright hostile.

In addition, the opposite condition has begun to occur. In the wake of the quincentennial, it has become fashionable once again to mythologize Native American culture. Our history is sometimes transformed into an impossibly serene, all knowing, cooperative, gender-sensitive enterprise that is then held as a shining example for the rest of the world to follow. White culture, corrupted by civilization, could supposedly learn much from our heritage. This benevolent, though misguided, viewpoint again places Native Americans in a category other than human. At times it seems easier to contend with clear-cut ignorance rather than well-intentioned romanticization.

Archaeology classes are generally much better, but they often fail to make the connection between living Native American groups and the "prehistoric" past. In most of my archaeology classes, little or no mention has been made of the modern Indian tribes who are related to the various aspects, chiefdoms, and phases being studied. One gets the idea that living Indian people are irrelevant to the study of North American prehistory, and maybe within the current formulation of prehistory, we are. But I believe that this merely illustrates the need for a reconsideration of what we have defined as archaeology. Are we uncovering the past for its own sake or for reasons of our own? We may be trying to be objective and scientific, but isn't there a sense of wanting to connect with the ancient peoples that drew all of us into this profession? It seems to me to be dangerous to define a past that does not possess a human soul.

COMMUNICATION

Communication between archaeologists and Native American groups has increased over the years, especially after the passage of the **Native American Graves Protection and Repatriation Act.** However, this term—communication—may involve different actions and have different meanings. If discussions only take place within the boundaries of legally mandated sharing of information, a true dialogue may not result. Let us consider the various Indian communities and ways in which archaeologists can open less formal communication with them.

Information about archaeological research need not be distributed only in cases where excavations take place on Indian lands. Members of tribes who are culturally or spatially related may be fascinated by studies that seem commonplace in departments of anthropology. It is vital that archaeologists come to view sharing information with Indian groups as an integral part of conducting research.

The method of transmission of information is also important. Sending a copy of the published report may be useful, but many of those who are interested may find it difficult to interpret. While technical reports may be useful to members of tribes who are considering archaeology as a career, academic language may obscure information fascinating to the general Indian community.

One interesting report has been published by the U.S. Department of the Interior's Fish and Wildlife Service about burials found at the Stillwater National Wildlife Refuge (Raymond 1992). This report discusses the project and the information learned from the burials in nontechnical language. It even describes paleopathological research in a clear manner. Because of financial constraints, reports like this one may be rare, but similar efforts should be undertaken where possible.

Other approaches to consider are giving talks at community centers, or tribal meetings, or inviting people to visit labs or excavation sites. I once arranged the NASO to take a tour of the Texas Archaeological Research Laboratory. In an apparent long-standing tradition, members of the Caddo Tribe of Oklahoma regularly attend an annual conference on Caddo archaeology. The level of communication that takes place at the conference may be questioned, however; at the last meeting, a Native American student commented to me that "It all looks very interesting, but I didn't understand a word of it."

When considering a connection to the Indian community, archaeologists often overlook intertribal organizations. Texas has many organizations that enable Indian people of all backgrounds to come together to discuss common concerns. These groups should not be dismissed in attempts to educate the native public about archaeology just because they are composed of people from many different tribes. The majority of the 65,000 Indians in Texas don't live on tribal lands (Reddy 1993).

I have been privileged to be a speaker at the American Indian Resource and Education Coalition's annual conference on Indian education in Texas. At the 1995 conference, I gave a short talk on skeletal research, discussing what is actually done and the sorts of information that can be learned. I had been quite nervous about making that speech. On other occasions I have been made to feel like a traitor for studying human remains. In fact, the listeners seemed quite interested and asked thoughtful questions. It became clear to me that many had not known what could be learned from skeletal analysis. To me, this incident represents a clear breakdown in communication because this group has been one of the more active in Texas to push for repatriation.

I do not mean to state that with a little more education members of groups such as this would change their minds about reburial, rather I think that they should be fully informed about the nature of archaeology and about what can be learned. As Lynne Goldstein states, "Since Native

Americans often have little idea of what we do, they may invent our culture for us, based on the limited information they have on hand" (Goldstein 1992:61).

NATIVE AMERICAN ARCHAEOLOGISTS

There have been many calls for an increase in the numbers of Native Americans in archaeology, and in fact our ranks have grown. However, the number of Indians who acquire a college education remains small, and the number of Indian graduate students remains even smaller. At the University of Texas at Austin, 182 students out of 48,000 are listed as American Indian or Alaska Native. Native Americans are not considered a minority group with regard to recruitment efforts (Office of Admissions, University of Texas at Austin, personal communication 1996). In Texas, Native Americans are not considered minorities when applying for state-regulated financial aid specifically available to minority students (Red Elk 1995). NASO has made efforts to recruit Native American graduate students, but it is nearly impossible to recruit undergraduates since we receive no support for this from the university.

Calls for an increase in the number of Native American archaeologists are easy to make, but can be much harder to answer. In stating a desire for more practicing native archaeologists, we must address what it is the discipline really expects of us. We are capable of bringing perspectives to our work that go against standard archaeological knowledge about the peoples of North America. Will these be accepted, or rejected as nonscientific?

For example, we know that at one time these lands were inhabited only by our ancestors. This country was Indian for at least 20 times as long as Europeans and their descendants have been here. This knowledge can provide modern Indian people with a feeling of kinship that transcends tribal boundaries. I have found that my own studies in archaeology reflect an emotional connection that is a result of being related somehow to the "prehistoric" peoples of North America.

I think the best way to explain this is to relate an experience I had as an undergraduate at Rice University. I was visiting the Houston Museum of Natural Science to study an exhibit of precolumbian Central American artifacts. I remember wandering happily through the exhibit, comfortable in the feeling of kinship with the ancient makers of the objects. When I examined a case of personal adornment items, I stared into a black obsidian mirror and was struck by a deeply satisfying thought: the owner of the mirror had probably seen a sight similar to the one I was seeing when he or she looked into the polished glass.

As Native Americans, when we study the past, we see our ancient selves, living and acting in a world not yet impacted by 504 years of colonial confusion. When we work at archaeology, we do so with a sometimes. unspoken responsibility: we know why we need to preserve the memories of those who went before us. It might be argued that this can lead to unobjective results; how can one scientifically study prehistory if one is also reverent of the ancestors? This question points me toward another difficulty of belonging to both groups. Is it reverent to the ancient peoples to pursue one of my interests, the study of health conditions in a "prehistoric" community through examination of their skeletal remains?

SKELETAL RESEARCH

I believe that one can attempt to maintain appropriate reverence toward the ancients while continuing to learn from their material remains. For many of our ancestors, skeletal analysis is one of the only ways that they are able to tell us their stories. The forthcoming information may not be as clear as it is from other sources; it seems that it is difficult to speak with a voice made of bone. Nevertheless, while so much has been lost, these individuals have found one last way to speak to us about their lives.

While working on my dissertation research, I have observed many different people and their approaches toward skeletal analysis. Many appear to work quite casually, and I know that I have irritated some by insisting on following rules about working conditions to the letter. In doing so, I find that I am attempting to foster an awareness of the heavy responsibility of working with human remains. Bioarchaeological research is a privilege. It must not be taken lightly.

I could not conduct skeletal research against the wishes of a related Indian community. If possible, I would make known to concerned individuals the types of studies that could be done and what could be learned, as well as my willingness to follow procedures that address religious needs. In the end, however, I would be forced by my own ethics and humanity to comply with their wishes. One of the basic common beliefs among native peoples is respect for elders and their wisdom.

CONCLUSION

As a Choctaw and an archaeologist, I am often forced to defend my own work and my choice of archaeology as a profession to members of various Indian groups. This is one of the more difficult aspects of being a Native American archaeologist. As a member of both groups, I can't help getting drawn into various conflicts. Although this leaves me quite cynical at times, I still feel that more Native Americans are needed for the future of archaeology. It has been hard sometimes to clearly articulate why this is necessary, but I think it has something to do with the image I saw in the obsidian mirror.

When we study the people of the past, we do so with a frame of reference that is constructed in the present. However unknowingly, we carry our own perspectives and experiences into our studies, and this affects to various degrees our conclusions about the past. The next people to come along in the precolumbian exhibit I mentioned above were an older, white couple. They also stared appreciatively into the mirror, but I knew there was little chance that their images were comparable to the owner's. Yet there must be similarities; we share common, human characteristics.

I believe that Native American archaeologists can study the past in ways that are both divergent and complementary to the more traditional canon. For us, the past is strong. The precolumbian past of this continent is a powerful, almost mythic time that illustrates the accomplishments of native peoples: it serves as a source of strength when confronted with the struggles of the present. This is the perspective that influences my own attitudes and activities in archaeology.

In continuing my studies of the past, I do so gratefully, with the tools developed by generations of archaeologists, most of whom are not Indian. It is necessary, however, to recognize that Native American archaeologists may see some areas of the past more closely. We look through an emotional lens that is knowingly constructed through our blood, the genetic characteristics of which echo in the bones of our ancestors.

I do not think that it is impossible to know the American past without being related to the peoples being studied. In fact, if we consider the history of North America when we define our profession, we may recognize a justice of a sort. While so much of our native history was lost through the actions of European peoples, it is perhaps fair that so many of their descendants strive so hard to restore it. White archaeologists might try to consider their work as a sort of penance rather than a right.

We must reconsider what our purposes are when we conduct archaeological research. We must recognize that our actions do affect native peoples on many levels. Acknowledging this fact need not compromise a scientific study of the past, it should merely force one more step toward active communication. Archaeology must also consider what is implied in calls for an increase in the numbers of Native American archaeologists. How much of a native perspective is to be incorporated? How easy is it for a Native American to choose archaeology considering the social and economic pressures that may be involved? Increasing the numbers of Indians practicing archaeology is certainly desirable, but it should be just as necessary to educate tribes and intertribal groups.

Finally, I do not maintain that the Native American perspective on the past be privileged to the exclusion of any other approaches, merely that it be recognized as an existing canon. There should be room in this discipline for a variety of viewpoints. After all, we are all human. We all share genetic characteristics and fundamental concerns, and when we look in the mirror we all see basically the same thing: our very human selves.

REFERENCES

Goldstein, L. 1992. The potential for future relationships between archaeologists and Native Americans. In *Quandaries and Quests: Visions of Archaeology's Future,* edited by LuAnn Wandsnider, pp. 59–71. Center for Archaeological Investigations, Southern Illinois University at Carbondale.

Hubert, J. 1989. A proper place for the dead. In *Conflicts in the Archaeology of Living Traditions*, edited by R. Layton, pp. 131–266. Unwin Hyman, London,

Lippert, D. 1992. Skeletons in our closets: Archaeology and the issue of reburial. Unpublished M.A. thesis, Department of Anthropology, University of Texas, Austin.

Raymond, A. 1992. Who were the ancient people of Stillwater National Wildlife Refuge, Nevada? U.S. Department of the Interior, Fish and Wildlife Service, Stillwater Wildlife Refuge, Fallon, Nevada.

Reddy, M.A., editor. 1993. *Statistical Record of Native North Americans*. Gale, Detroit.

Red Elk Hardman, R. 1995. Presentation at the 1995 Conference on Indian Education in Texas, San Antonio.

Trigger, B. 1989. *A History of Archaeological Thought*. Cambridge University Press, Cambridge.

The Homegoing

Michael Alan Park

EDITOR'S INTRODUCTION

Imagine being a forensic anthropologist. Most of the time your research focuses on the dead, on your attempt to tell the story of people long gone by listening to, as Dorothy Lippert phrased it in the previous article, their "voice made of bone." It is amazing to be able to give voice to those bones, to be able, at least in a general way, to identify not just bones, but the once-living, breathing person represented by those bones, to know if they were man or woman, how old they were when they died, and maybe even to identify the cause of their death. As fascinating as that might be, now imagine what it's like to have a name and a face and a family to associate with a set of those bones, buried in Cornwall, Connecticut. Finally, imagine being able to help the descendants of that person recover their ancestor and bring him home. Michael Park shows how archaeology and biological anthropology can work together to provide closure in a family's quest to return a prodigal son to his home. This article should also serve to remind students that all of the individuals archaeologists excavate, like Henry Opakahaia, had names and families who cared for them and grieved their passing.

POINTS TO PONDER

1. Why were archaeologists concerned that they might not be able to find Henry Opakahaia's bones, even though his grave was marked?
2. How did the techniques and skills of archaeology assist in the recovery of Henry Opakahaia's bones?
3. How did the techniques and skills of forensic anthropology assist in the recovery of Henry Opakahaia's bones?
4. What are the lessons that can be gleaned from the work exemplified here in the aid provided by archaeologists and forensic anthropologists to the family of Henry Opakahaia?

On a hot July afternoon in 1993, I found myself standing over an open grave in a peaceful hillside cemetery in the small Connecticut town of Cornwall—waiting for a colleague to unearth the remains of a native Hawaiian who had lain interred there for 175 years.

A few weeks before, Nick Bellantoni, the Connecticut state archaeologist, had phoned me with a fascinating story, one I had never heard, although I had lived in the state for twenty years. In 1808, a sixteen-year-old Hawaiian named Opukahaia (Oh-poo-kah-hah-EE-ah) escaped the tribal warfare that had killed his parents and younger brother—reportedly before his eyes—by becoming the cabin boy aboard a Yankee sailing ship, the *Triumph*. Two years later, sailing by way of China and the West Indies, he landed in Connecticut where he was taken under the care of the president of Yale University. He learned English, took the name Henry, and converted to Christianity, becoming a Congregationalist. He is said to be the first Christian Hawaiian. In 1817 he helped build a missionary school in Cornwall. His dream was to return to Hawaii (then known as the Sandwich Islands) and bring his new faith to his people.

Henry's dream was never realized. On February 17, 1818, at the age of twenty-six, he died during a typhoid fever epidemic that swept through Connecticut. His vision, however, helped inspire the missionary movement that would profoundly change the history of the Hawaiian Islands—including a role in their annexation by the United States in 1898. Henry's grave in Cornwall became a shrine both for the people of his adopted town and for visiting Hawaiians, who would leave offerings on his headstone. The inscription on the stone reads: "Oh, how I want to see Hawaii! But I think I never shall—God will do right. He knows what is best."

Then, in the fall of 1992, Deborah Liikapeka Lee, a descendant of Henry's family, awoke from a dream convinced that Henry wanted to return to his homeland. A family association garnered the necessary funds and legal documents, and the next summer Henry's "homegoing" took place. And this is where anthropology comes in.

Old New England cemeteries vary in the precise placement of headstones relative to the bodies beneath them. Moreover, the acidic, often wet New England soil is unkind to organic remains. The recovery, removal, and accurate identification of whatever remained of Henry Opukahaia required the methodologies of archaeology and forensic anthropology. Nick wanted my help with the latter—making sure anything recovered was indeed Henry. He also wanted my help, it turned out, in moving several tons of stone.

First in 1818, and then with modifications later, Henry's tomb had been carefully and lovingly assembled by the people of Cornwall's Congregational Church. They had placed a large horizontal headstone or ledger (the only one of its kind in the cemetery) on a pedestal of fieldstones and mortar several feet high. When we arrived, the headstone was covered by offerings—shells, flowers, candy, and coins. We removed and boxed these and then carefully separated the stone from the pedestal, locking it away in the cemetery sexton's tool shed. We dismantled the pedestal, carefully labeling and diagramming the position of each stone because the portion of the tomb above ground was to be rebuilt by a stone mason. Under the pedestal, and going down about 3 feet into the ground, we uncovered, as we dug, three more layers of fieldstones that acted as a foundation for the monument above and as protection for the coffin and remains we hoped were still below. All the stones were removed, labeled, and set aside. When we were into a layer of sandy soil about 52 inches down, Nick worked alone in the excavated pit, delicately scraping away the dirt inch by inch with a trowel and a brush.

Late on the second day of our excavation, a dark stain became visible in the soil. The wooden coffin itself had long since decayed, but the dark shadow of its six-sided outline could be seen. At that point we began to despair of finding much else. Indeed, the Hartford funeral home that was to prepare the remains for re-burial had provided us only with a metal container about the size of a single file cabinet drawer. The family had been cautioned not to expect much.

But then something truly exciting came to light. It was a small portion of the wooden coffin lid, preserved (even to the inclusion of some black paint) possibly by the action of metals from the brass tacks that had been driven into it in the shape of a heart. This was not an uncommon practice for that time period in New England. Inside the heart shape, more tacks spelled out "H.O.," "ae" (from a Latin phrase for "age at the completion of life"), and the numerals "26"—Henry's initials and age at death. After another hour of careful scraping and brushing, Nick's trowel grazed something hard, and within a few minutes the apparent remains of Henry Opukahaia saw the light of day for the first time in 175 years.

To our surprise, the skeleton was virtually complete. The elaborately constructed tomb and the sandy soil with good drainage had kept the bones dry enough for excellent preservation. Apparently, a regular coffin was going to be needed for Henry's eventual reburial after all.

Nick carefully freed each bone from the soil and identified it as he handed it up to me. I confirmed the identification, and the bone was checked off by one of our colleagues from a list of the 206 bones of the normal adult human skeleton. Each bone was wrapped in acid-free paper to prevent any surface damage and then placed in the metal box, which barely managed to accommodate all the bones. We all worked with surgical gloves because harmful pathogens have been known to persist even in old remains, and Henry had died of an infectious disease. (Later in our investigation we ran out of gloves and ignored the caution, but with no ill effects.)

Everything to this point clearly indicated we had recovered Henry's bones, but verification was still necessary. As we identified, recorded, and wrapped each bone, we compared important diagnostic bones with what we knew of Henry from written descriptions and a single drawn portrait. The skeleton was clearly that of a male and, at least at my brief first glance, seemed to conform to that of a person in his late twenties. Henry had been described as being "a little under six feet." We did not have precision measuring instruments with us in the field, but using my own six-foot-one stature as a gauge, I held several of the arm and leg bones up to my limbs and guessed that they belonged to someone a few inches shorter.

As Nick brushed the dirt away from the skull (saving it for last), the face of Henry Opukahaia emerged—the very image of his portrait. The skeleton is more than just a bony foundation for the body's soft tissues. The bones themselves are living tissue, connected in many ways to muscles, blood vessels, nerves, and skin. The shape of the outer body is reflected in the skeleton, and vice versa. With training, one can "see" the face of a person in the bony visage of the skull. The skull in the grave, with its prominent nose, high forehead, and heavy, squared jaw was clearly that of the man in the portrait.

We spent two more days with Henry, this time in the garage of the Hartford funeral home. With the bones laid out in anatomical orientation on a gurney, we were able to conduct a more thorough scientific analysis, cleaning, photographing, measuring, and describing the bones. The family graciously gave us their blessing to do this.

Henry's skeleton was indeed surprisingly complete. The only bones missing were the hyoid, a horseshoe-shaped bone in the throat, and five finger bones. The coccyx (tail bone) and xyphoid process (the pointy bone at the bottom of the breastbone) were badly decomposed and identifiable only by the place in which we found them relative to the other bones. Other than that, the only damage was some deterioration of the back and underside of the skull and to some of the cervical (neck) vertebrae. We hypothesized that Henry's head may have been laid on a pillow, which retained moisture that speeded decomposition.

The size and robusticity of the bones (as well as the perfect match with the portrait) all identified the skeleton as that of a male. The cranium had the typical male traits of brow ridges, a sloped forehead, a protruding, square chin, and rounded upper borders on the eye sockets. The angle at the back of the jaw (the gonial angle) was about 120 degrees—relatively large for males, who more typically have angles close to 90 degrees—and the mastoids (the bony humps behind the ears) were small for a male.

The pelvis, however, was unequivocally male. Essentially, everything about a female pelvis is wide and broad (an obvious adaptation to pregnancy and childbirth), whereas corresponding features of a male pelvis are narrow. The pelvis before us was as good and as typical an example of a male pelvis as any of us had seen.

There are several skeletal traits used to determine age at death. They are all based on changes that take place with regularity in the development of portions of the bones. The latest change that has *already* taken place, and the next change in the chronological order that has *yet* to take place, mark the minimum and maximum age at which the individual died. In Henry's case, the ends of all the long bones, which initially develop separately from the shafts, were almost all completely fused to form a single bone. The exceptions were the crest of the pelvis and the end of the collar bone where it meets the breastbone. Fusion was still taking place at these sites. This indicated an age at death of between eighteen and thirty.

The internal surfaces of the pubic bones (where the pelvic bones meet in front) change appearance at different ages. Henry's matched the standard for an average age of twenty-eight. Similarly, the front ends of the ribs undergo regular changes, and Henry's indicated an age range of nineteen to thirty-three, with a mean of 25.9. All these data coincided well with his documented age at death of twenty-six.

Traditionally, the closure of the cranial sutures has been used as a common method of determining age at death. It is based on the fact that the cranial vault begins as four separate bones that fuse, along suture lines, at certain ages. The method, however, has fallen from favor because there is too much individual variation. Henry's sutures were a case in point. At twenty-six all his major suture lines should have been open or in the process of fusing. In fact, they had all prematurely closed. Some sites were completely obliterated, a condition only seen in the very elderly. There is no indication why this occurred in Henry, nor is there any evidence that it caused any problems sometimes related to premature closure, such as cranial deformation.

There are a number of formulas for estimating overall stature from the measurement of one of the major long bones. Applying four of these to Henry's skeleton gave us an average stature estimate of five-foot-eight—a bit shorter than "a little under six feet"—but these estimates do not take into complete account differences in individual proportions. Henry could have been a bit taller than these calculations indicate.

Henry's skeleton displayed only a few abnormalities. The joint where his jaw met his cranium (the temporomandibular joint) was oddly shaped and noticeably worn. He may well have had some discomfort at this joint during his life. Both hip joints, where the femur articulates with the pelvis, were also oddly shaped, but here there was no indication that this condition caused him any pain or malfunction. Both joints were similarly shaped, and there were no other abnormalities of the bones involved.

Henry's right ribs, numbers 3 through 10, however, showed a striking and very noteworthy condition. On the inside surface between the head of the ribs, where they attach to the vertebral column, and at the angle where they curve toward the front of the body, we observed an ashy, porous texture. On rib 7, this abnormal texture was 44 mm long. This condition is called osteomyelitis, and it occurs in about one percent of cases of typhoid fever, usually in precisely the area where we observed it on Henry's ribs. In the midst of our scientific investigation, this observation served to remind us of the nature of the subject of our study—another human being whom we had come, in only a few days, to know very well indeed.

Toward the end of our analysis, a coffin arrived from Hawaii. It was a fairly plain wooden box but was covered in a layer of koa wood, which is native to the islands. The family requested that we lay out Henry's bones in the coffin in correct anatomical orientation. To do this we lined the bottom of the coffin with heavy foam rubber into which we cut spaces to hold each bone. The family kindly agreed to let us place the wrist, finger, ankle, and toe bones together in four bundles at the ends of the arms and legs. Cutting individual spaces for all those bones would have been quite time consuming.

The following Sunday about 200 people, including those of us who had helped exhume Henry's remains, gathered at the Congregational Church in Cornwall for a "homegoing" celebration. A local Congregational minister, himself a native Hawaiian, spoke over Henry's coffin, which was surrounded by ti leaves, flower and yarn leis, and bouquets of anthuriums. Henry's portrait faced the congregation. The next day Henry Opukahaia was flown home to Hawaii, taken by canoe to Kealakekua Bay on the "Big Island" where he had first boarded the *Triumph* in 1808, and, finally, buried in a cemetery overlooking the bay.

Except for two days of labor under the hot summer sun (and perhaps cutting those spaces in the foam rubber), this was not a particularly difficult endeavor. The archaeological and forensic applications and analyses were fairly straightforward. But in the Cornwall church that Sunday, as we lined up in front of Henry's coffin for photos and the family warmly thanked us for our help, I knew this was one of the most rewarding bits of anthropology I would ever participate in.

Section 3

A USEFUL PAST

We usually think of modern technologies, including those related to agriculture, as being manifestly better—both far more efficient and far more productive—than past technologies. Our modern version might appear to represent the pinnacle of the evolution of technology. That being the case, and although investigating ancient technologies might be worthwhile in an effort to satisfy our curiosity about past ways of life, one might think that such studies offer little in the way of practical benefit to us in the modern world. Certainly, when I sit down and work on my new computer and compare it to my first machine (low-resolution black-and-white screen; there was no hard drive, two 5.25-inch floppy bays, one of which was used to load the operating system every time you booted up the computer!), there seems little of value in my DEC (Digital Equipment Corporation) Rainbow except, perhaps, as a museum piece. However, the two articles included in this section show clearly that this conceit about modern technology isn't always true. Ancient responses to problems can sometimes offer viable solutions that modern technology can't provide and might even make things worse.

Sometimes people in the past responded to existential challenges, reacted to significant changes in their environment, or solved a vexing problem that threatened their way of life. People in the past sometimes needed to provide food for a burgeoning population. Sometimes they needed to react to changes in their environment. Ancient people faced drought, soil erosion, salinization of farmland, pollution, population growth, urban decay, and war. Sometimes they had to find new ways of accomplishing existing tasks and sometimes they needed to come up with ways of responding to new challenges. And sometimes these strategies, responses, reactions, and solutions can be applied, either directly or indirectly, by us in the modern world when we are faced with similar challenges.

Walk down the aisles of any fancy supermarket—Whole Foods comes immediately to mind—and take a look at the section labeled "ethnic" or "world" foods. There you will find a host of foods that once offered subsistence to large chunks of the world's people—foods like amaranth, quinoa, chenopodium, jicama, ulluco, and oca. In all likelihood, most of you have never heard of these foods and fewer still have eaten any of them. But there's plenty of protein, carbs, and calories in those foods and many thrive under conditions that challenge our more significant modern crops. Perhaps some of these ancient foods, when more fully embraced in modern agricultural contexts, will help feed the world's hungry.

One of the articles presented in this section shows how a world region (the Lake Titicaca Basin in South America) once supported a larger population than it does currently. The ancient people of the Lake Titicaca Basin developed an agricultural technology largely ignored in the modern world—raised field agriculture—that provided for a carrying capacity for human beings higher than what has been accomplished with more "modern" methods (at least without a substantial financial investment). Perhaps by applying this ancient technology in the present, more mouths can be fed and the hunger can be lessened or even eliminated in those world areas where the technique can be applied.

Raised Field Agriculture in the Lake Titicaca Basin

Putting Ancient Agriculture Back to Work

Clark L. Erickson

EDITOR'S INTRODUCTION

I was always disturbed by the public service ads for some government or private agency whose strategy for helping people of the third world was to take young American college kids with little practical experience and probably even less experience in rural, agricultural environments, send them to Africa or Asia or South America, and have them teach the backward indigenous folks how to dig a well for water or how to plow, irrigate, or fertilize their fields to improve their food production. I mean really; those indigenous folks have been digging wells, plowing, irrigating, and fertilizing their own fields for decades, centuries, and even millennia, without the assistance of a bunch of well-meaning American college kids. If the locals were going hungry, it almost certainly was the result of colonialism, political repression, economic inequality, land grabs by corporations, and perhaps even climate change and none of these issues can be addressed by the Peace Corps or other organizations. Perhaps, instead of thinking we can or should teach native people how to increase their agricultural productivity, we should become the students ourselves and investigate how they, for those aforementioned decades, centuries, and millennia, solved those problems on their own. Clark L. Erickson's paper here does precisely that by examining an agricultural strategy developed by the native people of the Andes in Bolivia, Peru, and Ecuador that allowed them to increase both the acreage and the productivity of the land they had under cultivation.

POINTS TO PONDER

1. What technique was used by the people of the Andes to increase the acreage and productivity of the land they had under cultivation?
2. How did that technique work?
3. What were the results of a modern test of the strategy?
4. What lessons can be derived from the analysis and replication of an ancient agricultural strategy?

The remains of an extensive ancient agricultural system built and used by Andean peoples centuries ago are found throughout the vast high plain surrounding Lake Titicaca in the Andean countries of Peru and Bolivia. Raised fields are large elevated planting platforms which provided drainage, improved soil conditions, and improved temperatures for crops, The remains of prehistoric raised fields, elaborate sunken gardens, and agricultural terraces cover tens of thousands of hectares in the region, and provide evidence of the impressive engineering abilities of the peoples who lived there in pre-Columbian times.

Our recent investigations of raised field agriculture demonstrate not only the technological expertise of the past cultures, but also that these systems could be re-used today to make high altitude lands more productive. In a region such as the Andes, where conditions of soil and climate greatly limit agricultural potential, technological methods to augment productivity have been increasingly necessary to support the growing populations of Quechua and Aymara farmers who live there today. The reuse of raised fields may be an economical and ecologically sound alternative to agricultural development based on expensive imported technology.

Until recently, very little was known about the origins and evolution of raised field technology in the Lake Titicaca Basin. Observant Spanish chroniclers in the 16th century described many aspects of the indigenous agriculture, such as terraces and irrigation canals, but they did not mention raised fields. This omission suggests that raised fields had probably been abandoned before the arrival of the Spanish. Questions such as who constructed the fields, when were they built, what crops were cultivated, why the fields varied so much in size and shape, and how raised field agriculture functioned needed to be answered.

Between 1981 and 1986, I directed a small team of researchers investigating prehistoric raised field agriculture in the community of Huatta in the northern Lake Titicaca Basin of Peru. Huatta is located in the center of the largest block of raised field remains, estimated to cover 53,000 hectares. The project, combining archaeology and agronomy, addressed the important questions raised above, as well as those more relevant to modern agriculture, such as estimating the potential productivity of the raised fields and investigating their effects on the local agricultural environment. The investigation was based on archaeological survey and excavation of prehistoric raised fields and selected habitation sites, together with the construction and study of experimental raised field plots (see box). To apply the results of this research, a small-scale development project involving local Quechua farmers was begun in 1982 to put raised fields back into use.

RAISED FIELD AGRICULTURE AND THE LAKE TITICACA ENVIRONMENT

Raised fields are constructed by excavating parallel canals and piling the earth between them to form long, low mounds with flat or convex surfaces. These raised platforms increase soil fertility, improve drainage in low-lying areas, and improve local micro-environments, primarily by decreasing frost risk. The canals between raised fields provide vital moisture during periods of short- and long-term drought. Water in the deep canals might have been used to cultivate aquatic plants and fish, as well as attract lake birds that were an integral part of the prehistoric diet. The raised fields of the Lake Titicaca region are diverse in form and in size, but generally range from 4–10 m wide, 10 to 100 m long, and are 1 m tall.

The prehistoric raised fields, covering some 82,000 hectares of low-lying land around Lake Titicaca in both Bolivia and Peru, have been badly eroded by a combination of wind, rain, flooding, and modern urbanization, but their remains can be seen clearly on the ground and in aerial photographs. They were specifically adapted to the particular environment, crops, and technology available to the indigenous farmers. Most of the land lies above 3800 m (12,500 feet), and nights can be bitterly cold, despite warm sunny days. The year is divided into distinct wet and dry seasons of roughly six months each, but even this situation may vary greatly from year to year, producing an unpredictable, high-risk agricultural environment. Frosts are most common during the dry season, and at the beginning and end of the growing (wet) season, but may occur locally at any time without warning, especially in low-lying depressions at the bases of hills.

The land immediately adjacent to Lake Titicaca has a somewhat more favorable environment for cultivation, mild enough for special races of corn to be grown in sheltered valleys and on the islands and peninsulas of the lake. The stored heat of the massive body of lake water warms the areas around it, an especially important effect at night when frosts are common. Farther from the lake, this warming effect diminishes, but the entire region around the lake benefits from a slightly higher than average annual rainfall. The major obstacle to lakeside agriculture is that most of the surrounding land is either rocky steep slope or flat, waterlogged lake plain which may be seasonally inundated. Both areas have relatively poor soils and are classified as areas of limited agricultural potential in government studies. Today, large rural populations are located in areas that have better drainage, favorable temperatures, and good soils, combined with access to the lacustrine resources of Lake Titicaca

The rich and varied biotic resources of the region would have made it an excellent location for prehistoric experimentation with domestication of plants and different cultivation techniques. Once local peoples learned to protect fields from inundation, the *pampa* (the grass-covered low-lying lake plain) would have been a relatively good area for crop production. In fact, botanical and archaeological research indicate that the potato, quinua and cañihua (two seed crops rich in vegetable protein), and many other important Andean crops were probably first domesticated in the Lake Titicaca region. Selection of special traits has produced crop varieties that can withstand harsh environmental conditions, such as high altitude, intense solar radiation, low nocturnal temperatures, and crop pests. The nocturnal cold was put to use by the prehistoric inhabitants in an elaborate freeze-drying technique which enabled vast amounts of agricultural surplus to be preserved and stored indefinitely. This Andean crop complex and its accompanying preservation technology, combined with the herding of llamas and alpacas and exploitation of lacustrine resources, provided a sound subsistence base for the civilizations that developed in the Lake Titicaca Basin.

The indigenous Andean agricultural tool inventory appears limited in technological complexity, but is more than adequate for the needs of the Andean farmer. Traditional tools include the Andean footplow, hoe, and clod breaker which are still the basic tools today, although the stone and wooden blades have been replaced by metal blades. The footplow, a remarkable implement which is excellent for turning over blocks of tough pampa sod for construction of lazy beds for tubers and for plowing stony ground on steep hillslopes, played a major role in the development of raised field agriculture.

THE ARCHAEOLOGY OF RAISED FIELD AGRICULTURE

Our trenches excavated through the prehistoric raised fields showed that those seen today in the pampa (Fig. 3) are only the badly eroded remains of fully functioning prehistoric field systems. The field surfaces were' originally much higher, with deep canals between them, which have now become filled with sediment. In some trenches, several distinct phases of construction, use, reconstruction, and re-use of the fields can be delineated. Some early fields were narrow ridges of 5 m wavelength (distance from canal center to canal center) which at a later time were expanded to larger fields of 10 m wavelength. From each stratum of the trench profile, samples were obtained for pollen and soil laboratory analyses. The data obtained from these analyses provide interesting insights into prehistoric agriculture.

Soil analysis indicates that the canal sediment, composed primarily of organic matter, is rich in nutrients, much more so than the average pampa soil. In addition, soil alkalinity, a major constraint on agriculture in the lake edge soil, is markedly lower in the canal sediments. These rich sediments were periodically removed from the canals and added to the raised fields to improve the crop soils. Pollen samples from these excavations have been analyzed by Dr. Fred Wiseman of the Massachusetts Institute of Technology. He finds that pollen grains of quinua and potato are present in many soil samples from the raised fields, indicating that these may have been the crops grown on the fields. Unfortunately, there is no way to distinguish between the pollen of the domesticated and wild strains of these plants.

The precise dating of raised fields presented a problem. Radiocarbon dating of material recovered from the excavation of two prehistoric habitation mounds associated with raised field agriculture indicated that most of the garbage midden and construction fill of these sites dates to the period from 1000 B.C. to A.D. 400 (corresponding to the Qaluyu and later Pucara cultures), with a smaller occupation after A.D. 1000 (related to the Aymara kingdoms and subsequent Inca occupation). However, direct dating of the raised fields themselves has proven to be much more difficult.

Aymara: the indigenous peoples of present-day Peru and Bolivia who speak the Aymara language

canihua: an Andean grain crop related to our weed lambsqcarters; high in protein

chakitaqlla: the Andean foot-plow, composed of a handle, shaft, and footpeg of wood with a heavy metal cutting blade bound by leather tongs

flotation: a water separation process used by archaeologists for the recovery of small plant and animal remains from the soils of archaeological sites

pampa: a grass-covered, treeless plain which may be seasonally inundated or waterlogged

pollen analysis: the study of microscopic pollen grains which may give information on past climatic conditions, local environments, or crops cultivated

Quechua: the indigenous peoples of present-day Peru and Bolivia who speak the Quechua language

quinua: an Andean grain crop related to our weed lambs-quarters; high in protein

raised fields: large elevated planting platforms with intervening water-filled canals designed to improve drainage, maximize soil fertility, prevent frosts, and/or provide irrigation

Changes in field use were determined through relative dating of the field stratigraphy, but the duration of each phase could not be ascertained through stratigraphic analysis alone. Carbonized remains for radiocarbon dating were not present in raised fields, but six pottery samples recovered from stratigraphic contexts in both the construction fill and the canals could be dated by the thermo-luminescence technique. This technique determines the time elapsed since the original firing or last exposure to fire of the ceramic vessel. These dates give us a secure chronology for the raised fields and correlate nicely with the dates from the occupation mounds. The surprisingly early dates between 1000 B.C. and the beginning of our era, and the successive building stages and abandonment periods, demonstrate that the raised field system was not a brief late phenomenon as previously suspected. It appears to have been a relatively early agricultural development which was expanded gradually and was used by many generations of Andean farmers.

Our archaeological survey focused on locating the sites occupied by farmers who constructed and maintained the raised fields around Huatta. Most sites on the pampa in direct association with raised fields were earthen mounds that had once been small farmsteads or hamlets. Several larger sites both on the pampa and in the hills overlooking the plain were once towns with rustic public architecture. All that remains now are the stones that served as the foundations for the adobe structures. The number and distribution of habitation mounds indicate a rather dense population in the raised field area throughout the prehistoric period of raised field use, much larger than that of today, surprisingly.

Two of the larger sites (those mentioned above for which dates were obtained) were partially excavated, and showed evidence of long-term occupation. These mounds were the cumulative result of continual rebuilding atop the remains of older, eroded structures. Many of these mounds are still considered to be ideal habitation locations due to their elevation, especially during the seasonal flooding of the pampa. Their garbage middens yielded information about prehistoric subsistence strategies, agriculture, and ceramic and weaving technology.

Plant fragments, direct evidence of agricultural crops preserved by accidental carbonization, have been recovered by the screening and flotation processing of soils from the garbage midden and mound fill of habitation sites. These samples include fragments of potato and possibly other tubers, and quinua. Also identified were aquatic lake plants and other wild plants that could have been used for making mats, nets, and bags, as thatching material, or as forage for domestic animals. Fish, camelids (probably the domesticated alpaca and llama), guinea pig, and various aquatic birds are represented in abundant bone material recovered in the excavations. The floral and faunal remains are found throughout the sequence of occupation and indicate a remarkable economic stability. All of this evidence indicates a prehistoric subsistence pattern similar to that still practiced today by lake-edge dwelling Aymara and Quechua farmers, a pattern based on a combination of potato and quinua cultivation, herding, fishing, and intensive gathering of wild lake resources. The recovery of thousands of basalt hoe fragments, polished through years of use, attests to their importance in the tool inventory of the ancient agricultural technology. These stone hoes were among the implements used to construct the raised fields. Pottery remains included utilitarian serving and cooking vessels, in addition to ceremonial or fine wares decorated with burnishing, incision, and painting. One nearly complete house structure belonging to the Pucara culture (300 B.C.-A.D. 400) was excavated (Fig. 5), and it has many features similar to those of adobe houses with thatched roofs constructed today in the area.

INTERPRETATIONS OF THE EXCAVATIONS

Our research results show that large farming villages were settled throughout the lake area by 1000 B.C. By 300 B.C., Lake Titicaca society had evolved sufficiently to support large ceremonial and population centers. The site of Pucara in the northern lake basin has approximately 42 km of urban sprawl, complete with pyramidal platforms and temples with semi-subterranean courtyards (see K. Chavez, this issue). Tiahuanaco (A.D. 300-1000), one of the most impressive Andean sites, probably had its humble beginnings at this time and rapidly grew to influence most of southern Peru and the Bolivian highlands by A.D. 500 through its control of long-distance trade, its colonies, and religious missionization (Brow-man 1978). Tiahuanaco subsequently collapsed and was replaced by several competing Aymara kingdoms around A.D. 1000. These in turn were conquered by the Inca empire around A.D. 1450. Earlier hypotheses suggested that construction of raised fields and terracing was related to the later cultures, when population stress resulted in the development of labor-intensive agricultural technology, and a centralized bureaucracy was available to plan, direct, and manage the agricultural systems (Smith et al. 1968; Kolata 1986).

Our investigation suggests some alternatives. The growth of the Andean polity of Pucara at the north end of the lake basin was certainly related to the expansion of raised field agriculture; however, this agriculture was well established several centuries earlier. As Pucara's power as a ceremonial center was usurped by Tiahuanaco in the southern lake basin, raised field use appears to have declined in the north, but it was probably never completely abandoned. New research indicates that, as might be expected, raised field construction at the southern end of the lake was related to the growth of Tiahuanaco (Kolata 1986). A later resurgence of raised field construction occurred when a number of independent Aymara kingdoms were established around the lake after the collapse of Tia-huanaco sometime after A.D. 1000. Limited raised field use may have continued during the brief period of Inca domination of the lake basin, sometime after A.D. 1450.

Why was the use of raised fields discontinued in the northern basin after the decline of Pucara and before the arrival of the Spanish? Many ideas have been put forward to account for the abandonment of the system, such as climate change, devastating droughts and floods, and tectonic uplift. I find none convincing. In my opinion, the raised field construction, expansion, and abandonment relate less to environmental factors than to the changes in the relative importance of various ceremonial centers in the Lake Titicaca area. As ceremonial and population centers grew, agriculture expanded to keep pace with them. When power and influence shifted to other areas, production needs dropped and fields were removed from production. Some of the prehistoric communities in the raised field zones may have been depopulated and the inhabitants perhaps even forcibly removed to other locations. Although the area and intensity of cultivation were reduced at various times in the past, raised fields were probably never completely abandoned until the severe depopulation of the region that followed the arrival of the Spanish.

Raised field technology enabled the prehistoric inhabitants of the Lake Titicaca Basin to effectively maximize crop production. The earliest raised fields documented in our project do not appear to have developed as the result of population stress, nor do the earliest phases of field construction and use appear to have been planned and directed by a centralized authority. This technology may have been one of the earliest forms of intensive agriculture, a logical outgrowth of early fishing, gathering, and hunting settled life based on the exploitation of rich lake resources. This subsistence strategy permitted a dense population of wetland-oriented peoples to maintain sedentary lives.

Simple cultivation on the floating islands as practiced today by the Uru of the Bay of Puno would have been a preadaptation to raised field agriculture, which was later expanded to include lake and river edge cultivation. Population appears to have grown along with agricultural expansion. Labor figures calculated from the experimental raised fields indicate that construction was not necessarily

EXPERIMENTS IN RAISED FIELD AGRICULTURE

More detailed information about raised fields as an agricultural technology was gained from the construction and cultivation of several experimental fields. An excavated archaeological trench provides original canal depth and ridge spacing, and the experimental fields were constructed to these specifications by local Quechua farmers using traditional agricultural implements available in all households (foot-plow, hoe, clodbreaker, shovel, and pick). The traditional Andean tools proved to be excellent implements ideally suited for the preparation of raised fields, It was found that the easiest, most efficient method of construction involved teams of three people; two used footplows to cut blocks of sod from the old canals between the ridges (Fig. 6). while the third tossed the sod blocks onto the old field surface, In this way, a thick layer of rich organic topsoil, a perfect medium for cultivation, was rapidly built up on the eroded field surface. It was calculated that for each hour of work, the team could move three cubic meters of earth, a construction rate much faster than had been expected.

Major crops native to the Andean highlands were cultivated on the experimental raised fields. Of the crops planted, potatoes, quinua, and cañihua (Fig. 7) produced the greatest yields. Potato production during five years of experimentation was between 8 and 16 metric tons per hectare, with an average of 10 metric tons. This figure is much larger than today's average potato production figures of between 1 and 4 metric tons per hectare for the Department of Puno. These larger yields are especially significant because we used local and improved potato varieties without fertilizers in the experiments (Fig. 8), while most of the potato fields upon which the current regional estimates for Puno are based were fertilized, We have also demonstrated that high yields can be sustained for several years of con-tihuous cropping. Green manure produced in the canals, including nitrogen

labor intensive, especially if fields were built and used over many generations. Field maintenance was found to be minimal in the experiments, but may increase after several years of cultivation. If fields can be continually used, with fertility maintained through the periodic application of decomposed organic matter from the canals, the initial labor investment for field construction is offset by the long-term benefits of continuous fertility combined with a high yield.

RAISED FIELD TECHNOLOGY AND RURAL DEVELOPMENT

Countries such as Peru and Bolivia often use models from more technologically advanced nations to develop their agriculture and industry. A succession of apparently sophisticated development fixing algae, can be used to replenish depleted soil nutrients on the fields after several years of continuous cropping. The canals were also productive in another way. Various useful aquatic plants, valuable resources in prehistoric times, rapidly colonized the water. Fish might have been raised in the deeper canals, providing a useful source of protein to supplement a diet based on starchy tubers while at the same time increasing the nitrogen content of the canal muck.

The value of raised fields in the cold Lake Titicaca Basin was dramatically demonstrated during a severe local frost in 1982. Crops in nearby fields were severely damaged, while potatoes cultivated on our experimental raised fields suffered only minimal damage and quickly recovered. Several investigators have hypothesized that raised field micro-topography tends to drain heavy, dense cold air from the elevated field surf: aces into the canals, Frost drainage may have played a role in this effect, but the data indicate that the presence of water in the canals was most important. In order to test this hypothesis, we conducted an investigation of the local climate of the experimental raised fields. Continuous records of incoming and outgoing energy were collected using sensitive meteorological instruments both for an experimental raised field and for nearby non-raised field areas, The study indicated that during a night of light frost in the growing season, soil and air temperatures on the raised fields were al couple of degrees Celsius higher, and the frost was of several hours shorter duration than on nearby regular fields. The water temperatures in the canals between the raised fields were even warmer than that of the soil and air, indicating that the water acts as a heat sink for storage of solar energy. We suggest that this energy is released slowly at night, when frosts are most common, blanketing the surrounding fields in warmer air. Although the increase in temperatures is only slight, our experience indicates that it was enough and that it may have been very important in minimizing the risks due to frosts for the prehistoric farmers of the zone, both lessening crop damage during the growing season and actually extending the season.

projects in the Lake Titicaca region have failed and in some cases we can determine why. For instance, certain projects have attempted to introduce capital-intensive agriculture that depends primarily on petro-chemical fertilizers, heavy farm machinery, imported seed, irrigation pumps, or special animal forage, none of which the small-scale farmer can afford. Other projects have been oriented towards producing cash crops, but small farmers who produce a cash crop on their land often cannot make enough profit to buy food for their family, food they would otherwise produce themselves. In most cases, the majority of the farmers have not benefited from such development projects.

A more effective approach to development is through what is referred to as "appropriate technology." This approach stresses the use of traditional forms of technology and ecologically sound modern forms that are not capital intensive. In the Andes, there is a large work force available, but little capital. Since communal work forces are the traditional form of labor organization, an appropriate technology that is more easily adopted by peasant communities would involve cooperative labor. Besides increasing productivity of land now under cultivation, time-tested agricultural systems such as raised fields could be used in areas that are not currently farmed, such as on the vast pampa of the Lake Titicaca Basin.

In order to make the information collected through our archaeological and agronomic studies available as appropriate technology to the present-day Quechua and Aymara farmers of the area, a small-scale development project, the Raised Field Agricultural Project, began in 1982. We formed a multidisciplinary team, combining archaeology, cultural anthropology, agronomy, and agricultural communications that worked directly with indigenous farmers for over five years to rehabilitate the raised field system. Working with the small farmers of communities in Huatta and Coata, 10 hectares of raised fields that had been abandoned or underutilized for centuries were put back into use on communal lands. The Project, in cooperation with the Swiss government and the Peruvian Ministry of Agriculture, designed and prepared a intensive video training program in Quechua, in addition to written textbook materials, to rapidly disseminate the ancient technology.

Our applied archaeological program has finally begun to have an impact. In 1986–87, Ignacio Garay-cochea, an agronomist who conducted many of the experiments, directed a government-sponsored project in collaboration with 10 Quechua communities. In our recent 1989 evaluation, we calculate that 100 hectares are now in production. A measure of the success of this project is that many individual farmers have begun to build raised fields on their own private land.

Not only can the Quechua- and Aymara-speaking peoples take great pride in the sophisticated agricultural technology of their ancestors, but they can actually apply it to solve some of the contemporary economic and agricultural problems of Peru and Bolivia. The farmers of the communities participating in rehabilitating raised fields are taking that step. The high productivity of raised field technology not only helps to support the growing populations of the towns and cities of the region where many small farmers have had to migrate in search of a livelihood, but also helps us to understand and preserve this technology for the future. It is ironic that such an immensely important and productive technology is being destroyed in many areas around Lake Titicaca by modern plow farming, urbanization, and road-building.

BIBLIOGRAPHY

Browman, David L.
1978 "Towards the Development of the Tiahuanaco (Tiwanaku) State." *In Advances* in *Andean Archaeology,* ed. David L. Browman, pp. 327349. The Hague: Mouton.
Erickson, Clark L.
1985 "Applications of Prehistoric Andean Technology:

Experiments in Raised Field Agriculture, Huatta, Lake Titicaca; 1981-2." In *Prehistoric Zntensive Agriculture in the Tropics,* ed. Ian Farrington, pp. 209–232. British Archaeological Reports, International Series no. 232. Oxford.

1986 "Agricultura en Camellones en la Cuenca del Lago Titicaca: Aspectos Técnicos y su Futuro." In *Andenes y Camellones en el Peru Andina: Historia Presente y Futuro,* ed. Manual Burga and Carlos de la Torre, pp. 331–350. Lima: CONCYTEC.

1987 "The Dating of Raised-Field Agriculture in the Lake Titicaca Basin, Peru." In *Pre-Hispanic Agricultural Fields in the Andean Region,* ed. William Denevan, Kent Mathewson, and Gregory Knapp, pp. 373–384. British

Archaeological Reports, International Series, no. 359. Oxford.

Garaycochea, Ignacio

1986 "Agricultural Experiments in Raised Fields in the Lake Titicaca Basin, Peru:

Preliminary Considerations." In *Pre*-Hispanic *Agricultural Fields in the Andean*

Region, ed. William Denevan. Kent Mathewson, and Gregory Knapp, pp. 385–398. British Archaeological Reports, International Series, no. 359. Oxford.

Lennon, Thomas J.

1983 "Pattern Analysis in Prehistoric Raised Fields of Lake Titicaca, Peru." In *Drained Field Agriculture in Central and South America,* ed. J. Darch, pp. 183–200. British Archaeological Reports, International Series no. 189. Oxford.

Kolata, Alan

1986 "The Foundations of the Tiwanaku State, A *View* from the Heartland." *American Antiquity* 51(1):748–762.

Smith, Clifford, William Denevan, and Patrick Hamilton

1968 "Ancient Ridged Fields in the Region of Lake Titicaca." In *The Geographical Journal* 134:353–367.

ACKNOWLEDGMENTS

The author would like to especially thank Kay Candler, Dan Brink-meier, Ignacio Garaycochea, and the communities of Huatta and Coata. The raised field project could not have been done without their help. The Instituto Nacional de Cultura graciously gave permits to conduct the archaeological research. The field work was supported by a fellowship from the Social Science Research Council and a dissertation improvement grant from the National Science Foundation. Logistical support was provided by the Convenio Peru-Canada, CARE, the Cooperación Técnica Suiza, the Proyecto de Investigación de Sistemas Agropecuarias, and the Peruvian Ministry of Agriculture.

In addition to the applied research on raised field agriculture in the Lake Titicaca Region (1981–1986) as part of a doctoral dissertation project (University of Illinois, Champaign-Urbana), **Clark L. Erickson** has been involved in a number of archaeological projects in Peru, Bolivia, and

Ecuador He has conducted surveys in the western montaña of Ecuador (1979) and the savanna\ and tropical forests of the Llanos de Mojos of the eastern Bolivia (1978). His deep interest in Andean archaeology began with participation as an archaeological assistant and archaeobotanist for Bolivian Institute of Archaeology-U'ashington University excavations at the site of Chiripa, on the Bolivian shores of Lake Titicaca (1974-1975). He is currently Assistant Curator in the American Section of The University Museum and Assistant Professor in the Department of Anthropology at the University of Pennsylvania.

Extinction Isn't Always Forever

Biodiversity and Prehistory

Paul E. Minnis

EDITOR'S INTRODUCTION

We usually think of ourselves in the modern world as representing the pinnacle of technological and intellectual sophistication, including how this relates to agriculture. People in the past may have been smart, the argument goes, they may have been highly motivated, and they may have worked hard at it, but there's little we in the modern world can learn that might be of practical consequence in our efforts to solve current world problems. The implications of the article written by archaeologist Paul Minnis should put that bit of temporal conceit to rest. As Minnis points out, thousands of ancient societies have, over the course of many millennia, successfully responded to adaptive challenges, domesticated plants and animals, and developed strategies for increasing food production. It is, in fact, little more than conceit to maintain that there is not much to glean from those accomplishments represented by thousands of adaptive experiments that supplied food to millions of past people under a broad array of environmental conditions.

POINTS TO PONDER

1. Minnis mentions the study of several indigenous crops used by ancient people in the American Southwest. How has the use of those crops changed? How were they used aboriginally? How have they been used more recently?
2. Minnis lists four ways in which the study of prehistoric human ecology is of practical value to modern people. What are those ways?
3. What is the potential value to modern people of crops that once were significant parts of ancient diets?
4. What lessons can be learned from the perspective provided by Minnis about the potential of ancient farming technology to modern people?

The ancient past has been all too easily ignored by those concerned with environmental issues and economic development. After all, it is gone; looking back only wastes precious effort that must focus on building a sustainable future in the face of critical environmental problems at the cusp between the industrial and post-industrial ages. This is a peculiar and largely indefensible view, since ecological relationships are the outcomes of evolutionary, and hence historical, processes. To understand modern ecology, one must understand the past. To understand current relationships between humans and natural environments, one must understand humanity's past. One can ignore ancient peoples only if they were irrelevant in shaping what are called "natural" environments or if their lives have no relevance today. This view is adequate only for areas without indigenous peoples, say Antarctica.

There are many ways in which understanding prehistoric ecology is relevant for pressing environmental issues today. How, for example, does one understand changes in the desert environments of the North American Southwest experiencing a population boom without examining the effects of past human population expansions in these areas? While I will mention four ways in which prehistoric human ecology is valuable, here I will emphasize one use of the prehistoric human ecological record that is too often neglected, even by those concerned with the past's bearing on current environmental issues. There is intensifying alarm over the reduction of crop and cultivar diversity. Much of this reduction has occurred among small-scale traditional societies, the very repositories of crop variation developed over thousands of years of genetic manipulation. Oddly, crop variability in the archaeological record has not been considered important by the various governmental and nongovernmental organizations dedicated to the preservation of poorly known crop landraces. Too bad, because this past inventory of crops and agricultural strategies can be ignored only to society's detriment. No one knows how much knowledge of ancient crops or agricultural systems may be useful now and in the future.

IGNORING PREHISTORY

Before considering the value of prehistoric human ecology, it is instructive to explore why prehistoric human ecology is undervalued. There are a number of reasons for this, but I believe a chain of commonly held, but rarely expressed, assumptions impede the use of the past for the future. These assumptions are at the least overstated and more likely just plain wrong. Their impact is such that the prehistoric human experience—an incredible record of adaptation, ingenuity, and problem solving—is slighted.

The first assumption is that indigenous knowledge simply accumulates through time. Traditional groups with historical roots in a locality are believed to be the storehouse of centuries of accumulated folk wisdom. This may be partly true, but it is then further assumed that this storehouse is simply additive; newly acquired knowledge is heaped onto older knowledge. If so, then folk knowledge—of agricultural practices, medicinal plant usage, ecological interactions, and plant uses, and so on—is a record of prehistoric and protohistoric human ecology inversely proportional to the degree of outside "contamination" or "disruptions" by colonial, capitalist, or industrial contacts. This expectation is related to the assumption that folk knowledge is exceptionally brittle, especially for groups with a nonliterate tradition. Once the chain of traditional knowledge is broken, it is extinct—lost for good.

These views, while quite common and commonsensical, are erroneous for several reasons. First, there is no simple progressive and lineal accumulation of folk knowledge, a view that I suspect is largely based on the equally false premise that much of human prehistory was largely unchanging. True, indigenous peoples today are living repositories of ancient knowledge, but it was not a static knowledge. Prehistory and protohistory were dynamic; environments and societies change, now and in the past.

One example will suffice to illustrate this point. Several years ago, I studied ethnographically documented famine foods of the American Southwest and northern Mexico (Minnis 1991). Many of the plant resources ethnographically documented as famine foods, such as *ricegrass (Oryzopsis hy-menoides), pigweed (Amaranthus spp.), goosefoot (Chenopo-dium spp.)*, and prickly pear (Opuntia spp.), were also among the most commonly consumed food plants prehistorically (e.g., Minnis 1989). There is clear evidence of a substantial change in the use of the same plants through time from seasonal staples to famine foods. The plants did not change, but rather the economic and political context of plant use changed from prehistory to history. With outside exploration and domination of the region came alterations in land-use patterns, population sizes and locations, and the addition of economic activities. New food became available, and traditional seasonal staples were relegated to less frequent use. Human history and prehistory is dynamic, and modern indigenous groups are not necessarily the repositories of unchanging ethnobiological knowledge.

The second assumption that the chain of accumulated indigenous knowledge is easily lost could be true to a degree. It may be fragile, but one should not conclude that once the chain of knowledge is broken it is gone for forever. Can the past be resurrected, at least in part? The answer is "yes," but for some it is an unsatisfying "yes."

Strangely, the unfortunate absence of the human past in issues of biodiversity and resource conservation are not simply the results of a few faulty assumptions held by those who formulate and execute environmental policies. Some of the problem arises from the current context of pre-historichuman ecology. Too much archaeobiological research is highly technical and focused on narrow methodological issues. While methods, techniques, and protocols are essential, they are not what is most important about research in prehistoric human ecology. On the other extreme is an emergent and overly faddish set of archaeological approaches that have returned to an older view that human-environmental interactions are at worst irrelevant and at best simply background for the real business of humanity politics. We could easily return to a day when human ecology is dismissed as a vestigial form of 19th-century "vulgar materialism." If this view prevails, then many of the important intellectual gains in understanding human ecology made during the past 30 years will have to be relearned by future generations of scholars. But we do not have time, given the acute and chronic ecological problems affecting all peoples of the world.

FOUR RELEVANCIES OF PREHISTORIC HUMAN ECOLOGY

When I speak of the relevance of prehistoric human ecology and archaeobiology, I am not talking about the "Jurassic Park scenario," that we can literally resurrect whole organ isms from fragments of ancient DNA fortuitously preserved in the archaeological record. Shredded sequences of genetic information have been retrieved from archaeological specimens and may well be useful in the future, but for now this scenario remains a fantasy: Rather, I want to briefly consider: (1) *the role of prehistoric environmental reconstruction*, (2) *the importance of prehistoric economic biological knowledge*, (3) *the value of ancient farming techniques*, and (4) *the potential of ancient craps to expand the world's larder.* 1 will spend a disproportionate time on the last issue because it is one usually overlooked when discussing the relevance of human ecology.

Mapping Environmental Dynamics

Mapping environmental change across space and through time is complicated. The task is even more complex when humans affect the natural environment. It is gratifying to see that archaeological data are used more widely to understand environmental change. For example, several articles in issues of *BioScience* discussed prehistoric environments, as did recent issues of *Scientific American*. Similarly, prehistoric human-caused changes in Pacific Island ecology and biogeography, such as those at Easter Island and Hawai'i, are widely cited in the biological literature. Paul Martin's (Martin and Klein 1984) hypothesis of Pleistocene megafauna extinctions is another possible example of prehistoric anthropogenic environmental change that has found a wide audience outside of archaeology and paleontology. E. O. Wilson's (1992) *Tile Diversity of Life*, a popular volume, features these examples. The recognition that nonindustrialized populations were an active and creative force in their environment is a pleasant and important change from the image of an all too Edenic prehistory dominant for so long. As George Collier points out:

> Because of popular conceptions of "primitives" as mystically more "natural" than "civilized" peoples, anthropological literature is often cited as evidence that human society is capable of a finely tuned, balanced harmony with its environment, comparable to that achieved in a successional climax. Unfortunately, it is all too easy to discover examples of native populations living in obvious disequilibrium with their environment. (Collier 1975:12)

There are a number of examples of anthropogenic environmental changes in one relatively small area of the world, the US. Southwest and far northwestern Mexico (heretofore call the Desert Frontier). For example, as discussed in Chapter 11 of this volume, the Hohokam altered their environment. I have argued on the basis of multiple data sets that the prehistoric puebloan Mimbres of southwestern New Mexico denuded their floodplain because of expanding field clearance during a time of significant population growth (Minnis 1978, 1985). Various studies have documented the impact of the prehistoric inhabitants of the Colorado Plateau on their natural environment (e.g., Betancourt and Van Devender 1981; Kohler 1992; Kohler and Mathews 1988).

Understanding prehistoric environmental change is significant for more than simply appreciating the fact that environments are dynamic. How does one measure the effects of humans on environments without a historical perspective, or more to the point here, a prehistoric one? How do you distinguish directional environmental changes, cyclical changes, natural oscillations, and anthropogenic effects without understanding the prehistoric human ecology? What is the susceptibility of natural communities to human manipulation and overuse? Prehistory can address these questions. True, even the largest prehistoric community in ancient North America would have had only a fraction of the impact of today's industrial economy Prehistoric peoples are hardly perfect analogies for urbanized populations with an expansive economic base in the industrial age. Nonetheless, you have to gather your information where and when you can. The thousands of years of prehistoric human/ natural environmental interactions are available now.

Prehistoric Use of The Environment

Drug companies have spent and continue to spend large amounts of research funds to gather ethnobiological information about the indigenous use of medicines, and economic botany texts regularly enumerate the many modern drugs ultimately derived from traditional medicines. The search for new drugs and other plant uses continues (e.g., Farnsworfh 1988; Plotkin 1988, 1993). This is recognition, even by hard-headed business leaders, that there is value in indigenous knowledge of the environment. Such is not the case for prehistoric environmental knowledge. *The collective fund of knowledge accumulated by millions of ancient peoples in thousands of now extinct "cultures" that faced untold numbers of adaptive challenges for millennia must surely hold many important uses of plants and animals for the modern world.* If ethnographic information is an incomplete record of past human experience, then evidence of the use of biotic resources by prehistoric peoples has practical value. As an example, Karl Reinhard et al. (1985) show a correlation between the presence of goosefoot seeds and the absence of intestinal worms in paleofeces from the Colorado Plateau of the Desert Frontier (see also Reinhard etal. 1991).

Ancient Farming and Storage Technologies

Two categories of prehistoric environmental knowledge deserve special mention: *prehistoric cultivation strategies and storage techniques. Our prehistoric ancestors often developed ingenious techniques for growing and storing crops in areas not well suited for agriculture. Such strategies constitute a valuable source of information.* Human populations are expanding. Marginal lands are becoming more important. Peasants are having to use more and more marginal land as population increases and as wealthier farmers and corporations use prime farming land exclusively. Furthermore, farming practices can lead to the degradation of soils and water, making what were once first-choice field locations less desirable. Under these circumstances, it is quite likely that ancient agricultural techniques for farming less-than-ideal fields could provide models for the future. The reintroduction of prehistoric Tiwanaku farming strategies to modern peasants is an exemplary model of the value of prehistoric farming techniques (Kolata 1996).

I know of no example of archaeological data on prehistoric storage technologies being used today to develop ways to eliminate postharvest losses, but there may be great potential here. Archaeologists have noted many examples of storage facilities used by prehistoric peoples with materials and techniques easily available to peoples in the Third World.

The Value of Prehistoric Crops

The fourth practical value of prehistoric human ecology is usually overlooked. Scholars and policy makers in many disciplines have raised an alarm over the reduction in the genetic diversity of cultivated species and of the reliance on fewer and fewer cultigens to feed the world's expanding population. Programs to increase yields through the introduction of new cultivars have led to the extinction of indigenous varieties that are well adapted to local environmental conditions and that store a treasure of genetic diversity necessary to develop new varieties (e.g., Fowler and Mooney 1990; Oldfield and Alcorn 1991). Consequently, there have been concerted efforts by governments and nongovernmental organizations to preserve traditional cultivars before they become extinct. Archaeologists should applaud such efforts.

Overlooked, however, are now extinct prehistoric crops. While the living descendants of such plants may now exist only as native or "wild" plants, the archaeological record clearly demonstrates that these species are amenable to domestication by the very best evidence possible: They once were crops. As research on the origins of agriculture continues to expand beyond the better-known regions of Mesoamerica and Mesopotamia, our knowledge of plant manipulation and of the ubiquity of such plants grows. There is a rapidly expanding inventory of historically unknown prehistoric crops, some of which could be redomesticated.

The best North American example of now-extinct indigenous crops comes from the Eastern Woodlands, although this area has not been considered a "'center" of domestication from before

Table 13.1 Documented and possible native cultigens of eastern North America

TAXON	COMMON NAME	USE
Helianthus annuuis	Common sunflower	Seeds (achenes)
Helianthus tuberosus	Jerusalem artichoke	Tubers
Iva annua var. *macrocarpa*	Sumpweed or marshelder	Seeds (achenes)
Cucurbita pepo var. *ovifera* (or *C. texana*)	Gourd	Fruit and seeds
Chenopodium berlandieri var. *jonesianum*	Goosefoot	Seeds; possibly greens
Polygonum erectum	Knotweed	Seeds
Hordeum pusillum	Little barley	Seeds (caryopses)
Phalaris caroliniana	Maygrass	Seeds (caryopses)
Ambrosia trifida	Giant ragweed	Seeds (achenes)
Passiflora incarnata	Maypop	Fruits
Carya sp.	Hickory	Nuts
Various fruit trees such as honey locust, persimmon, paw paw, plum		

Sources: Cowan (1978), Yarnell (1987), and Smith (1992b).

Vavilov to more recent scholars. While it is true that a couple of composites, the common sunflower *(Helianthus annuus)* and the Jerusalem artichoke *(H. tuberosus),* were first domesticated in this vast region, only the former has become a staple, a minor staple to be sure, in the world's economy. Archaeobotanical research over the past 30 years, however, has shown that there was a suite of native plants domesticated by prehistoric peoples of the Eastern Woodlands (e.g., Scarry 1993; Smith 1992a, 1992b; Smith and Cowan 2003) (Table 13.1).

The suite of native indigenous crops includes some interesting plants. For example, the domesticated status of marshelder or sumpweed *(Iva annua* var. *macrocarpd)* has been documented clearly for several decades (e.g., Asch and Asch 1978; Smith 1992a, 1992b; Yarnell 1978) The seeds of this plant are produced in abundance and yield edible oil. The domestication of sumpweed is apparent in the archaeo logical record, as is its geographic spread throughout eastern North America.

Prehistoric native crops in eastern North America have been studied in most detail, but there is increasing potential for western North America. Little barley *(Hordeum pusilum)* and sunflower are the only species that appear to have been native crops in both the Eastern Woodlands and western North America. Otherwise, the assemblages are separate. There is a growing corpus of indigenous crops from the Desert Frontier, even though the economic foundation of this region's prehistoric farmers depended on Mesoamerican-derived crops (Ford 1981). Several historically known crops, such as devil's claw *(Proboscidea parviflora)* and panic grass *(Panicum sonorum),* may have been cultivated preliistoricaUy but" data regarding their prehistoric presence are sparse (Nabhan and de Wet 1984; Nabhan et al. 1981).

The best example of a native cultigen in the Desert Frontier documented in the archaeological record is a century plant, *Agave marpheyi,* Paul and Suzanne Fish and their collaborators (see Fish et al. 1985; Chapter 11, this volume) have demonstrated that this plant was cultivated extensively north of Tucson by the prehistoric Hohokam of the Sono-ran Desert, and it now appears that cultivated agaves were spread widely.

A number of authors (e.g., Fowler 1986; Minnis and Plog 1976; Winter 1974; Winter and Hogan 1986; Yarnell 1965, 1977) have suggested that many other plants may have been cultivated or at least manipulated by native populations of the Desert Frontier and adjacent Great Basin, and some of these may have been cultivated during prehistory. These pliants include *Cleome serrulata, Nicotiana attenuata, N. trigonophylla, Solanum jamesii, S. trifolum, Lycium pallidum, Physalis longifolia, P. hederaefolia, P. foetnens* var. *neomexicana, Rumex hymenosepalus, Ascelpias* spp., *Cirsium neomexicana, Sphaeralcea coccinea, Lepidium* spp., *Allium* spp., *Datura* spp., *Amaranthus powelli, A. lecocarpus, Mirabilis multiflora, Helianthus* sp., *Chenopodium berlandieri, Atriplex argentea, Dichelostemma pulchellum, Cyperus* sp., *Eragrostis orcuttiana, Agropyron trachycaulum, Elymus* sp., *Rorippa curvisliqua, Echinochloa* sp., *Sophia* sp., *Agave parryi*, and *Oryzopsis hymenoides*. No doubt the inventory of cultigens will expand greatly with more research in western North America, especially in California where we know prehistoric plant manipulation was intense.

DISCUSSION AND CONCLUSION

Analysis of prehistoric human ecology can offer more than an understanding of the past, as useful as that may be. It has the potential to refine models of ecological change, expand the inventory of useful plants and animals, augment agricultural and storage techniques, and enlarge the world's crop base. However, three issues impede the full potential of archaeological research to increase biodiversity and improve resource conservation. The first is the role of ethnographic analogy. The second concerns the nature of archaeological data and interpretations. The third issue centers on the ethics of intellectual property rights.

If society is to make full use of the record of prehistoric human ecology, then archaeologists must go well beyond ethnographic analogy. Typically, the use of plants and animals by ethnographically documented peoples is the primary basis for inferring the prehistoric use of the same plants. The report of plant taxa from archaeological sites is often accompanied by a paragraph or two enumerating their known uses by traditional peoples of the region. This ethnographic information then offers a smorgasbord of analogies to interpret how the plant was used by prehistoric peoples. The danger, of course, is that one can then not only misinterpret the past, but that the human ecologist can also miss novel behaviors and ecological relationships. With this approach, one sees only the present in the past, and the possible uniqueness of ancient history is lost. This problem is well known in archaeology hut rarely considered in prehistoric human ecology.

The second issue focuses on the nature of understanding of the past. Others make the useful distinction between biodiversity and biological integrity. The concept of "integrity" recognizes that environmental preservation is not simply a matter of counting species or crop diversity but rather of understanding the structure and organization of communities.

As in any historical science like paleontology or geology, archaeology cannot observe the integrity of past human ecology in its full rich and subtle texture. This is counterbalanced by having a long-term perspective. Still, archaeologists will never be able to model the integrity of prehistoric human ecological relationships with the same precision as they can in studies of modern living peoples. Prehistoric human ecologists study bits and pieces—critically important bits and pieces that provide information about change through time that cannot be known any other way—but bits and pieces nonetheless. Fully modeling ancient biological integrity is an impossible goal. They have to do the best they can and use their data as creatively and wisely as possible.

Accepting incomplete interpretations in historical sciences is not a fundamental problem for those doing the research. It can be exceptionally frustrating for those accustomed to working with more detailed synchronic ecological information. They must recognize that archaeology is still the only way to investigate a whole range of important topics. Knowing, for example, that many potential crops from eastern North America and elsewhere are available for re-domestication is worthwhile, even if one does not know all the ecological, economic, political, and cultural factors involved in their first domestication.

The final issue involves ownership of the past and the concern about proper compensation for intellectual properties. If prehistoric human ecological information has value, then who owns it? Intellectual properties of living indigenous groups have been legally and economically contentious. What happens to prehistoric intellectual properties when one party no longer exists or where historical relationships with modern groups are difficult to trace? Who, for example, should profit—yes, literally profit—from the first modern cultivated marshelder marketed as "the mystical grain of the Mound Builders" in some New Age Yuppie breakfast cereal? How do archaeologists help ensure that public knowledge of the past remains public and at the same time understand that the commercialization of ancient crops or technologies could be for the general good? They also recognize that some groups have special claims to the past. Do, or should, the recognized descendants of ancient peoples have special claim to ethnobiological knowledge? These questions now seem remote, but in light of changing biogenetic technologies and altered political relation they may not in the near future.

I am not arguing here that one should be silent to the pressures faced by indigenous peoples due to unwelcome changes, environmental destruction, and cultural genocide. The fact that archaeologists study such situations in the past does not mean that they take pleasure in or anticipate the premature and accelerated formation of the archaeological record through the destruction of peasant and tribal peoples at the beginning of the 21st century. Nor am I suggesting that there is no intrinsic worth in simply "knowing" the past, a view I hold dear. Nor am I arguing that archaeology and the study of prehistory is the most important analytic dimension for the issues of biodiversity and resource conservation. In fact, archaeology's contribution may be small, hut it can and should be larger than it is, in light of the fact that prehistory encompasses the majority of human experience. Fortunately, the past is not gone for good, and extinction isn't always forever.

ACKNOWLEDGMENTS

An earlier draft of this chapter was presented as the keynote address of the 1995 Annual Meeting of the Society of Ethnobiology, Tucson. Thanks go to organizers of the meeting. Pat Gilman and Charles Redman read draft and provided comments.

LITERATURE CITED

Asch, D., and N. Asch
1978 The Economic Potential of *Iva annua* and Its Prehistoric Importance in the Lower Illinois Valley. In *The Nature and Status of Ethnobotany*, edited by R. I. Ford, 300–341. Anthropological Papers No. *67*. Museum of Anthropology, University of Michgan, Ann Arbor.

Betancourt, J. L., and T. R. Van Devender
1981 Holocene Vegetation in Chaco Canyon, New Mexico. *Science* 214:*656–658*.

Collier, G. A.
1975 *Fields of the Tzotzil: The Ecological Bases of Tradition in Highland Chiapas,* University of Texas Press, Austin.

Cowan, C. W.
1978 The Prehistoric Use and Distribution of Maygrass in Eastern North America: Cultural and Phytogeographical Implications. In *The Nature and Status of Ethnobotany*, edited by R. I. Ford, 263–288. Anthropological Papers No. 67. Museum of Anthropology, University of Michigan, Ann Arbor.

Farnsworth, N. R.
1988 Screening Plants for New Medicines. In *Biodiversity*, edited by E. O. Wilson, 83–97. National Academy Press, Washington, D.C.

Fish, S. K., P. R. Fish, C. H. Miksicek, and J. H. Madsen
1985 Prehistoric Agave Cultivation in Southern Arizona. *Desert Plants* 7:107–113.

Ford, R. I.
1981 Gardening and Farming before A.D. 1000: Patterns of Prehistoric Cultivation North of Mexico. *Journal of Ethnobiology* 1:6–27.

Fowler, C. S.
1986 Subsistence. *In Handbook of North American Indians*, vol. 11, *Great Basin*, edited by W. D'Azevaedo, 64–97. Smithsonian Institution Press, Washington, D.C.

Fpwler, C, and P. Mooney

1990 *Shattering: Food Politics, and the Loss of Genetic Diversity.* University of Arizona Press, Tucson.

Kohler, T. A.

1992 Prehistoric Human Impact on the Environment in the Upland North American Southwest. *Population and Environment* 13:255–268.

Kohler, T. A., and M. H. Mathews

1988 Long-Term Anasazi Land Use and Forest Reduction: A Case Study from Southwestern Colorado. *American Antiquity* 53:537–564.

Kolata, A. L.

1996 *Tiwanaku and Its Hinterland: Archaeology and Paleoecology of an Andean Civilization: Agroecology.* Smithsonian Institution Press, Washington, D.C.

Martin, P. S., and R. G. Klein (editors)

1984 *Quaternary Extinctions: A Prehistoric Revolution.* University of Arizona Press, Tucson.

Minnis, P. E.

1978 Paleoethnobotanical Indicators of Prehistoric Environmental Disturbance: A Case Study. In *The Nature and Status of Ethnobotany,* edited by R. I. Ford, 347–366. Anthropological Papers No. 67. Museum of Anthropology, University of Michigan, Ann Arbor.

1985 *Social Adaptation to Food Stress: A Prehistoric South western Example.* University of Chicago Press, Chicago.

1989 Prehistoric Diet in the Northern Southwest: Macroplant Remains from Four Corners Feces. *American Antiquity* 54:543–563.

1991 Famine Foods of the Northern American Desert

Borderlands in Historical Context. *Journal of Ethnobiology* 11:231–257.

Minnis, P. E., and S. E. Plog

1976 A Study of the Site Specific Distribution of *Agave parryi* in East Central Arizona. *Kiva* 41:299–308.

Nabhan, G. P., and J. M.J. De Wet

1984 *Panicum sonorum* in Sonoran Desert Agriculture.

Economic Botany 38:65–68.

Nabhan, G. P., A. Whiting, H. Dobyns, R. Hevley, and R. Euler

1981 Devil's Claw Domestication: Evidence from South-western Indian Fields. *Journal of Ethnobiology* 1:135–164.

Oldfield, M. L., and J. B. Alcorn

1991 *Biodiversity: Culture, Conservation, and Ecodevelopment.* Westview Press, Boulder,

Plotkin, M.J.

1988 The Outlook for New Agricultural and Industrial Products from the Tropics. In *Biodiversity,* edited by E. O.Wilson, 106–116, National Academy Press, Washington, D.C.

1993 *Tales of a Shaman's Apprentice.* Viking, New York.

Reinhard, K.J,J. R. Ambler, and M. McGuffie

1985 Diet and Parasitism at Dust Devil Cave. *American Antiquity* 50:819–824.

Reinhard, K. J., D. J. Hamilton, and R. I. Hevley

1991 Use of Pollen Concentration in Paleopharmacology: Coprolite Evidence of Medicinal Plants. *Journal of Ethnobiology* 11:117–132.

Scarry, C. M.

1993 *Foraging and Farming in the Eastern Woodlands.* University of Florida Press, Gainesville.

Smith, B. D.

1992a Prehistoric Plant Husbandry in Eastern North

America. In *The Origins of Agriculture: An International Perspective,* edited by C. W. Cowan and P.J. Watson, 101–119. Smithsonian Institution Press, Washington, D.C.

1992b *Rivers of Change: Essays on Early Agriculture in Eastern North America.* Smithsonian Institution Press, Washington, D.C.

Smith, B. D., and C. W. Cowan

2003 Domesticated Crop Plants and the Evolution of Food Production Economies in Eastern North America. In *People and Plants in Ancient Eastern North America,* edited by P. E. Minnis, 105–125. Smithsonian Books, Washington, D.C.

Wilson, E. O.

1992 *The Diversity of Life.* W. W. Norton, New York.

Winter, J. C.

1974 *Aboriginal Agriculture in the Southwest and Great Basin.* Unpublished Ph.D. dissertation, Department of Anthropology, University of Utah, Salt Lake City.

Winter, J. C., and P. F. Hogan

1986 Plant Husbandry in the Great Basin and Adjacent Northern Colorado Plateau. In *Anthropology of the Desert West: Essays in Honor of Jesse D. Jennings,* edited by C. J. Condie and D. D. Fowler, 117–144. Anthropological Papers No. 10. University of Utah, Salt Lake City.

Yarnell, R. I.

1965 Implications of Distinctive Flora on Pueblo Ruins. *American Anthropologist* 67:662–674.

1977 Native Plant Husbandry North of Mexico. In *Origins of Agricidture,* edited by C. Reed, 861–875. Mouton Press, The Hague.

1978 Domestication of Sunflower and Sumpweed in Eastern North America. In *The Nature and Statuscf Ethnobotany,* edited by R. I. Ford, 285–299. Anthrological Papers No. 67. Museum of Anthropology, University of Michigan, Ann Arbor.

1987 A Survey of Prehistoric Crop Plants in Easter North America, *Missouri Archaeologist* 47:47–60

Section 4

HELPING HISTORY: CLEARING THE AIR AND SOLVING MYSTERIES

We have all heard the stories a hundred times, read about them in a social studies or history course, seen the exposé presented in a cable documentary: famous and even infamous stories where cruel fate combined with human frailty, pride, and even stupidity led to tragic consequences. If only the travelers hadn't followed the new, untested and virtually untried trail; if conceit and presidential aspirations hadn't clouded the judgment of an ambitious colonel; if circumstances had been different, a villain might have been a hero; if a fictional account of a real king had been written differently, he might not be thought of today as an evil madman. But history is, well, history. Half of the people in the Donner Party searching for a new life in California died in the winter of 1846–7 and some resorted to cannibalism to survive. Researchers are still investigating their stories. More than 210 US cavalrymen met their deaths in the face of an enormous force of Indian warriors, leaving traces of the battle in the form of bullets, arrow points, and even their bodies. Similarly, the lives of an Australian outlaw and a British king are being reconsidered and re-evaluated on the basis of the archaeological record they left behind. In each case, archaeology is attempting to fill in the gaps in our knowledge of what happened. Four articles present the stories of the archaeological investigation of the historical truths behind these events and people.

In a very general sense, all archaeology strives to collect physical evidence, to recover remains left behind by human beings, and to understand the circumstances surrounding not just the scene of a crime but the scene of a life. While forensic archaeologists work as literal detectives, the practitioners of archaeology in general work as metaphorical detectives of the past, attempting to illuminate the lives of those who have preceded us on this planet.

In some cases, these detectives of the past apply their investigative skills in the assistance of historians examining historical events and personalities. These are events that have occurred in, and people who inhabited, the not-too-distant past and about which and whom, often, much has been written.

Archaeology can help to illuminate these historical events and people because, as all historians know, just because people in past times were literate and often wrote accounts of the events that happened in their own lifetimes, we do not by any means today have a perfect understanding of the actual nature of those events. History, for example, isn't inclusive. Accounts written at the time of an event do not necessarily tell the whole story. Depending on who controls the printing presses, the newspapers, magazines and, yes, even the radio and television stations in more recent history, a version of history is told, recorded, passed down, and made "official" that does not necessarily reflect a complete and accurate transcript of what actually occurred. The victors of ancient battles got to write the official accounts of the war; the losers often were silenced and silent.

Napoleon Bonaparte is supposed to have asked: "What is history but a fable agreed upon?" He recognized that the accounts that he sponsored of his own victories on the battlefield were self-aggrandizing, self-serving statements intended to solidify support back home and, perhaps, written with an eye to how future people might view this ruler of France. Another great leader, Winston Churchill said it, perhaps even more directly; when commenting on his place in history Churchill was quoted as maintaining, "History will be kind to me for I intend to write it." In a similar manner, slave owners and not slaves wrote the accounts of plantation life; in the American south, it was difficult and dangerous for slaves to tell their stories because, at least in some states, it was illegal to teach them to read and write. Their historical voice is muted as a result and our histories are at best, incomplete and at worst, badly biased.

That written accounts may be incomplete or even untrue is the case even when we are examining very well-known historical events and people, the kinds of events and people that we are all exposed to even in elementary school. Archaeology, with its focus on material evidence can provide assistance to historians interested in such physical evidence related to events for which most previous information has been literary. Written records may be incomplete, biased, or intentionally inaccurate; the physical record may be incomplete, but it is hardly ever intentionally skewed. Physical evidence of the sort collected by archaeologists can be used to test history, to verify or refute or merely add details to the official versions of events as they have been handed down to us. And in some cases, where history provides us with no official version and where the actual nature of the events and the disposition of the historical personages remain a mystery, archaeology can help solve the riddles and allow us to know with varying degrees of certainty what actually transpired. The articles in this section of the reader provide examples where archaeological investigation has complemented history by adding to our understanding of historical events and people, where archaeology has challenged the official version and caused us to change how we interpret those events and how we view those people, and, in some instances, where archaeology has provided the physical evidence necessary for the solution of historical mysteries where the written record has, by itself, not offered a solution.

A New Look at the Donner Party

Julie M. Schablitsky

EDITOR'S INTRODUCTION

The story of Donner Party has become so entrenched in American history that it has become the punchline for a series of bad jokes, all related to cannibalism. Named the Donner Party for George Donner, the man selected to lead the group, more than 80 immigrants made their way to California from the Midwest in 1846, hoping for a better life. Their trip was a perfect example of Murphy's Law in practice: virtually anything that could go wrong did. There was a delay at the beginning of the journey as an elderly woman lay dying. The group made a terrible mistake in following a new, ostensibly faster and easier trail that was, in fact, far more difficult and longer. Provisions were lost, pack animals escaped, and they arrived at the foothills of the Sierra Nevadas just as the earliest recorded blizzard erupted, making climbing those mountains impossible. More than half the group died and some of the survivors resorted to cannibalizing their comrades in order to survive. Understandably, the versions of the tale written by those who experienced it (in journals written at the time or in later reminiscences) and historical versions written by observers are incomplete and inconsistent. This is a perfect opportunity for the material evidence offered by archaeology to contribute to our understanding of what happened to the doomed people of the Donner Party.

POINTS TO PONDER

1. Why is archaeology necessary to help us more completely understand what happened to the members of the Donner Party?
2. Why couldn't the Donner Party make it over the Sierra Nevadas before the first snows of winter?
3. What does the research of archaeologist Julie Schablitsky tell us about the cannibalism recorded by contemporary observers of the Donner Party?
4. What are the lessons of the archaeological research of the Donner Party?

Julie Schablitsky, "A New Look at the Donner Party," *Archaeology*, vol. 65, no. 3, pp. 53-54, 56, 62. Copyright © 2012 by Archaeological Institute of America. Reprinted with permission.

n late October 1846, an early snowstorm stranded 22 men, women, and children in Alder Creek meadow in California's Sierra Nevada. The squall came on so fiercely and suddenly that the pioneers had just enough time to erect sleeping tents and a small structure of pine trees covered with branches, quilts, and the rubber coats off their backs. Living conditions were crowded, and their wool and flannel clothes were useless against leaks and the damp ground. As time passed, seasoned wood became so hard to find that the stranded pioneers, known as the Donner Party were often without fire for days. Huddled under makeshift shelters, the migrants ate charred bone and boiled hides until they turned to more desperate measures to survive. Today the people of the Donner Party are remembered for cannibalizing their dead in a last-ditch effort to survive.

Almost 10 years ago, I arrived at Alder Creek meadow, a few miles outside of Truckee, California, with my excavation codirector Kelly Dixon, of the University of Montana, and a team of colleagues to search for archaeological evidence of that miserable winter. The story of the Donner Party is a familiar tale, well known from the accounts of survivors and rescuers. But, as in many cases, archaeology provided a different perspective and forced us to reevaluate what we thought we knew about this dark chapter in Western history

The Donner Party was a wagon train of about 80 pioneers who set out for California from Springfield, Missouri, in 1846. Hoping to make the Sacramento Valley by autumn, they fell behind schedule after taking an untried shortcut through the Great Salt Lake Desert. When an October snowstorm hit, the party was just 100 miles from their destination. Most of the migrants sought shelter in cabins near Truckee Lake (now Donner Lake), while the families of brothers George and Jacob Donner, their teamsters, and trail widow Doris Wolfinger made the decision to winter at Alder Creek.

By the time the pioneers were found in late February 1847, half the members of the Donner Party had died. Both survivor and rescue party accounts note human bodies disarticulated and butchered. Survivor Jean Baptiste Trudeau, George Donner's hired hand, admitted to eating the remains of his employer's four-year-old nephew Even before the last survivor made it out of the mountains, the *California Star* newspaper wrote, "A woman sat by the body of her husband, who had just died, eating out his tongue; the heart she had already taken out, broiled, and eat [*sic*]!" But as with many tales of the Wild West, there are deeper and more complex truths to be found in the four months the Donners spent trapped. Our archaeological investigations revealed the nuances of daily life, the party's mounting desperation, and, surprisingly that these unfortunate migrants were not alone in the mountains.

The approximate location of the Donner Party encampment at Alder Creek has been known since the late nineteenth century, but the precise camp spot had never been pinpointed. Don Hardesty an archaeologist and professor emeritus at the University of Nevada, Reno, searched for the site in the 1980s and early 1990s. Using metal detectors, he found a mid-nineteenth-century site there, but was cautious about declaring it the Donner camp in the absence of human bones or any remains of a campfire. Building off his work, my research focused on the layout of the camp, close study of the pioneers' fragmented belongings, and identifying evidence of cannibalism. One can imagine the morbid appeal of discovering human bones with butchery marks among other, more genteel artifacts such as floral decorated teacups, but I felt uncomfortable and even guilty about considering the grim possibilities.

Part of this anxiety comes from being a Generation X archaeologist trained in the age of NAGPRA (Native American Graves Protection and Repatriation Act), a federal law that protects Native American graves. Both the government and my mentors taught me to avoid burial sites. Though I understood the legal and logistical reasons for this, only when I began to work as a professional archaeologist did I appreciate the Native American perspective. My work with Pacific Northwest tribes taught me a respect for their culture that changed my approach to human remains, regardless of ancestry. So before digging at Alder Creek, I turned to the person who taught me the most about Native American culture, Jeff Van Pelt, a member of the Confederated Tribes of the Umatilla Indian Reservation in Oregon.

Van Pelt knows the story of the Donners, but he held a different viewpoint than I did. From my European-American perspective, the Donners were an unfortunate, hard-luck chapter in the otherwise heroic tale of pioneers who settled the American West. I pictured hundreds of wagons, packed full of provisions, with calico-clad children bouncing along the Oregon Trail to a better life. Not unexpectedly, Van Pelt saw the story of the Donners—and all westward expansion, for that matter—as a self-serving expedition for land and wealth. To him, their troubles were symptomatic of greed rather than bad luck

Van Pelt urged me to seek out the *wel mel ti,* or the tribe now known as the northern Washoe, to ask what their oral history says of the Donners. "They were there, and probably saw them," he said. Van Pelt also warned me against the negative energy that lingers in such places of suffering. He removed from his neck an elaborately carved shell pendant given to him by a Florida shaman. On it, two animal spirits, called *spilya* ("coyote" in the Sahaptin language), danced, actively creating order from chaos. It would protect me through the turmoil of the Alder Creek dig, Van Pelt said.

Months before arriving in California, I studied maps, historical narratives, and the notes from earlier archaeological investigations. Hardesty had found the eastern edge of the site, but not its western extent, so we planned to move from the known to the unknown. The first shovelfuls of dry soil were sterile, but inches below, we began to find glass shards, once part of beverage and sauce bottles, mixed with fragments of decorated and blue shell-edge teaware. We also discovered a particularly riveting artifact—a small piece of writing slate, possibly used by the Donner children or adults in camp to make notes, figure math problems, practice letters, or just doodle. This nineteenth-century notepad may have helped the children pass the time, and perhaps even made their situation feel a little more normal. Deeper in the soil, just below these more recently discarded objects, we found Native American stone tools—large basalt flakes and bifaces that reminded us who was there first.

The soil that held pioneer-era artifacts contained occasional pockets of ash and charcoal that gave me hope that an elusive Donner hearth might be near. As our team pushed south through the site, the soil became more ashy, and larger pebbles and pieces of lead shot appeared. My trowel followed the edge of a dark charcoal stain with a thin layer of ash: the hearth. Shannon Novak of Syracuse University one of the team's bioarchaeologists, knelt beside me with a whisk broom, further delineating the feature. She exposed bone fragments that appeared larger than any we had seen before, and some exhibited cut, saw, and chop marks. As my trowel continued to scrape the edge of the charcoal, I discovered a large ceramic plate sherd, face down. Everyone gathered around as I picked up the fragment from the exact place it was broken by one of the Donners. A "hooray" rang out as I turned the artifact over to reveal a scalloped edge rimmed with a vibrant cobalt-blue glaze. The hearth feature, approximately two by two-and-a-half feet, anchored our collection of artifacts that fanned out to the east. In addition to delicate ceramics—seemingly out of place in the wilderness, but right in line with a Donner campsite—the assemblage included wagon hardware, even horseshoe nails and oxen shoes, clear evidence that the animals that pulled the pioneers into the meadow never left it. At last, we had found our long-term pioneer campsite, but we were still looking for evidence of starvation and desperation. So we turned to the most abundant artifact on the site, bone.

The dig crew picked out thousands of tiny calcined (burned) bone fragments from the site. Whenever we found a "big" bone—a piece at least the size of a thumbnail—I handed it over to our faunal analyst, Guy Tasa of the Washington State Department of Archaeology and Historic Preservation. I waited for each of his verdicts as he turned the bones around in his hand a few times, but all he ever said was, "Medium to large mammal." This frustratingly broad category includes everything from goats to buffalo, but in this region and context more likely represents cow, horse, deer, elk, bear ... and human. We know from survivor accounts that the Alder Creek pioneers consumed the animals they brought with them, including cattle, horses, and perhaps even their faithful dog, Uno. When the last of the meat was gone, they turned to boiling animal hides and charring bone so they could eat the pieces by crunching them between their teeth.

Back at the laboratory with his collection of comparative bone samples at hand, Tasa listed the cuisine on the Donner Party desperation menu: small rodent, rabbit-sized animal, canine, cow, and deer. But no human. Only a very small percentage of the bone could be visually identified. Out of 16,204 bone fragments (5.03 pounds), over 13,000 pieces remained unidentified. Because I knew the faunal analysis would be a challenge, I sacrificed a few bone fragments to a DNA laboratory in California, but the results were inconclusive. The bone had been cooked and boiled before it spent over 150 years in acidic soil, degrading the DNA beyond detection even by twenty-first-century forensic technology Tasa had another idea. Gwen Robbins Schug, an anthropologist at Appalachian State University, can identify animal species by observing bone structure. It is not a common method for archaeologists, but was worth a try.

Using an optical microscope to observe osteons, or the fundamental structural units of bone, Schug found 85 bone fragments that belonged to cow, deer, horse, and dog. But again, there were no human bones. This, of course, does not mean that the Donners did not practice cannibalism. Our excavations might have missed the human remains, or if the Donners ate only organs and flesh, leaving the bone unprocessed and unburned, the skeletons may have decomposed in the acidic soil. A third possibility is that the human bone simply remains undetected in our collection. Although the absence of identifiable human bone was an interesting problem, I was much more intrigued by what we *did* find: None of the survivor accounts from Alder Creek mention successfully hunting and killing rabbit or deer. We also found lead shot and sprue from lead casting, suggesting the pioneers had attempted to make ammunition for their guns. Perhaps one of the Donner Party members or rescuers had been successful at hunting wild game. But if the Donners found themselves too weak to hunt in the deep snow, or their aim was off, how could they have ended up eating these animals?

After the dig I returned home to Oregon, but there was one thing left to do. We still needed to check in with the *wel mel ti,* the northern Washoe, to learn if their ancestors passed down stories about the Donner Party The *wel mel ti* are thought to have lived in that region for centuries, and Alder Creek was just miles from one of their villages. Although they usually wintered in lower elevations, living off food stores gathered throughout the year, it would not have been unusual for a *wel mel ti* to strap on a pair of round snowshoes, or *shumélli,* and go ice fishing or hunting on higher ground. We asked ethnographer Penny Racks, who has more than twenty years of experience with the local tribes, to ask the *wel mel ti* if the pioneer tragedy had survived in their tribal narrative. Rucks reached out to Jo Ann Nevers and Lana Hicks, who agreed to share the *wel mel ti* story with the understanding that they diq so to honor their ancestors.

Until now the Native American perspective has been left out of the telling of the Donner tragedy, not because the *wel mel ti* did not remember the pioneers, but because they were never asked, or perhaps were not ready to share. Their oral tradition recalls the starving strangers who camped in an area that was unsuitable for that time of year. Taking pity on the pioneers, the northern Washoe attempted to feed them, leaving rabbit meat and wild potatoes near the camps. Another account states that they tried to bring the Donner Party a deer carcass, but were shot at as they approached. Later, some *wel mel ti* observed the migrants eating human remains. Fearing for their lives, the area's native inhabitants continued to watch the strangers but avoided further contact. These stories, and the archaeological evidence that appears to support them, certainly complicated my interpretation of the Donner Party event. The migrants at Alder Creek were not surviving in the mountains alone—the northern Washoe were there, and they had tried to help.

Historical archaeologists combine anthropology history, and science to reconcile the human experience with archives, oral history and physical evidence. More often than not, there are contradictions in these data, reminding us that we can never truly *know* the past. But when the pieces fit together, we are provided with possible scenarios of what may have taken place hundreds of years ago. In this case, the absence of cannibalized bone forced us to give up trying to answer who was butchered and how it was done. Instead, we had to find answers to questions about life in camp from the crumbs of domestic debris and animal bone. Our intense desire for information drove us to seek out cutting-edge technology and reach out to a group of people who I thought played only a peripheral role in this pioneer tragedy When I considered the subtle archaeological findings within their proper cultural landscape, an unexpected narrative was born. This new perspective is one that I believe gives us a better understanding of what the Donners experienced and whom they met in the mountains during that notorious winter.

Archaeology of the Battle of the Little Bighorn

Douglas Scott

EDITOR'S INTRODUCTION

Depending on which side of history you fall on, the Battle of the Little Bighorn has been told as a tale of great military bravery in a doomed attempt to fight off an implacable and much larger enemy, or comeuppance for the oppression of a people who merely wanted to be left alone. The facts are pretty simple: late in June of 1876, a group of about 210 US Cavalry attempting to enforce their removal to a reservation came upon a large force of Lakota, Northern, Cheyenne, and Arapaho warriors near the Little Bighorn River, attacked them, and were wiped out utterly. There were no written accounts of the battle, no embedded journalists to record the flow of the battle, no eyewitnesses wrote of the deaths of Custer and his men on the grass-covered hills of southern Montana. The only survivors of the battle were Native American warriors and some of their eyewitness accounts were collected substantially after the fact. But, as archaeologist Doug Scott tells the story, the battlefield itself is an archaeological site where the recovery of bullets, military hardware, arrow points, and even the remains of some of the people killed during the battle provide us with a detailed picture of the ebb and flow of the battle, including the movement of troops and even the strategies of the soldiers on both sides of one of the most famous battles fought on American soil.

POINTS TO PONDER

1. What was Custer's point in attacking a clearly much-larger contingent of Indian warriors?
2. What happened to reveal the wealth of artifacts left in place at the battlefield sometimes known as Custer's Last Stand?
3. What strategies were employed by the archaeologists working at the site of the Battle of the Little Bighorn to recover and analyze the artifacts from the battle?
4. What lessons about the battle have been learned through archaeology?

INTRODUCTION

June 25th marks the anniversary of the Battle of the Little Bighorn. The anniversary of the day George Armstrong Custer led approximately 210 men to their deaths in the Montana wilderness. Since that day, the story of Custer and the Battle of the Little Bighorn has assumed legendary, if not mythological, proportions in American culture.

The battle epitomizes the clash of cultures—the Native American versus the Euro-American—that is so much a part of our heritage. These two cultural systems clashed in hundreds of ideological and practical concepts—their ideas of land ownership, their ideas of treaties and boundaries, their leadership, their concept of how to fight a war.

At the battle of the Little Bighorn, these differences produced a conflagration which has illuminated these differences for the American public from 1876 to the present.

From that fateful Sunday in June, 1876 until the present, Custer's movements, after a messenger left him and until his defeat, have been the subject of hot debate. No white survivors lived to tell the tale, and Indian accounts of the battle have often been discounted, suggesting that the Indian's fear of retribution and the language barriers combined to create inaccuracies.

A literal conflagration in August 1983 produced the opportunity to examine the battlefield in a new way when a wildfire scorched the Little Bighorn Battlefield National Monument, administered by the National Park Service. Recently, a series of multidisciplinary studies have combined to provide fresh interpretations of the battle and its significance in American history.

Archeological investigations have used physical evidence, artifacts, to interpret specific elements of the battle. In turn, the archeological studies spurred historians and other researches to re-evaluate the documentary record, Native American oral tradition, and ethnohistorical accounts.

The results are a significant reinterpretation of the battle events. Some of the reinterpretation is particularistic in nature, literally following combatant movements across the field or revealing physical evidence that combined with oral tradition identifies the site and occupants of a previously unknown Lakota camp circle on the west side of the Little Bighorn river. Other elements allow a broader re-evaluation of the events.

In an attempt to make the battlefield speak for itself, archeological procedures were applied during the summers of 1984, 1985, 1989, 1993, 1994, and 1996. This has resulted in the accumulations of over 5000 artifacts, and much new data on the battle. The multidisciplinary work clearly demonstrates that Custer divided the Seventh Cavalry into three elements during the early phases of the battle and then subdivided his immediate command into wings. This division of his troops in the face of an overwhelming number of Indians may not have been his best decision, but it was an accepted and field tested military tactic that was successful until this battle.

The Lakota and Cheyenne warriors, although surprised by the army's attack, quickly rallied and put all elements of the Seventh Cavalry's attack on the defensive. The Indians fought in a prescribed cultural manner as is demonstrated by oral tradition and physical evidence. Ramifications of the

event aside, it is clear from the newly reinterpreted multidisciplinary sources that the Lakota and Cheyenne warriors outnumbered, outgunned, and outfought the soldiers of the Seventh Cavalry, giving the army its worst defeat of the entire Indian Wars.

HISTORY

To put the battle in context requires returning to 1868 when the Treaty of Fort Laramie was signed. This treaty granted the Black Hills area to the Indians. However, in the early 1870s, rumors spread of gold in the Hills, and white miners began slipping into the reservation area. In 1874, the U.S. government decided to determine the validity of these rumors and sent a geological team, under Custer, to examine the minerals in the area. Gold was among the minerals found, and not Caesar himself could have stopped the barbarian hordes of miners flowing into the reservation.

In the spring of 1876, a three pronged campaign was launched to shepherd the Sioux and Cheyenne back to the reservation. The first prong, under General John Gibbon, marched east from Fort Ellis (near present-day Bozeman, Montana). The second prong, led by General Alfred Terry (and including Custer) headed west from Fort Abraham Lincoln near Bismark, North Dakota. The third prong consisted of General George Crook's men moving north from Wyoming into Montana.

Unknown to Terry and Gibbon, Crook encountered the Indians near the Rosebud Creek in southern Montana, and was defeated by them about a week before Custer's battle. After this, his force withdrew to Wyoming, breaking one side of the triangle.

Meanwhile, Terry was moving west up the Yellowstone River to the Little Bighorn. The 7th Cavalry, under Custer, was to scout ahead and departed Terry's command on June 22. On the morning of the 25th, the 7th Cavalry was at the divide between the Rosebud and the Little Bighorn Rivers. From a spot known as the Crow's Nest, they observed a large Indian camp.

Worried the Indians might escape, Custer decided to attack and descended into the valley of the Little Bighorn. At the Crow's Nest, Captain Frederick Benteen was ordered to travel to the southwest with three companies to block a possible southern escape route. A few miles from the Little Bighorn, Custer again divided his command, as Major Marcus Reno was ordered to take three companies along the river bottom and attack the Indian village on its southern end. The remaining five companies would follow Custer in support of Reno.

Custer, in the meantime, followed the top of the ridge to an ephemeral tributary of the Little Bighorn. He must have finally realized the gravity of the situation as the north end of the village came into view. From here, he sent a message back to Benteen: "Benteen, Come on. Big village, be quick, bring packs. P.S. Bring pacs (sic). W.W. Cooke." The messenger, bugler John Martin, was the last to see Custer and his command alive and Custer's movements after this are a point of speculation.

In the meantime, the Indian warriors had forced Reno and his men to retreat across the river, and up the bluffs to a defensible position. Reno and the men on the hilltop were joined by Benteen's forces and the pack train, both moving along Custer's line of march in order to bring up the ammunition packs.

All were pinned down by the Indians until June 27th, when the village retreated as General Terry, joined by General Gibbon's column, arrived. For that day and a half, Reno, Benteen and the men fought to keep their defensive position and wondered when Custer would relieve them. Reno sent two men to meet the advancing column, and they found Terry and Gibbon near the abandoned Indian village. Here, a scout brought the news. Custer and his men lay dead on a ridge above the Little Bighorn.

METHODS

The project archeologists chose to view the battlefield as a crime scene and by using a combination of forensic techniques such as studies of firing pin marks on cartridge cases and rifling marks on bullets, and standard archeological field, laboratory, and analytical techniques they have been able to determine the variety of weapons used by the various participants.

By combining crime lab methods with the archeological constructs of spatial patterning and individual artifact analysis, they have been able to discover evidence for the movement of individual firearms over the field of battle, verify cavalry positions, and define previously unknown Indian fighting areas.

Forensic studies on the human skeletal remains have revealed information about the wounds the men received, as well as their general health and condition at the time of death. The archeological work consisted of three parts. The first was a metal detector inventory of the battlefield. Volunteers, experts in the use of detectors, walked about 5 meters apart covering the field.

When their detectors 'beeped', they marked the area with a pinflag. Behind them came the recovery crew. These people would excavate cautiously, searching for the object that caused the detector to signal. When found, the object was carefully left in place. Finally, the survey crews came along.

Using either a transit or theodolite, these crews would set up on a predetermined datum point and determine the angle and distance of the surrounding artifacts from that point. This crew would make notes on the depth of the artifact below ground surface, and in the case of bullets and cartridges, also note the orientation and the declination of the piece. Only then was the artifact collected.

Another phase of the archeological work was the excavations, which were centered on a series of marble markers. The marble markers which dot the battlefield were placed to commemorate the location where one of Custer's men fell. However, they were set in place fourteen years after the battle, and more than nine years after the bodies were disinterred and placed in a mass grave near where Custer's body was found on Last Stand Hill.

EXCAVATIONS

The excavation units added more detail to the findings of the metal detector inventory. They suggest that the majority of markers were placed were a soldier fell, as indicated by pieces of uniforms, weapons and human bone. Paired markers, markers placed by twos around the battlefield, usually indicate a single soldier, thus identifying many of the probable spurious markers.

Bone was the major class of artifact found in the excavations. Despite the fact that the men were reburied in a mass grave in 1881 it was not unusual to find small bits of human bone around a marker.

Dr. Clyde Snow and Dr. P. Willey, physical anthropologists who interpreted the bones found at the battlefield, say this is typical of a modern crime scene where bone has been gathered by untrained lay people. Small bones, such as hand and feet bones, are either not recognized as human or overlooked and left behind. Indeed, these were the majority of the bones found.

In the excavations where skull fragments were uncovered, they were all just that, fragments. They had been broken while the bone was green indicating what is called "perimortem blunt instrument trauma". An Indian warrior, Black Elk, recounted the final moments of the battle, describing how the Indians used hatchets and clubs to finish off the surviving soldiers. The evidence of trauma on the recovered human bone supports these recollections

While some of the trauma was undoubtedly induced at the time of death, other trauma, such as cut marks and crushed skulls, may have occurred after death. The mutilation of the dead was a normal cultural expression of victory for the Sioux and Cheyenne in battle. This battle was no exception, but to the soldiers who buried Custer's dead on June 28, 1876 the field was a scene of ghastly and sickening horror.

Remains consistent with those of a minimum of 44 individuals were uncovered during archeological investigations. The combination of skeletal and artifactual material reveal some of the most poignant pictures of the battle. The examinations revealed the men had poor dental health as a rule, although one man had several gold and tin fillings indicating the quality of dental care available in the 1870s was good, if people only went to the dentist.

The men's teeth also revealed the widespread use of coffee and tobacco. Other skeletal elements demonstrate broken bones, as well as significant back problems. The bones demonstrate these men led a rugged and hard life, certainly not the romantic one so-often portrayed in books and film.

FIREARMS

A primary analytical tool of the Little Bighorn Archeological project was Firearms Identification. The comparative study of ammunition components is known as firearms identification analysis. Firearms, in their discharge, leave behind distinctive metallic fingerprints or signatures on the ammunition components. These signatures, called class characteristics, allow the determination of the type of firearm (i.e., model or brand) in which a given cartridge case or bullet was fired. This then allows determination of the number of different types of guns used in a given situation.

Further, they allow the identification of individual weapons by comparing the unique qualities of firearm signatures (individual characteristics). This capability is very important because coupled with the precise artifact locations, identical signatures can be used to identify specific combat areas. This can be done with cartridge cases and bullets even though the actual weapons are not in hand. With this information, patterns of movement can be established and sequences of activity can be more precisely interpreted.

The comparison microscope is critical to the analysis of ammunition. Simply, the microscope is constructed so that two separate microscope tubes are joined by a bridge with prisms mounted over the tubes. Two separate images are transmitted to the center of the bridge, where another set of prisms transmit the images to central eyepieces. The eyepieces are divided so that each image appears on one-half of each eyepiece. Movable stages allow the objects under scrutiny to be manipulated so that they can be directly compared for class and individual characteristics.

The firearms analyses has verified 47 different types of guns used by the warriors. A forty-eighth weapon is represented by metal arrowheads, showing that the stereotypical bow and arrow was also used. By using modern crime laboratory firearms identification techniques it was possible to discover that a minimum number of 415 guns were used by the Indians.

This is a conservative estimate as groups of round balls, on which these techniques are not as effective, were counted as one gun per caliber.

Indian arms included the .44 caliber Henry, .44 caliber Model 1866 Winchester, and the .44/.40 caliber Model 1873 Winchester, all repeating rifles. The army in 1876 did not issue repeating rifles

The army's single shot Springfield was simply not as fast as the repeating rifles, although it was more powerful and more accurate than the majority of the Indian arms. Indian arms also included the army's Springfield carbine and Colt revolver. These arms could have been captured either in the Rosebud fight or the valley fight against Reno and, in addition, some were no doubt taken from Custer's men during the battle. Antiquated muzzle loading firearms were also well represented.

BIBLIOGRAPHY

Applied Ground Imaging

1996 Little Bighorn Battlefield, Montana, Non-Intrusive Characterization Survey Field Project, Ground Penetrating Radar Survey. Manuscript report on file Midwest Archeological Center, Lincoln, Nebraska. *Applied Ground Imaging conducted experiments with new geophysical remote sensing instruments to see if they were capable of finding any features that might be associated with the soldiers reportedly buried in Deep Ravine. An anomaly was located that is consistent with a deeply buried disturbed area in the same location as that predicted by earlier geomorphological studies.*

Bennett, Connie

1977 Preconstruction archeological investigations at Custer Battlefield National Monument. Memo report on file, National Park Service, Midwest Archeological Center, Lincoln. *A short report on monitoring utility work in the park. No cultural resources were found.*

Bozell, John R.

Non-Human Vertebrate Faunal Remains from Custer Battlefield National Monument. In Archaeological Perspectives On the Battle of the Little Bighorn, by Douglas D. Scott, Richard A. Fox, Jr., Melissa A. Connor, and Dick Harmon, pps 283-298. Norman, University of Oklahoma Press. *Identifies horse and mule bones found during the archeological investigations.*

Bray, Robert

A report of archeological investigations at the Reno-Benteen site Custer Battlefield National Monument June 2 - July 1, 1958. Ms on file Midwest Archeological Center, Lincoln. *The first archeological report on the battlefield. Excavations of riflepits and three soldier burials are described.*

Coleman Research

1996. Little Bighorn Measurements II Processing Results. COR/96-101. Manuscript report on file Midwest Archelogical Center, Lincoln, Nebraska. *Coleman Research also conducted experiments with new geophysical remote sensing instruments to see if they were capable of finding any features that might be associated with the soldiers reportedly buried in Deep Ravine. An anomaly was located that is consistent with a deeply buried disturbed area in the same location as that predicted by earlier geomorphological studies.*

Connor, Melissa

Exhumation of Grave 402, Block B, Custer Battlefield National Cemetery. Rocky Mountain Region Archeological Project Report, dated April 8, 1986. On file, National Park Service, Midwest Archeological Center, Lincoln. *A short report on the exhumation of some soldiers remains for identification.*

The Application of Comparative Bone Histology to Fragmented Archeological Bone from the Reno-Benteen Dump, Custer Battlefield National Monument. Appendix B of Archeological Investigations at the Reno-Benteen Equipment Disposal Site, in Papers on Little Bighorn Battlefield Archeology: The

Equipment Dump, Marker 7, and the Reno Crossing, edited by Douglas D. Scott, pps 148-166. Reprints in Anthropology Volume 42, J and L Reprint Co., Lincoln.

A report of microscopic examination of small bone fragments found in the equipment dump excavations, and the identification of cow and pig as remains of meals eaten by the soldiers.

Exhumation of Human Remains on the Pitsch Property Near Little Bighorn Battlefield National Monument, Montana. Midwest Archeological Center, National Park Service, Lincoln, NE.

Describes the excavations, on private property, of some human remains that were missed in a 1928 exhumation.

DeVore, Steven L.

2002a. Search for the Horse Burial Pit: Conductivity and Magnetic Gradient Investigations at Last Stand Hill, Little Bighorn Battlefield National Monument, Montana. Appendix B in Archeological Investigations of the "Horse Cemetery" Site, Little Bighorn Battlefield National Monument, by Douglas D. Scott. Midwest Archeolgical Center, National Park Service, Lincoln, NE.

This report details the use of geophysical remote sensing instruments as part of an effort to locate the 1881 horse burial pit. The work was conducted in support of construction of the new Indian Memorial access trails.

2002b Trip Report – Inadvertent Discovery of Remains Related to Fort Phil Kearney reinterments. Memorandum on file, Midwest Archeolgical Center, National Park Service, Lincoln, NE.

During construction of a new traffic island in the parking lot at Last Stand Hill some human bone and possible burial box nails and wood were uncovered. These proved to be parts of a human skeleton from the Fort Phil Kearny burials that were placed on Last Stand Hill around 1890 and moved again to Custer National Cemetery in the early 1900s. The remains were reburied with the Fort Phil Kearny dead.

Fox, Richard A., Jr.

Discerning History Through Archaeology: The Custer Battle. Ph.D. Dissertation, Department of Archaeology, University of Calgary, Calgary, Alberta.

Uses the archeological data to analyze the progress of the battle.

Archaeology, History, and Custer's Last Battle. University of Oklahoma Press, Norman.

The published revision and reinterpretation of his dissertation, which suggests Custer moved further north and west than previously thought.

West River History: The Indian Village on Little Bighorn River, June 25-26, 1876. In Legacy, New Perspectives on the Battle of the Little Bighorn, edited by Charles E. Rankin, pp 139-166, Montana Historical Society Press, Helena.

A study of oral history sources and limited archeological data to suggest where the Indian camp circles were located before and during the battle.

Fox, Richard A., Jr. and Douglas D. Scott

The Post-Civil War Battlefield Pattern. Historical Archaeology 25(2):92-103.

A theoretical model of how to do battlefield archeology and what can come from the study of conflict sites.

Glenner, Richard A., P. Willey, and Douglas D. Scott

Back to the Little Bighorn: Remains of a 7th Cavalry Trooper, Recovered at the Little Bighorn battlefield in 1903, Provide A Glimpse of Nineteenth Century Dental Practices. Journal of the American Dentistry Association, 125:835-843.

The description and analysis of gold and tin dental fillings in the remains identified as Corporal George Lell.

Greene, Jerome A.

Evidence and the Custer Enigma: A Reconstruction of Indian-Military History. Reno, Nev.: Outbooks.

The classic reconstruction of the battle from oral history and relic finds around the battlefield.

Haynes, C. Vance Jr.

Archaeological Geology of Deep Ravine, Custer Battlefield National Monument. In Archeological Perspectives on the Battle of the Little Big Horn. by Douglas D. Scott, Richard A. Fox Jr, Melissa A. Connor, and Dick Harmon, pp. 224-242, University of Oklahoma Press, Norman.

Uses the principles of geology to explain the changes in Deep Ravine since the battle.

Geoarcheological Investigations at Custer Battlefield National Monument. Appendix C. of Archeological Investigations at the Reno-Benteen Equipment Disposal Site, in Papers on Little Bighorn Battlefield Archeology: The Equipment Dump, Marker 7, and the Reno Crossing, edited by Douglas D. Scott, pps 167-184. Reprints in Anthropology Volume 42, J and L Reprint Co., Lincoln.

Uses the principles of geology to explain the changes at the Reno-Benteen equipment dump site since the battle.

Heinz, Ralph

Tack rivets. pp. 205-206. In Archaeological Perspectives on the Battle of the Little Bighorn. University of Oklahoma Press, Norman by Douglas D. Scott, Richard A. Fox Jr., Melissa Connor, and Dick Harmon, University of Oklahoma Press, Norman.

Description and identification of the saddle and tack rivets from the battlefield.

Cavalry Equipment From Reno/Benteen Dump Site (1989). Ms on file Midwest Archeological Center, Lincoln.

Description and identification of the saddle and tack from the Reno-Benteen equipment dump site.

Nickel, Robert K.

2002 A Ground-Penetrating Radar Search for a Horse Burial Pit Associated with the 1876 Battle of the Little

Bighorn, Appendix A in Archeological Investigations of the "Horse Cemetery" Site, Little Bighorn Battlefield National Monument, by Douglas D. Scott. Midwest Archeolgical Center, National Park Service, Lincoln, NE.

This report details the use of geophysical remote sensing instruments as part of an effort to locate the 1881 horse burial pit. The work was conducted in support of construction of the new Indian Memorial access trails.

Phillips, Patrick

Tin Cans. In Archaeological Perspectives on the Battle of the Little Bighorn by Douglas D. Scott, Richard A. Fox Jr., Melissa Connor, and Dick Harmon, pp. 215-221. University of Oklahoma Press, Norman.

Describes and analyzes the tin cans found on the battlefield. Most post-date the battle.

Cannibalism, Combat and Post Battle Mutilation: Observed Similarities Between Cannibalism Criteria and Human Remains From Custer Battlefield. Master of Arts Thesis, Department of Anthropology, University of Nebrasaka, Lincoln.

A comparison of cut marks on human bone that is often described in physical anthropological reports as evidence of cannibalism to known mutilation marks from the battlefield. Concludes that care should be exercised in making blanket statements that cut marks equal evidence of cannibalism.

Scott, Douglas D.

1987a The Recovery and Replacement of a Cremated Burial at Custer Battlefield National Monument. Rocky Mountain Region Archeological Project Report, dated February 27, 1987. On file, National Park Service, Midwest Archeological Center, Lincoln.

Reports on finding an unreported recent cremation deposition site at the battlefield.

1987b Prehistoric Resources of Custer Battlefield. Rocky Mountain Region Archeological Project Report, dated April 1, 1987. On file, National Park Service, Midwest Archeological Center, Lincoln.

Describes and interprets the archeological evidence of the park's prehistoric occupation.

1987c Surviving the Second Battle of the Little Bighorn: Effective Means of Dealing with a Media Blitz. In Captivating the Public through the Media While Digging the Past. Technical Series No. 1, Baltimore Center for Urban Archaeology. (edited by Kristen Peters, Elizabeth A. Comer, and Roger E. Kelly).

Describes the manner in which project personnel dealt with a barrage of media contacts during the field work in 1984 and 1985.

Testing and Evaluation of Two Prehistoric Sites at Custer Battlefield National Monument. Rocky Mountain Region Archeological Project Report, dated September 1989. On file, National Park Service, Midwest Archeological Center, Lincoln.

Determines the prehistoric sites in the park have little integrity remaining.

Interpreting Archaeology at Custer's Last Stand. In What's Past is Prologue Our Legacy Our Future, edited by David L. Kulhavy and Michael H. Legg, pp 159-163. National Interpreters Workshop, Center for Applied Studies, School of Forestry Stephen F. Austin State University, Nacogodoches.

Describes some of ways project personnel and park rangers interpreted the field investigations to the park visitors.

Archeological Investigations at the Reno-Benteen Equipment Disposal Site, in Papers on Little Bighorn Battlefield Archeology: The Equipment Dump, Marker 7, and the Reno Crossing, edited by Douglas Scott. Reprints in Anthropology Volume 42, J and L Reprint Co., Lincoln, pp 1-184.

Describes and interprets the remains of boxes and saddle gear found in the Reno-Benteen equipment dump.

1992a Exhumation of Little Bighorn Battle-related Human Remains from the Custer Battlefield National Cemetery. Rocky Mountain Region Archeological Project Report, dated May 20, 1992. On file, National Park Service, Midwest Archeological Center, Lincoln.

Describes the excavation of several graves in the national cemetery which contained remains from the battle. The purpose of the excavations was to recover remains for identification purposes.

1992bDeep Ravine Overlook Site Little Bighorn National Battlefield, Montana. Rocky Mountain Region Archeological Project Report, dated July 14, 1992. On file, National Park Service, Midwest Archeological Center, Lincoln.

A short report dealing with the archeological potential of developing a Deep Ravine overlook near the national cemetery. No archeological resources were found.

1993a Archeological Mapping of the Pitsch Property: The Valley Fight Segment of the Battle of the Little Bighorn, Montana. Rocky Mountain Region Archeological Project Report, dated August 31, 1993. On file, National Park Service, Midwest Archeological Center, Lincoln.

A report on mapping of archeological finds on the Pitsch property located in the area of the Reno Valley fight. This report is not available without the landowners' permission.

1993b Trip report on the Reno-Benteen Walkway fill project, Little Bighorn National Battlefield. Memorandum to Chief, Midwest Archeological Center, dated September 20, 1993. On file, National Park Service, Midwest Archeological Center, Lincoln.

This short report documents the absence of archeological battle artifacts in the area of the concrete walkway at the Reno-Benteen defense site.

Archaeological Perspectives on the Battle of the Little Bighorn: A Retrospective. In Legacy, New Perspectives on the Battle of the Little Bighorn, edited by Charles E. Rankin, pp 167-188, Montana Historical Society Press, Helena.

This chapter reviews the accomplishments of the archeological project and points out how this effort has stimulated other battlefield archeological work.

A Look at Cedar Coulee and Sharpshooter Ridges: Archeological Inventory of the Faron Iron Property Near Little Bighorn Battlefield National Monument. Midwest Archeological Center, National Park Service, Lincoln, NE.

Describes the archeological finds related to the retreat from Weir Point on some private property near the Reno-Benteen defense site.

Final Resting Place of an Outlaw

Samir S. Patel

EDITOR'S INTRODUCTION

It may always be the case that one person's terrorist is another person's freedom fighter, or that one person's outlaw is another person's populist hero. Was Robin Hood nothing but a common thief, or was he champion of the poor, taking from the rich only that which they had stolen from the poor? Were Bonnie Parker and Clyde Barrow (Bonnie and Clyde) and perhaps the most famous of the Depression-era icons, John Dillinger, nothing but talented, media-savvy bank robbers and killers, or were they soldiers in a populist war against the pernicious bankers? Were the Australian Ned Kelly and the other bushrangers all murderers and thieves, or were they merely reacting to the pervasive oppression against the descendants of the convicts, many of them Irish, who had been sentenced to Australia in the nineteenth century? Was Ned Kelly a villain or a hero? Archaeology may not settle this issue, but at least the work reported on here shows that he has been found. Executed at the Old Melbourne Gaol (a prison) on November 11, 1880, Kelly's body was buried, then moved to the grounds of Pentridge Prison in 1929 whereupon its precise location was lost for decades. A combination of good archaeological detective work and genetic testing shows that a relatively intact skeleton found at Pentridge Prison in 1996, in fact, is the remains of the hero-outlaw, Ned Kelly.

POINTS TO PONDER

1. How were Ned Kelly's remains traced to the grounds of Pentridge Prison?
2. How do we know that the skeleton found at Pentridge Prison really is that of Ned Kelly?
3. What happened to Ned Kelly's skull?
4. What are the lessons of the Ned Kelly story? Was he a hero or a villain? Or a little of both?

n the photo taken the day before he was hanged in November 1880, Ned Kelly's eyes are fixed in a firm, defiant gaze. Though much of his face is hidden beneath a thick beard, it is possible that a little smile plays about his lips. But it's hard to tell for sure.

Kelly is one of the most iconic and polarizing figures in Australian history He is the most famed of the guerilla bandits known as bushrangers, some of whom, in their day personified revolt against the colony's convict system ("Australia's Shackled Pioneers," July/August 2011) and against the excesses of wealth and authority There's no real non-Australian analogue for Kelly—he was part Clyde Barrow, part Jesse James, part Robin Hood, but with media savvy and a strong political sense. To some, particularly Australians of Irish descent, he's a populist hero. To many others, he's a cop-killer, and his lionization is distasteful at best. He is, at the very least, an enduring subject of fascination.

For all that is known about his life and the crime spree that ensured his immortality theories have long abounded about what happened to Kelly's remains after his execution. "Whilst he was an outlaw, there's a lot of interest in how he was treated by, the qolice, the courts, and judicial systems." says David Ranson, a pathoiogist at the Victorian Institute of Forensic Medicine. In the place of certainty, there was rumor, supposition, and endless questions. Had his skeleton been taken apart by trophy hunters? Was his skull put on display and then stolen in the 1970s? Had doctors conducted a clandestine autopsy and taken his remains away for study? It has taken a decade of archaeological, forensic, and historical sleuthing to understand the convoluted story of Kelly's remains—and those of more than 40 other executed criminals—and learn that everything we thought we knew about that history was wrong. Finally, many of the mysteries surrounding Kelly's bones can be laid to rest. But not all of them.

In 1929, construction had begun on a school that would become the Royal Melbourne Institute of Technology (CRMIT) at the site of the recently closed Old Melbourne Gaol. It was known that around 30 executed criminals had been buried there between 1880 and 1924. The graves were located in a long, narrow yard at the base of a wall that held markers for each burial, including one grave marked "E.K." with an English broad arrow, signifying the grave of Edward "Ned" Kelly The construction workers expressed misgivings about digging through a graveyard, but were told that the remains had been covered with quicklime and would have disintegrated Even though some of the remains had been in the ground for only a few years, workers were still shocked when bodies started turning up.

Plans were made to exhume and rebury the bodies at Pentridge Prison, about five miles away On April 12, 1929, the first graves were opened, including the one thought to contain Kelly. Onlookers were seized with desire for a souvenir from the great outlaw "As soon as this gruesome discovery was made a crowd of boys who had been standing around expectantly while eating their luncheons rushed forward and seized the bones," read a story in the newspaper the next day. Authorities retrieved most of the bones that were taken, reports said, but the process can charitably be described as disorganized. The remains in the graveyard were moved to a series of mass graves at Pentridge in 1929 and, in 1937, four more were relocated there from the jail's hospital grounds.

In 2002, archaeologists from La Trobe University were monitoring landscaping work at RMIT when they were surprised to find a grave—one had apparently been missed in 1937. Archaeologists believe this was the only body that had been left behind. But they also knew the reburial of the others had been haphazard, leading them to speculate whether these remains moved from the old jail were where they were supposed to be—including the remains of Kelly if there were any left. Pentridge, where they were reburied, was used as a prison from the 1850s until 1997, but the precise location and layout of the cemetery within its sprawling grounds had been forgotten, and the government had recently sold portions of the site to private developers.

"We decided we really needed to be confident that we knew everything about [Pentridge]—particularly about its archaeology and particularly about the burials," says Jeremy Smith, an archaeologist at Heritage Victoria, the state's historical authority which oversaw a series of excavations there between 2006 and 2009. Somewhere at this site, unmarked amid the remains of dozens of other criminals, might be the remains of Kelly himself

Ned Kelly was born in Beveridge, north of Melbourne, in 1855, the son of an Irish convict. Young Kelly ran afoul of the law throughout his teens, but his bushranging career didn't really begin until April 1878, when a constable arrived at the family home to arrest Ned's brother Dan, and afterward claimed that the Kelly family had attacked him. The brothers, who denied the accusation, took to the bush. Their mother, Ellen, was charged with attempted murder for the incident and sentenced to three years, fueling Ned's hatred of the police and distrust of government. Ned and Dan joined up with friends Joe Byrne and Steve Hart, forming the Kelly gang, which consistently tried to one-up itself over the next 21 months.

In October 1878, Ned killed three constables at Stringybark Creek. The reward for the gang's capture went from £100 to £500 per man, dead or alive. In December, they took 22 hostages at a sheep station and then robbed the National Bank in Euroa of £2,000. The reward doubled. In February 1879, the gang took over a police station in Jerilderie, locking up two officers while they robbed the Bank of New South Wales (wearing police uniforms) of another £2,141 pounds, after which they rounded up 60 people at the Royal Hotel next door. There, Ned dictated a fiery, quasi-political, 8,000-word manifesto about his Irish roots and the injustice of the courts and convict system. The reward was doubled again and Aboriginal trackers were brought in to find them. In late June 1880, the gang took over the Ann Jones Inn in Glenrowan, holding another 60 people hostage, and attempted to derail a special police train sent to bring them in. Surrounded by police at the inn, the gang donned armor made from metal plows. Ned fled the hotel and flanked the cops, coming out of the shadows in his mailbox-like, but no less intimidating for it, armor. His legs weren't protected, so Ned was taken down with low shots. In the hotel, Byrne was killed in the shootout and Dan Kelly and Hart took poison before the police set fire to the building. On November 11, 1880, Ned, the last surviving member of the gang, was hanged at Old Melbourne Gaol.

Reportedly 8,000 fans and sympathizers turned out at a rally for his reprieve. His last words are said to have been, "Ah well, it has come to this." It's the stuff of legends. (And movies—both Mick Jagger and Heath Ledger played him on screen.)

According to historical records, 44 bodies had been buried at Pentridge—30 moved there in 1929, another four in 1937, and 10 prisoners executed at Pentridge between 1932 and 1967. One version of the Pentridge cemetery plan showed that the remains moved in 1929 were buried in three mass graves, but wasn't clear on where they were actually located.

In 2006, Heritage Victoria had private company Terra Culture conduct test excavations at what was thought to have been Pentridge's cemetery but they found only one set of remains— those of Ronald Ryan, the last man to be executed there in 1967. "I remember thinking that day" says Heritage Victoria's Smith, "we've got more than 40 bodies unaccounted for, including some of the most notorious and infamous Australians that there are, including the most famous of all Australians, Ned Kelly"

The team then found a 1955 aerial photograph that showed a rectangular, overgrown, fenced yard that appeared to match the dimensions of the cemetery plan. Archaeologists found the area muddy covered in weeds, and surrounded by the prison's massive, intimidating bluestone buildings. "As an archaeological site, it's quite unusual. It almost had echoes of a Bronze Age site. You had these large monolithic structures looming over these equally large open areas," says Smith. "It still very much had that sense of isolation and remoteness even though it's only 10 kilometers [six miles] from the center of Melbourne."

The excavations first uncovered the more recent graves, and later located two of the three mass graves from 1929—roughly where the plan indicated they might be. But the last and largest of the mass graves, containing the remains of 15 more men, probably including Kelly was not where the plan indicated. In February 2009, the owners of the site phoned Heritage Victoria to say they had uncovered a deeply buried box. Archaeologists investigated and found the third mass grave, 100 feet from where it was indicated on the plan. It contained two layers of burials, with 24 coffins and boxes that held the remains of 15 men (some spread across multiple boxes). It is thought it might have been relocated—without documentation—during drainage work in the 1960s. Somewhere among this jumble of bones and boxes may have been evidence of Ned Kelly himself "Kelly's important," says Smith. "If it wasn't for the notoriety the significance, the profile of Ned Kelly probably the project would have trickled along."

Most unidentified human remains in Australia go to the coroner, who must determine whether an inquest is required. With so many sets of remains, an inquest would have been lengthy and costly so it was incumbent on the archaeologists to establish a clear history of the site. "It was all about demonstrating to the coroner, through the archaeological processes, that we were confident that these were late-nineteenth-century executions that had been done as part of the judicial process, and that the stratigraphy showed no signs of recent disturbance," says Smith.

ANATOMY OF A SHOOTOUT

NED KELLY'S LIFE ENDED on the gallows, but it climaxed at the Ann Jones Inn in Glenrowan in June 1880. Equipped with metal armor made from plows, the four members of the Kelly gang held off the police ' who peppered the rustic building with shots for hours.

Adam lord, founder of archaeological consulting firm DIG International, led a 2008 excavation of the site where the inn once stood. The plot had seen three different structures: the first Ann Jones Inn, which burned down at the end of the siege; a second hotel built by Jones, which was also lost to fire; and a brick wine shanty (a sort of unlicensed watering hole) that was demolished in the 1970s. Ford worried that construction and decades of artifact collection—which began feverishly immediately after the siege—would leave little evidence behind. "I was quite fearful that I'd get there and there wouldn't be any remains left," Ford says. But the site was surprisingly intact: Around and beneath the foundations of the wine shanty were carbonized wall and floor timbers, bits of ceramic and melted glass, and, most importantly nearly 100 pieces of ammunition.

Ford and his team approached the site as a battlefield, looking for patterns that might say something about the shootout between the gang and police. The archaeologists found a line of some 40 deformed bullets where there had been a wall separating the inn's front and back. rooms. Behind that wall, in just one square yard of space, the team found approximately 30 cartridges and percussion caps, including one that matched a gun said to he Kelly's. The pattern suggests that the gang found little protection in the inn's three front rooms, so they retreated to the back rooms to reload before coming out to resume firing. "We were able to identify the actual movements, and perhaps even the motivations, of the members of the Kelly gang in their final hours," says Ford. "It is a powerful vision of these four young men who, for whatever reason, had got themselves into a situation they were never going to get out of"—S.S.P.

The oldest remains were sent to the coroner at the Victorian Institute of Forensic Medicine (VIFM). "This is a very unusual case. It was old skeletal remains and they are difficult to examine, but in addition, there was a very large amount of historic interest among the general public and also at a political level," says Fiona Leahy Senior Medico-Legal Officer at VIFM. While the excavations were taking place and the remains were being examined by forensic pathologists, anthropologists, and odontologists, another mystery was unfolding. "We had the long-standing, quite interesting, scandalous story of the alleged Ned Kelly skull," says VIFM pathologist David Ranson.

In 2008, Heritage Victoria reached out to a man named Tom Baxter who claimed to know the whereabouts of Kelly's skull. A complete cranium thought to be Kelly's had a long and checkered history This skull was apparently not reinterred at Pentridge, but was given to government officials and then passed to Colin Mackenzie, first director of the Australian Institute of Anatomy in Canberra. The institute made a cast of the skull, and eventually turned it over to the National Trust in 1972, which put it on display in the museum of the Old Melbourne Gaol, next to a Kelly death mask (a postmortem plaster cast). This skull, which had been labeled "E. Kelly" at some point in its history was stolen in 1978.

Baxter, without saying how he came into possession of it, agreed to return the skull on November 11, 2009, 129 years to the day after Kelly's execution. With it in their possession, the experts at VIFM had any number of questions, and a sophisticated arsenal of techniques by which to answer them. Was this the skull held at the Institute of Anatomy? Was it the one on display and stolen from the Old Melbourne Gaol? And, perhaps most importantly was it Kelly's?

Researchers at the VIFM took photographs, X-rays, and CT scans, and conducted craniofacial superimposition—layering the new images of the skull over the replica made at the Institute of Anatomy and photos of it on display later at the old jail. All the images matched up. They also located a tooth—kept by the grandson of a workman present at the 1929 exhumation—and it fit perfectly The pathologists then superimposed the CT scan of the skull over CT scans of death masks from the executed men. While this process cannot provide conclusive evidence, and not all the executed prisoners had death masks, it helped reduce the number of possible candidates. These comparisons eliminated all but two men: Frederick Deeming, a serial killer who was suspected of having been Jack the Ripper, and Ned Kelly

By September 2010, the coroner had determined no inquest was necessary The VIFM, working with the experienced Argentine Forensic Anthropology Team, subjected the left clavicles from 30 sets of remains from the mass graves to mitochondrial DNA (mtDNA) testing. The Baxter skull was also tested, as was a sample from the living great-grandson of Kelly's sister. "It's about delivering certainty," says Smith.

The mtDNA from the surviving Kelly ancestor was a match to a set of remains from the third pit—and not a match for the Baxter skull. Surprisingly the matching remains were among the most complete of any of the Pentridge burials. They were missing only a few cervical vertebrae, some small bones, and the skull, except for a palm-sized fragment—further proof that the intact Baxter skull could not have been Kelly's. "The Kelly remains are almost complete. It's one of the best sets of remains from the entire site. That I did not expect at all," says Smith. "It contradicted the historical evidence that Kelly's burial had been targeted by trophy collectors."

Closer examination of the bones showed unmistakable evidence of Kelly's injuries from the shootout at the Ann Jones Inn. Injuries to the top of the right tibia, the left arm, and the right foot all matched those documented by prison surgeon Andrew Shields when he examined Kelly after arrest. Using an otoscope and dental instruments, Ranson even removed two lead pellets from the tibia. "We had genetic evidence and a lot of anthropological evidence, and then when we looked at

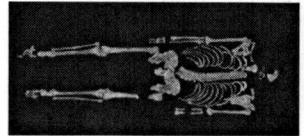 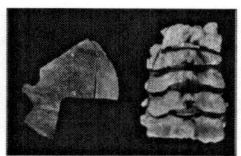 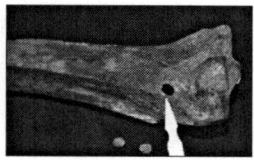

DNA was used to identify the mostly complete skeleton (left) of Ned Kelly. The remains included a bullet hole in the leg (right) consistent with his injuries. A fragment of skull (center left) and several vertebrae (center right) show evidence of saw marks, suggesting that Kelly's body had been examined postmortem to determine the effectiveness of his hanging.

the historical evidence as well, it really tied it all together," says Soren Blau, the forensic anthropologist who examined the remains. Smith describes the outcome as "staggeringly conclusive."

As for the Baxter skull, it actually matched another set of remains, one that was in the fragmentary condition that Smith expected of Kelly's. A closer look at plans from the original cemetery at the Old Melbourne Gaol suggests that Deeming— whose death mask is consistent with the skull—may have been buried close to Kelly This raises the possibility that the trophy seekers in 1929 simply raided the wrong coffin. But without Deeming family DNA, "we haven't been able to prove that conclusively," says Leahy

If the Baxter skull does not belong to Kelly and the mass grave contains only a palm-sized fragment, what happened to the rest of Kelly's head? A lurid account from 1880 refers to rumors that Kelly's remains were dismembered and taken away by "medical men" after execution. It is now known this didn't happen, and it is also known that Kelly told the prison surgeon Shields that he did not want his body dissected. Helen Harris, a historian working with the VIFM team, found evidence of a letter from the prison governor, John Castieau, stating that there was no truth to the dissection rumors. But Kelly's remains have a story of their own to tell, somewhere between rumors and official record.

The skull fragment with the Kelly remains came from the back of his cranium, and shows saw marks across the top and down the sides. The cuts clearly continue on the cervical vertebrae below A physician had explored the remains of Kelly with more than his eyes. In that era, authorities were concerned with whether hanging was indeed an instantaneous, humane form of execution. Hangings were known to have been botched, resulting in long, drawn-out choking rather than death from a hangman's fracture—a quick, decisive snap of the neck. "This piece of skull suggests the individual had been subject to a limited autopsy probably to investigate the interior back half of the neck following an execution," says Blau. "That was probably not uncommon given that there was interest in whether hangings were effective or not, and it was important for the jail to say that it was a successful hanging."

It is impossible to say what became of the rest of Kelly's skull, beyond the fact that any complete skull couldn't possibly belong to him. "Unfortunately we only have part of the answer," says Leahy "It could be sitting in someone's garage or it could simply have gotten lost, discarded, or disintegrated. We don't know"

"The mystery continues," she adds. "What exactly happened in the jail after his hanging has not been fully explained. We have our theories."

And theories are the coin of the realm for a figure as near mythic as Kelly The stories and speculation will continue-some even refuse to believe the definitive findings from Heritage Victoria and VIFM. Mythos notwithstanding, archaeology and forensic work have provided knowledge about the end of Kelly's life: The back of his skull was opened, he was buried at the Old Melbourne Gaol, his grave was not looted, and his remains were reburied at Pentridge Prison mostly intact. Almost all the remains of the executed prisoners will be reburied again in an official cemetery at Pentridge. But probably not Kelly's. Officials are still trying to decide his final resting place.

"It's introduced certainty" says Smith, "into a project where 10 years ago everything we knew about this was wrong."

A Notorious King's Life and Death, Revealed by His Mortal Remains

Rachel Ehrenberg

EDITOR'S INTRODUCTION

Clearly, William Shakespeare was not a big fan of English King Richard III. He described him as a mean-spirited, vile man whose body was almost as deformed as his soul. Hero or villain, historians do know that Richard died in battle in 1485. They also know that, in an attempt to avoid any reverential treatment given the dead king, Richard's victorious enemies unceremoniously disposed of his body on the grounds of Greyfriars Church. After that, the trail goes dark and, until 2012, no one knew where Richard III's body lay. But then, an archaeological investigation recovered the remains of a deformed man—a person who had suffered from a severe curvature of the spine—on the grounds of what had been the old Greyfriars church. The man had suffered a violent and ignominious death: researchers identified multiple wounds, several of which would individually have resulted in death. The back of the head had been dealt a crushing blow, another weapon had pierced the base of the head, multiple stab wounds were found on his ribs and pelvis. His enemies took apparent joy in killing this man and then, even after he was almost certainly dead, violating his dead body. Archaeological, historical, and genetic evidence reported here show with near certainty that this mangled skeleton is the remains of Richard III. Ultimately, his killers could not eliminate our memory of him and archaeological research has revealed the death of the fifteenth-century English king.

POINTS TO PONDER

1. How do we know that the remains found in 2012 on the grounds of what had been Greyfriars church are those of King Richard III?
2. How did Shakespeare describe Richard III?
3. How does genetic analysis contribute to the identification of the remains found at Greyfriars church?
4. What are the lessons we can learn from the discovery, excavation, and analysis of the body of King Richard III?

History and literature have painted England's King Richard III as a scoundrel who met a violent death in battle and was unceremoniously buried. Now that researchers have revealed some conclusions from a fast-paced scientific investigation of a skeleton and its DNA found under a parking lot in Leicester, England, that end seems all the more gruesome. The results announced February 4 by a team from the University of Leicester paint a picture that is remarkably consistent with both historical and fictional accounts.

The search for the king's body began in August 2012 in the parking lot of a Leicester city council building. An excavation there uncovered walls and other structures of Grey Friars church, where Richard III was buried after his ignominious death on August 22, 1485, in the Battle of Bosworth. Beneath the spot where the church stood, the researchers found a skeleton stuffed into what appears to have been a hastily dug grave, too small for the body it contained.

History says Richard III's final moments were brutal; Shakespeare portrays the king frantically calling for a new horse to carry him back into battle after being knocked off his mount, only to be killed by Henry, Earl of Richmond, who then takes the throne.

Though the bones can't reveal the king's final words, 10 wounds confirm a violent and chaotic end. A gaping wound in the back of his head suggests the death blow was delivered by a halberd, a bladed pole weapon favored in the 15th century. A second blade wound that would have been fatal on its own penetrated the base of the skull. Carefully examining the skull's interior revealed a mark opposite this entry point, suggesting the blade penetrated 10.5 centimeters.

Then there are the humiliation wounds. In battles throughout history, combatants have rushed to plunge weapons into the dead or mortally wounded bodies of enemy leaders. Cuts deep enough to penetrate bone litter the skeleton's skull, marring its jaw and right cheek. Richard's ribs bear signs of further attacks, Leicester osteoarchaeologist Jo Appleby reported. His pelvis was nicked, indicating that a knife or dagger was plunged into his right buttock. Many of these wounds would have been prevented if Richard III had been wearing a protective helmet and armor, leading the team to speculate that these injuries were inflicted after his death.

Historical accounts report that after his death in the final major battle of the Wars of the Roses, Richard III's body was tied up, thrown naked over the back of a horse and brought to Leicester for public viewing. The body was then buried unceremoniously in Grey Friars church. The arrangement of the skeleton's hands suggests they were still tied at burial.

"The last thing the victors wanted was to give him a nice tomb in Westminster Abbey and have people put pretty flowers on it," says Cornell's Paul Hyams, a specialist in conflicts and disputes of the Middle Ages.

Grey Friars church was demolished sometime after 1538. In the early 17th century, a mayor of Leicester lived in a mansion on the site. In the 19th century, excavations for a brick outhouse apparently severed the feet from the rest of the skeleton and came close to destroying the grave.

While it suffered minor damage from being buried for 500 years, the skeleton is well preserved, Appleby says. It shows Richard III was a slight man whose spine curved like a question

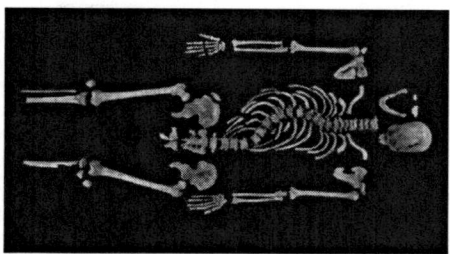

King Richard III's bones bear witness to his life and death. His remains show that severe scoliosis curved his spine; either of two wounds evident on his skull could have killed him.

mark—characteristics consistent with historical accounts. While Richard III was not "the foul bunch-backed toad" that Shakespeare made him out to be, his skeleton indicates he had scoliosis that developed sometime after about age 10. The condition would have reduced his height, caused one shoulder to stand higher than the other and may have caused him pain. Contrary to another Shakespearean description, neither of Richard's arms was withered.

Surviving portraits of Richard III depict him with a prominent chin and nose. Those features emerged when facial reconstruction experts added layers of muscle and skin to a digital scan of the skull, says Caroline Wilkinson of the University of Dundee in Scotland, who led the reconstruction team.

While the bones tell much of the story, genetic data bolster the case that the skeleton is Richard's. The researchers examined DNA from mitochondria, cellular energy factories that contain genetic material,that were extracted from the skeleton's teeth and right femur. Unlike nuclear DNA, half of which comes from each parent, mitochondrial DNA passes down only from mother to child. Previous research by historian John Ashdown-Hill had traced an all-female line through 17 generations from Anne of York, Richard's sister, to Michael Ibsen, a cabinetmaker from Canada. He agreed to have his DNA tested. The genetic work also included another individual in the maternal line who wanted to remain anonymous.

Ibsen's mitochondrial DNA and that of the anonymous donor matched the DNA extracted from the skeleton, says Turi King, who led the genetic work. Unlike nuclear DNA, mitochondrial DNA is not usually unique to individuals. But it is far more prevalent in the body and more likely to be found when remains are very old, or not much is left; hence it finds frequent use in forensic investigations. The DNA signature that the skeleton, Ibsen and the third individual shared, called haplotype J1c2c, is quite rare, says King, making the match a solid argument for relatedness. Only a small percentage of Europeans carry it.

"They've built a strong forensic case," says anthropologist John Hawks of the University of Wisconsin-Madison. The analyses of the remains have not yet appeared in a peer-reviewed journal, he notes. But none of the presented evidence calls into question the notion that the skeleton is indeed Richard's.

Genetic data from the Y chromosome, which passes from father to son, will provide more definitive evidence. Several male descendants of Edward III, Richard Ill's great-great-grandfather, have agreed to share their genetic data. (Richard III himself had only one legitimate son, who died as a child in 1484 without any descendants). The team plans to compare the skeleton's DNA with that from the descendants. Richard's Y chromosome is being analyzed now, says King.

"I'm dying to get on with it," she says.

Section 5

IF THE PRESENT WERE AN ARCHAEOLOGICAL SITE

The articles in this section represent a fascinating genre in archaeological writing; imagining what future archaeologists would make of our current, rather peculiar, modern material culture. One of the pieces suggests how future archaeologists would interpret the rather odd adult playground, Las Vegas. The Dig project goes a step further and actually concocts a mythical community and presents a modern archaeological analysis of its fake archaeological site.

There have been a number of attempts—primarily humorous, but informative, nonetheless—by archaeologists and others, to imagine what future archaeologists might make of the material record of our own present. For example, Robert Nathan's (1956) book, The Weans, presents a world some five or six thousand years in the future where African archaeologists are attempting to understand the ancient and extinct culture that once ruled the "Great West Continent." This greatly ancient civilization is called the "Weans" because it is believed, on the basis of inscriptions on found on their crumbling monuments, that they called their land the "We" or the "Us," to distinguish themselves from the rest of the world. Nathan's Weans are, of course, a clever, thinly veiled reference to the society of the United States in the mid-1950s.

These exercises, along with being entertaining, approach some important issues in archaeological epistemology and at the same time allow us to evaluate modern life through the lens of a mythical archaeologist from the future. In a sense, the theme here is the reverse of that presented in an earlier section of this reader. There, the question is asked: "can the study of the past provide insights into the study of the present?" Here the question is asked: "Can the 'archaeological' study of the present provide insights into our study of the past?"

It is instructive that in virtually all of the fantasies in which some future archaeologist attempts to analyze our modern material culture, they always manage to muck it up. It is a running joke in archaeology that when we are clueless concerning the function or meaning of some artifact recovered at an ancient site, we often fall back on the explanation that the object in question must surely have been ceremonial in intent. In the archaeological fantasies you are about to read, this is a common thread. Perhaps it is true—and certainly instructive; when archaeologists encounter the ordinary or mundane in ancient societies, we may too quickly ascribe some unwarranted ceremonial significance. Following this theme, when writer/illustrator David Macauley imagines what future archaeologists might make of the crumbling ruins of a place called Las Vegas, so much of what those imaginary archaeologists screw up rests in their insistence that objects that you and I recognize as being perfectly mundane and even silly—an artificial plant or, say, even a toilet seat—become terribly meaningful, ceremonially significant objects. Dutch performance artist Geert Hautekiet played on a similar theme when he went to the extreme of manufacturing an entire archaeological site of a mythical town on the very real Governor's Island in the harbor of New York City.

Part of the challenge here is that archaeologists do not just excavate individual objects; we recover artifacts in spatial contexts, in other words in spatial association with one another. We excavate sites so carefully and meticulously and keep accurate records of where everything was found because archaeological sites are far more than the sum of their constituent parts. An inventory of artifacts found at a site is only a part of the database. Where each object was found in relation to each other object tells us how these objects were used together to accomplish some task. The very same flaked stone object may have been a weapon for hunting big game animals, it may have been a weapon of war, or it could have served as a ceremonial grave offering to a deceased hunter. When such objects are found outside of their original contexts—for example, when the artifact was disposed of in a communal trash pit, or if it was removed from a site by an artifact collector who made no record of its context of discovery—determining function can be quite difficult. The same would be (will be) true for future archaeologists who attempt to understand the function of piles of rusting, compacted metal (crushed automobiles) or the interrelationships among items excavated at landfills.

It is useful to be reminded of such difficulties in archaeological interpretation of the past, especially those resulting from the problems inherent in having members of a particular cultural group in a particular time period (primarily western scientists in the present), attempting to explain the life ways of ancient people with very different cultures. The following articles together serve as a useful cautionary lesson.

Motel of the Mysteries

David Macauley

EDITOR'S INTRODUCTION

David Macauley is not an archaeologist. He is a brilliant, talented, and accomplished artist and author. Through exquisitely detailed pen and ink drawings, Macauley has trained his artist's eye on topics like medieval castles, cathedrals, cities, sailing ships, mills, and Egyptian pyramids. Instead of focusing on technology or architecture, his book *Motel of the Mysteries* is one of the very best send-ups of archaeology you'll ever find. His focus is Las Vegas, actually, the site of a sleazy motel off the Vegas strip. It is some time in the distant future and archaeologist Howard Carson has made the archaeological discovery of the century (that name is a play on "Howard Carter" who discovered the tomb of Egyptian pharaoh Tutankhamun). The excerpt from *Motel of the Mysteries* presented here is particularly hilarious if you know about the history of archaeology. Some of Macauley's words here are actual quote or near quotes from the writings of Howard Carter (Carter, like his mythical, future archaeological near-namesake, Carson, really did respond to the question when first gazing into Tut's tomb "Do you see anything," "Yes, wonderful things.") Reading *Motel of the Mysteries* can be humbling for an archaeologist. But it also can be a valuable reminder of the mistakes we can make when we impose a preconceived perspective on the archaeological record. And besides, it's pretty funny.

POINTS TO PONDER

1. Who is the mythical Howard Carson based on?
2. What has Carson actually discovered? What does he think he's discovered?
3. What really are Carson's "water trumpets," "sacred urn," and "sacred parchment?"
4. What lessons concerning archaeological interpretation are imparted by Carson's hilarious misinterpretations of the archaeological record of Las Vegas?

The ground below his feet suddenly gave way. He was precipitated headlong downward. When the dust had settled and he had recovered his spectacles, he found himself at the bottom of an ancient shaft, facing the entrance of a long-forgotten tomb. The shaft, probably dug by tomb robbers shortly after the tomb was sealed, had been covered initially by the natural vegetation of the surface. More recently, the whole area had been buried under vast quantities of soil from the adjacent excavation.

Unimpressed and rather annoyed at this inconvenience, [Howard] Carson's first thought was to call out for assistance, but, before he could utter a sound, light from the shaft caught the area around the handle on the tomb door. Upon closer inspection, he discovered that the sacred seal which was traditionally placed on the door following the burial rites was still in place. Staff artists' reconstructions of similar, but always defiled, tombs that had appeared in his most recent *National Geographic* flooded his mind. Thunderstruck, he realized he was on the threshold of history. His entire body trembled as he contemplated the possible significance of his find. The mysterious burial customs of the late twentieth-century North American were finally (and as it turned out, magnificently) to be revealed.

Less than a month later, aided by his companion, Harriet Burton, who "enjoyed sketching," and a dedicated group of volunteers, Carson began the first of seven years' work on the excavation of the Motel of the Mysteries complex, and most specifically on the removal and recording of the treasures from Tomb 26.

While Carson paced back and forth in a supervisory manner, Harriet numbered each of the items surrounding the entrance as well as those on the great door. Descriptions of the most significant discoveries are to be found in her diary:

> Number 21, "the gleaming Sacred Seal, which had first caught Howard's attention, was placed on the door by the officials after the burial to protect the tomb and its inhabitant for eternity."
> Number 28, "the Sacred Eye, which was believed to ward off evil spirits."
> Number 18, "the partially exposed Plant That Would Not Die. One of these exquisite plants, which had apparently been grown in separate pieces and then joined together, was placed on each side of the entrance."
> Numbers 19 and 20, "containers in which the sacrificial meal was offered to the gods of eternal life."

Once the exterior of the tomb had been recorded in detail, preparations for entering it were begun. With a steady hand, Carson, who had presumably picked up a few tricks in his time, jimmied the lock. With his helpers peering nervously from a safe distance, he cautiously pried open the door. The creaking of the ancient hinges, in Miss Burton's own words, "cut through the silence like

Figure 19.1. Sketch and labeling of the archaeological discoveries made in the outer burial chamber. (David Macaulay)

the scream of a ghostly fleeing spirit." Suddenly, to Carson's astonishment, the door stopped dead. A frantic but successful search for the obstruction revealed a beautifully crafted chain about two thirds up the inside of the door, linking it with the sturdy frame. Clearly this stood as the final barrier between the present and the past. Once the workers had sawed through the chain, they withdrew, and Carson continued to open the great door.

At first, everything was dark. Carson lit a match. Still everything was dark. Carson lit two matches. Still, everything was dark. Attempting to avoid a rather protracted delay, Harriet eased the large spotlight toward the entrance with her foot. As the blanket of darkness was stripped away from the treasures within the tomb, Carson's mouth fell open. Everywhere was the glint of plastic. Impatiently, the others waited for a response. "Can you see anything, Howard?" they asked in unison.

"Yes," he replied …

Figure 19.2. Detailed drawing of the fabulous discovery made in the inner burial chamber. (David Macaulay)

"WONDERFUL THINGS!"

Everything in the Outer Chamber faced the Great Altar(No. 1), including the body of the deceased, which still lay on top of the Ceremonial Platform(No. 5). In its hand was the Sacred Communicator (No. 3) and around its wrist was a flexible golden band (No. 4) bearing an image similar to that of the upper altar. Signs of the ancient burial ritual were everywhere. A variety of garments, including the ceremonial chest plate (No. 2) and shoes designed to hold coins(No. 6), were scattered about the chamber. Various containers (No. 9) which had once held libations and offerings stood on the altar and around the platform. A statue of the deity WATT, who represented eternal companionship and enlightenment, stood faithfully next to the platform. To ensure maximum comfort during eternal life, several pieces of beautifully crafted furniture were placed in the room, along with additional garments stacked carefully in a specially designed rectangular pod. Perhaps the single most important article in the chamber was the ICE (No. 14). This container, whose function evolved from the Canopic jars of earliest times, was designed to preserve, at least symbolically, the major internal organs of the deceased for eternity. The Yanks, who revered long and complex descriptions, called the container an Internal Component Enclosure.

Aware that the two pairs of shoes implied a double burial and having seen only one body, Carson immediately began searching for another chamber. By the time he had found the entrance to what eventually became known as the Inner Chamber, Harriet had already catalogued and numbered it. Quivering with excitement, Carson removed his shirt and began the delicate operation of dismantling the door.

Although it seemed hardly possible, the contents of the Inner Chamber were even more dazzling than those already discovered. Harriet immediately began tagging and identifying each item while Howard drew conclusions. As he had predicted, a second body was present, and this one appeared to have been buried with more care and ritual than the first. Wearing the Ceremonial Head Dress (No. 8), it had been placed in a highly polished white sarcophagus(No. 9), which had in turn been sealed behind an exquisite and elaborately hung translucent curtain(No. 10).

The proportions of the sarcophagus had been precisely determined to prevent the deceased from ever sliding down into a fully reclined position. The similar postures of the two bodies led Carson to the conclusion that the proper burial position had the chin resting as much as possible on the chest. Although the outer surface of the sarcophagus was plain, there were two sets of ceremonial markings on the inside. The first consisted of ten parallel rows of slightly raised discs along the floor of the sarcophagus over which the body had been placed. The second was an almost entirely faded line that ran all the way around the walls parallel to and about ten inches above the floor. Two water trumpets, one about five feet above the other, projected from the end wall facing the deceased. Some of the music required during the final ceremony was produced by forcing water from the sacred spring through the trumpets and out through a small hole in the floor of the sarcophagus. Other music came from the music box (No. 6) situated above the Sacred

Urn (No. 2). Articles No. 1 and No. 4 were used in preparing the body for its final journey and No. 5 was the Sacred Parchment, pieces of which were periodically placed in the urn during the ceremony. Carson was overjoyed to find that the Sacred Point was perfectly preserved on the sacred parchment. Very few had previously been uncovered, and none in such remarkable condition. The Headband, which bore the ceremonial chant, and the Sacred Collar (not numbered) were still in place on the Sacred Urn to which they had been secured following the ceremony.

The Archaeological Dig that Never Was on Governor's Island

Ken Feder

EDITOR'S INTRODUCTION

I met Belgian artist Geert Hautekiet on Governor's Island in Manhattan Harbor in October 2009 at his incredible art piece, which can be characterized only as archaeological performance art. His project called simply "The Dig" involved the creation of what appeared for all the world to be an abandoned and partially buried small town that had been home to a handful of residents who were at the hub of a completely fabricated and entirely ridiculous worldwide snow globe industry. An onsite museum displayed the fake artifacts that had been "excavated" at the site and visitors were provided hard hats to walk among the ruins of the town of "Goverthing." With its partially buried, steepled, foot pedal mill, abandoned convenience store, half-submerged automobiles, and the ruins of commemorative statuary, it was equal parts instructive and absurd. When I visited the site, Hautekiet confided in me that when he "performed" the dig in Europe, everyone understood that it was satire, but in the US version, about half of the visitors came away amazed at what they thought was a true but forgotten part of the history of New York City and, apparently, New York City's historical role in a worldwide snow globe industry. It truly was hilarious and wonderful.

POINTS TO PONDER

1. What was the point of Geert Hautekiet's "The Dig"?
2. What "hidden history" of New York was revealed in the archaeological excavations carried out on Governor's Island?
3. Why was the town of Goverthing abandoned?
4. What are the lessons provided by the fake site and fake excavation on Governor's Island?

The secret to good parody, I think, is that it appears absolutely absurd only in hindsight. Parody is at its best when the parodist creates a world that, at least at first glance, and without looking too closely or thinking too deeply, seems at least sort of plausible. If I am right about that, then the Belgian "archaeologist" (actually, he's an artist) Geert Hautekiet was completely successful with his art installation, "The Archaeological Dig," on Governor's Island in New York City. I visited The Dig in the fall of 2009 and, maybe especially because I am an archaeologist, I found it to be an absolute hoot.

The Dig was presented as an actual archaeological excavation site, complete with a museum and lots of artifacts and features left in place for visitors to examine and explore. The story behind the fabricated site was that it was the ruins of a now-forgotten settlement called Goverthing, located on a small island just a short hop from Manhattan. The bio of the faux community indicated that Goverthing was founded in the seventeenth century, abandoned in 1954, and at its peak had just 29 settlers. The village's claim to fame, if you can call it that, was that its existence depended on a single, rather interesting industry: snow globe manufacturing. Though the fictional village lasted a few centuries, apparently they never did get their fingers on the pulse of the snow globe purchasing public; some of the exquisitely bad examples were on display in the museum. I mean, who thought there would be a big market for snow globes depicting two polar bears about to consume a small, terrified boy running for his life as the shaken fake snow flurries prettily around him?

A walk around the site—all visitors were supplied with hard hats for no fathomable reason—brought the visitor past the island's abandoned gas station, a number of partially buried, rusted-out automobiles, the ruins of a foot-powered mill that, apparently, powered the snow globe plant, broken-down silos for the storage of the fake snow and water used in the snow globes, and a statue dedicated to the settlement's founder, appropriately covered with seagull feces. Artifacts exhibited in the on-site museum reflect the hard times and tribulations endured by island residents. Apparently, one particularly difficult episode in Goverthing's history, called "the Plague of Birds," involved the invasion by highly aggressive seabirds who viciously attacked the residents. To protect themselves

from bird attacks, the men of Goverthing fashioned protective "metal scrotum covers" that were recovered at the site and exhibited in the museum. OMG.

When I spoke to Hautekiet he was quite open in admitting that, of course, he had made the whole thing up. I asked if he had a sense that visitors recognized that The Dig was a joke. He revealed to me that he had conducted similar archaeological parodies in Europe where virtually everyone got the fact that he was kidding. He did admit to me, however, that among the visitors to the Governor's Island installation he had spoken to, about half weren't entirely sure about the reality of the dig and some left convinced they had encountered an unknown and admittedly peculiar episode of American history replete with silos filled with fake snow, foot-powered snow globe mills, and terrified men donning their protective scrotum covers before they left their homes in the morning. Really.

Section 6

FORENSIC
ARCHAEOLOGY

The articles in this section show how the application of standard methods of archaeological data collection and analysis can aid in solving crimes, both modern and historical, and illuminate tragedies that occurred, both in the historical and very recent past. The articles here tell the stories of archaeological methods employed in the investigation of Ground Zero immediately following the terrorist attacks on Manhattan on 9/11; the investigation of war crimes; a heinous murder in Connecticut; and a historical case of cannibalism in the American west.

Watch any news report where the police or FBI are investigating an unsolved murder from some time past where the body was never found. Then, weeks, months, or even years after the crime was committed and the trail has long since gone cold, a new piece of evidence is brought to light. Someone, perhaps a neighbor of the victim, remembers seeing a stranger in the woods. Or, perhaps, a dog digging gleefully in some loose soil, as dogs are apt to do, comes loping toward his or her master, wagging its tail, and in its mouth, a gruesome prize: a human bone. Next, the local police or FBI will descend upon the site (I use that common archaeological term consciously) to search for additional clues. Note the investigators' use of hardware cloth screens to separate fragmentary evidence from the surrounding soil matrix, and their reliance on trowels, dental picks, and brushes to gently move soil away from possible bone remnants; these all are items in the tool kit of every field archaeologist. Archaeologists often are called on by local and national law enforcement agencies to aid in such searches expressly because of our experience and expertise at recovering small, fragmentary bits of evidence from the earth. In a particularly infamous crime committed in Connecticut and reported on here—the so-called

Wood Chipper Murder, named for the tool used by the murderer to dispose of his wife's body (gross)—an individual trained and experienced in archaeology was called in to use the techniques of our craft in an attempt to recover identifiable remains of the accused's missing wife. A guilty conviction and a long prison sentence are both a testament to the usefulness of archaeological techniques in this case (the archaeologists found a small piece of the dead woman's tooth and a part of her finger mixed in with the debris produced by the wood chipper; think of the movie *Fargo*). Recovering clues from the scene of a crime or accident, after all, is not unlike recovering clues from the scene of an ancient life. Our skills here are not esoteric; they are directly relevant and useful for the task at hand.

For the same reason, the skills of the archaeologist have come in handy in the search for human remains at Ground Zero. Searching for the often meager remains of people killed under such tragic circumstances helps both to contribute to the legal investigation of a crime scene and to supply some degree of solace or "closure" to the friends and family of those who were killed.

Finally, for whatever reason, many of us are fascinated by cannibalism, especially when it occurs as the accidental result of starvation. Perhaps such incidents cause us to consider how we might respond if we were lost in the wilderness, without food and without hope. What would we do if one of those sharing our fate, perhaps a friend, maybe even our parent or our child, died and the only way to survive was to consume their flesh? One of the articles here addresses this issue except, in the historical case examined, the archaeological evidence proves that the sole survivor didn't wait for his compatriots to die natural deaths but actually killed them before he butchered and then ate them.

Forensic Archaeology and the Woodchipper Murder

Albert Harper

EDITOR'S INTRODUCTION

It is one of the more grotesque scenes in a movie *(Fargo)* chock full of graphically depicted murder and mayhem. One of the bad guys (the psycho) has just killed the other bad guy (the sleaze-ball) and is attempting to dispose of his body using a small wood chipper, the kind you can purchase or rent to convert brush or small branches into, well, wood chips. He hasn't quite finished and the dead guy's as-yet un-chipped lower leg and foot is sticking up out of the device when the extremely pregnant sheriff catches him in the act. *Fargo* was a terrific movie but, as the cliché goes, truth is stranger than fiction. A wood chipper figures prominently in one of the most infamous murder cases in Connecticut's recent history. The wood chipper in question was rented, and not one of the little ones seen in the movie. No, this was a large, professional grade machine of a kind used by loggers that can turn large chunks of wood into sawdust and chips nearly instantly. The murderer thought sure that this wood chipper was up to the task of utterly and completely disposing of all of the evidence of his heinous crime. Unfortunately for him, he didn't reckon on the investigative skills of forensic archaeologists, including my colleague Al Harper, who wrote this article.

POINTS TO PONDER

1. Why did the police call in forensic archaeologists to help solve this case?
2. What was the archaeologist able to find in the residue produced by the wood chipper? How was he able to find it?
3. What specific evidence connected the human remains found at the wood chipper site with the missing woman?
4. What valuable lesson can be learned here by anyone thinking they can get away with murder?

elle Crafts was last seen about 7 P.M. on November 18, 1986, when she was dropped off at her home in Newtown, Connecticut, by a friend and co-worker. Helle, a flight attendant for Pan Am, had completed an international shift and was home with her husband and children for Thanksgiving. Some forty days later, tiny fragments of human tissue and bone, which were later proven to be parts of Helle's head, hands, and feet, were found amidst hundreds of wood chips littered on the shores of the Housatonic River in western Connecticut. The case is most remarkable in demonstrating the scientific capacity of a team of forensic experts to collect, analyze, interpret, and reconstruct an event that a murderer so carefully and craftily tried to obscure.

HELLE'S DISAPPEARANCE

Helle's disappearance was suspicious from the start. She had returned home from an overseas flight and was not scheduled to leave again for several days. Helle had started divorce proceedings against her husband, Richard, but the couple nonetheless continued to reside together.

The night of her disappearance, an early winter snow and ice storm caused power outages in many parts of the state, including Newtown. About 6 a.m. on the morning of November 19, 1986, Richard took their three children and the nanny to his sister's home in Westport. He told the nanny that Helle had gone ahead and would meet them there. When they arrived and did not see Helle, Richard said that Helle had taken a flight to visit her mother who lived in Denmark.

Helle's friends were rightly concerned about her unusual absence, but at each inquiry Richard provided an excuse that delayed any additional investigation. Thanksgiving came and passed with no word of Helle. Finally, Helle's friends made their concerns known to Helle's divorce attorney who in turn alerted a private investigator, Keith Mayo, who had previously investigated Richard's amorous adventures, and serious inquiry began. Acting independently, Mayo uncovered a series of unusual events that eventually led the police to undertake the exhaustive investigation that led to the discovery of Helle's remains on the shores of the Housatonic River. Without Mayo's dogged persistence, Richard Crafts, who had beaten a state police polygraph, would have gotten away with murder.

THE FATE OF HELLE CRAFTS

Richard Crafts was an unusually thorough man in everything he did. A commercial airline pilot, Crafts was exacting in the details. He had plotted Helle's demise and disappearance for some time. Helle was scheduled home from her European tour on November 18. Not so coincidentally, Richard had arranged for the delivery of a new dump truck, the cash purchase of a new freezer, and the rental of a large commercial size woodchipper that could devour twelve-inch diameter logs, all for her November 18 homecoming. A series of unplanned events—the delay in delivery of the truck and the unexpected snow storm and power outage—crimped his plan, but only slightly. Crafts made quick arrangements to rent a U-Haul truck capable of towing the woodchipper, paid extra to have the chipper available after the eighteenth, and conveniently used the snow storm as an excuse to get his children and their nanny out of the house until he could complete the deed.

By chance a U-Haul truck towing a large woodchipper was seen by several witnesses along the shores of the Housatonic River during the night of November 20. Crafts was seen at various other locations with the U-Haul and chipper in tow. Armed with this evidence and a search warrant, police and Dr. Henry Lee, director of the State Forensic Lab, searched the Craft's home, finding a bloody mattress cover, several drops of human blood, and many other pieces of evidence that would eventually lead to Crafts' conviction.

It was, however, the evidence found in the wood chips along the river that led to Crafts' arrest for the murder of his wife on January 13, 1987. It was late December when the wood chips alongside the road skirting the Housatonic were discovered. The winter was typical for New England: rain, sleet, snow, followed by more rain, sleet, and snow. The ground was now frozen solid, as were the piles of debris, wood chips, and Helle's remains.

Archaeological excavation is carefully planned and executed research designed to provide complete control of a site's stratigraphy. In contrast, forensic recovery of human remains is often undertaken with due haste and records nothing more than the **provenance** of the body and evidence surrounding it. As Helle's body was not yet viable, the State Police Major Crime Squad constructed a makeshift laboratory, melted the ground with jet heaters, and began the arduous task of sifting through thousands of bits of wood chips. Dr. Bruno Frohlich, a biological anthropologist trained in archaeological methods, recovered many of the tiny fragments of bone using standard archaeological **flotation** methods. Each fragment recovered was assigned a field identification number, noting the location where the fragment was found, and packaged for additional analysis at the forensic laboratory.

Scattered among the leaves and wood chips recovered from the frozen mud on the shore of the Housatonic River were very small pieces of bone, hair, and tissue interspersed in the debris. Additionally, a crown of a human tooth and a lower premolar with a fractured root were also recovered. This was the evidence that was needed to obtain an arrest warrant for Richard Crafts. The police now had a body, such as it was, and evidence that the body had been subjected to very severe forces either before or after death.

ROLE OF FORENSIC ANTHROPOLOGY

The recovery of bone fragments immediately raised the need for a forensic anthropologist to determine whether the bone fragments were human, and if so, to whom did they belong?

The development of forensic anthropology as a subspecialty of **physical anthropology** has been an important trend in anthropology over the past several decades. Originally, the application of physical anthropology to legal issues was a mere sideline of the interests of physical anthropologists. Dr. William Krogman's (1962) book, *The Human Skeleton in Forensic Medicine,* and Dr. Lawrence Angel's work at the Smithsonian Institution for the FBI are hallmarks in the development of forensic anthropology. The foundations to the science were, of course, much earlier, but the disciplinary origins of forensic anthropology can be found in the 1960s and 1970s.

The role of the forensic anthropologist is to determine, first, that the remains are human. All vertebrate species have a skeleton that is adapted to the environment occupied by the species, and each species has a unique skeletal morphology. Although most anyone would surely recognize a human cranium as being human, identification of other bones of the human body can be difficult even for persons trained in medicine.

Once the forensic anthropologist has established that the bones are human, the analysis shifts to deciding class characteristics that might be useful in narrowing a search to a single individual. Usually the analysis first focuses on the age at death, which can be accurately determined in young persons but less accurately as age increases. The forensic anthropologist relies on morphological clues such as the appearance and union of the **epiphyseal bodies,** the development and eruption of the teeth, the metamorphosis of the face of the **pubic symphysis,** the closure of the **cranial vault suture,** and other morphological changes that occur with age.

Next, the forensic anthropologist decides whether the remains are male or female based on the shape of the pelvic bones, the morphology of the cranium, and the size and rugosity of the long bones.

Determining racial ancestry is a more difficult task because of the high degree of variation in the species. All humans are extremely similar, and most of the variation that can be attributed to ancestral origin occurs in the facial skeleton. Under the best of circumstances, the forensic anthropologist is often limited to an assignment of an individual's racial origins to the major continental races and then only with difficulty.

Regression equations relating long bone length to living stature permit reconstruction of body height. Determination of body weight is very difficult without nonskeletal evidence such as clothing.

Once the class characteristics of age, sex, race, and stature are determined, the forensic anthropologist searches for clues that might assist in determining actual identity of the remains. The most common method to detect identity is through comparison of dental records. Comparison of X-rays of the frontal sinus or trabecular patterns of the vertebra have been used to provide proof of identity.

Osseous pathology, including fractures and arthritis, is useful in providing clues as to the actual identity.

Finally, the forensic anthropologist determines the post-mortem interval. The rate of decomposition of the body depends on environmental circumstances, especially ambient temperature, surrounding the body after death. The post-mortem interval can be accurately determined only in large temporal units.

WHAT WAS LEFT OF HELLE?

The total morphological approach outlined here was impossible to apply in this case. All that remained of the body in the wood chips were sixty-nine tiny fragments of bone, the largest of which was 38 × 14 × 5 mm. Most of the fragments were much smaller, typically 10 × 8 × 4 mm. All were fractured in multiple planes and at multiple angles by an instrument exerting great force. Most of the fragments were rectangular in shape, with the long edge of the rectangle almost invariably cut at a straight, steep angle.

The degree of destruction was enormous and precluded identification of specific bone, species, age, sex, race, or body size for most of the pieces. Remarkably, some pieces—parts of the head, hands, and feet—could be identified as being an adult human female.

Most of the pieces were cortical or compact bone, which is found in the shafts of the long bones. Only two fragments were wholly trabecular or spongy bone located in the epiphyses or vertebra. Importantly, seven fragments could be identified as being part of the cranium because of the unique layering of the cranial bones.

Of the fragments that could be identified as human and from a particular bone, four fragments stand out as most important.

First, part of the ball joint of a human big toe was found, ligament and cartilage intact. The distal articular surface of the first metatarsal was severed in one plane, and the attached articular surface of the proximal phalanx was severed at a right angle to the metatarsal. The ball joint of the foot is a unique human adaptation to upright, bipedal locomotion.

Next, the recovery of the distal phalanx of the left thumb provided the clues that the remains were those of an adult human female. The epiphysis of the phalanx had united with the shaft, indicating skeletal maturity. The small size of the bone, nearly complete but severed into two pieces, was a sign that the thumb belonged to a woman.

Of the several pieces of cranial bone, one piece was especially informative as it was possible to ascertain that the fragment came from the parietal bone of a human. The inner surface of the human parietal is well marked with deep arterial grooves from the blood supply to the meninges of the outer surface of the brain. Moreover, the surface of the inner wall was larger than the surface of the outer table, proving that the fragment had been ripped out of the parietal bone by a force coming from the outside to the inside of the skull. This is important because although a person might survive a severed toe or thumb, no one could survive having a part of the parietal bone forced into the brain.

Finally, three tiny fragments of cortical bone were found not in the pile of wood chips by the river but in association with the U-Haul truck Crafts rented to tow the woodchipper. The three fragments were held together by strands of light brown-blonde human hair.

Many of the fragments were very greasy, and several were attached to bits of decaying nonosseous tissue. This observation suggested that the person had not been dead for a long period of time, perhaps for a few weeks or months at most.

In the final analysis, the sixty-nine tiny fragments of bone demonstrated that the remains were an adult human female, most likely of European origin, whose death had occurred only a short time before the remains were recovered.

IDENTIFYING HELLE CRAFTS

It was remarkable, given the enormous destruction of the skeleton, that it was possible to discern that the tiny bone fragments belonged to an adult, European woman, but this was not sufficient evidence to prove that the remains were those of Helle Crafts.

Here, as in most cases, the team approach to forensic science paid off. Forensic serologists were able to establish that the fragments that could not be identified morphologically were biochemically human. The blood type of the person was "O-positive," as was Helle Crafts.

DNA taken from the small bits of tissue adhering to the thumb and toe fragments was determined to be from the child of Helle's mother and the mother of Helle's children. This evidence was never presented in court because of the potential complication of DNA evidence in an already highly complex case. In 1988 the use of DNA in the forensic context was still quite novel. Under the laws of Connecticut then, introducing DNA evidence would have invoked a lengthy legal battle called a Frye hearing to decide whether DNA typing was generally accepted by the scientific community. A Frye hearing would have unnecessarily diverted the focus of the trial from the real issue of whether Richard murdered Helle.

Besides the blood, bone, and flesh, thousands of blond hairs were recovered from the wood chips, Crafts' car, the woodchipper, and from Crafts' chain-saw, which was found in the Housatonic River with the serial number filed off. Some 2,660 strands of hair were examined and determined to be human Caucasian head hair of blond color. The hair had been tinted and suggested that the owner had been a woman who visited a hair salon.

The real proof that the remains were Helle Crafts came from the remarkable analysis of Dr. Gus Karazulas, the forensic dentist who examined the tooth and crown found in the wood chips. Ordinarily, a forensic dentist will compare known dental records with the entire dentition of the deceased. Dr. Karazulas had a crown to go on. Thousands of X rays later he was able to prove that the crown was identical to the crown Helle Crafts had had made in Denmark.

The tooth, a lower premolar, was also Helle's tooth, and the root had been fractured with a force that Dr. Karazulas had never seen before.

CRAFTS ON TRIAL

As one might imagine, the "Woodchipper Murder" created enormous publicity, so great that the trial was moved across the state. State's Attorney Walter Flanagan carefully orchestrated the story of Helle's disappearance, the discovery of the wood chips, the forensic science evidence, and then Dr. Lee's reconstruction of the murder.

Crafts was defended by Daniel Sagarin whose blistering cross examination and suggestion that the state had framed Richard almost won the day. After three weeks of deliberation, one juror refused to continue, and the case was declared a mistrial.

A mistrial does not ordinarily confer the constitutional protection against double jeopardy. Crafts' second trial, this time without the aid of Sagarin, resulted in his conviction. His conviction was upheld by the Connecticut Supreme Court.

WHAT HAPPENED TO HELLE?

Richard Crafts is the only person who knows what happened to Helle. The crime scene reconstruction by Dr. Lee suggests that after the children had been put to bed, Helle and Richard perhaps discussed the divorce. Helle was wearing a blue nightshirt and was in the bedroom when she was struck with some heavy instrument, perhaps Richard's police flashlight. The blow probably killed her and resulted in the blood splatter found on the mattress and bedroom wall.

At this point Richard began the plan to dispose of her body. First, he placed Helle's body in the freezer, and then he began the process of cleaning up the blood in the bedroom. He moved the incriminating carpet and box spring to a nearby wooded lot, and he hid Helle's car.

After he had the children and nanny out of the house, he continued with his plan. Authorities believe that Crafts took Helle's dead and frozen stiff body to the wooded lot and dismembered her into smaller pieces with his chainsaw. Richard then took her dismembered body to the banks of the Housatonic River where he fed the parts to the woodchipper. Most of the tiny chips of frozen human flesh and bone disappeared into the river. Perhaps some were eaten by local carnivores. Sixty-nine tiny pieces of bone, a crown, and a tooth were all of Helle that was ever found.

Despite Crafts' best, and almost perfect, attempt to get away with murder, he was arrested, tried, found guilty, and sentenced to fifty years in prison. His conviction was the result of the efforts of the forensic science team in reconstructing the events surrounding the disappearance, death, and dismemberment of Helle Crafts.

REFERENCES

Herzog, Arthur, *The Woodchipper Murder,* 1989, Henry Holt, New York.

Krogman, William M., *The Human Skeleton in Forensic Medicine*, 1962, C. C. Thomas, Springfield, IL.

A Case of Historic Cannibalism in the American West

Implications for Southwestern Archaeology

Alison E. Rautman and Todd W. Fenton

EDITOR'S INTRODUCTION

I will grant you that I am not in the primary demographic that Trey Parker and Matt Stone aim for in their Comedy Central show *South Park*. Nevertheless, I am a huge fan of the show and their sense of humor. As a fan of *South Park* and of Matt and Trey, I heard about and purchased the DVD for a movie they produced when they were students at the University of Colorado. I wasn't expecting much from a student project filmed during spring break and funded by maxing out all of their friends' credit cards. I was more than pleasantly surprised to find the movie, called *Cannibal! The Musical,* was a brilliant send-up of Broadway shows including an absurd abundance of musical theatre clichés. The movie is loosely based on an actual event: a case of cannibalism among a group of travelers lost in the Wasatch Mountains in 1873–74 in territory that a few years later would become incorporated into the state of Colorado. Amazingly, and the reason I bring up the story of *Cannibal! The Musical* in the first place, the skeletal remains of those cannibalized by the only survivor of the expedition, Alferd Packer, were discovered and excavated. The results of that research are presented here. Oh, and by the way; there's an Alferd Packer Memorial Grill at the cafeteria at the University of Colorado in Boulder. Shpadoinkle! (Watch the movie to get that reference.)

POINTS TO PONDER

1. What happened to the crew of prospectors in the Wasatch Mountains in 1873–1874?
2. What forensic evidence is there for cannibalism of the five people whose remains were investigated in this study?
3. How does the evidence for Euro-American cannibalism compare to that of Native American practices in the same region?
4. What are the lessons gleaned from the forensic study of Packer's companions?

Discoveries of concentrated deposits of fragmentary human bone and their interpretation as evidence of cannibalism in the pre-Hispanic American Southwest have engaged archaeologists in a continuing debate. Forensic study of the victims in the historic Alferd [sic] Packer case from southern Colorado in the 1870s contributes to this discussion by providing detailed data regarding perimortem trauma, cut marks, and butchering patterns in a well-accepted case of mass murder and survival cannibalism. In particular, postmortem cut marks record a butchering strategy focused on filleting muscle tissue for immediate consumption; patterning of cut marks was structured by anatomy and also by cultural values. Contrasts between this historic case and the archaeological assemblages highlights the need for a more nuanced discussion of the cultural context and meaning of the archaeological cases. Interpretations of human skeletal remains arguably must begin with the view of "the body as artifact" and from a theoretical perspective defined largely by osteology and in comparison with zooarchaeological assemblages under various ecological conditions. At this point, however, the debate regarding Anasazi cannibalism would benefit from the addition of other anthropological perspectives, particularly those concerning the human body as a vehicle for the expression of cultural ideas and values.

THE ALFERD PACKER CANNIBALISM CASE

Alferd Packer (d. 1907) is relatively well known to students of western U.S. history as the "Colorado cannibal" who reputedly killed and cannibalized five companions during the nineteenth-century gold rush (Curry 2002; Starrs and Ramsland 2005). Documents show that he was a member of a party of 21 gold prospectors who left Utah in November 1873 for southwestern Colorado Territory. By January 1874, they sought shelter in an Indian winter encampment near the modern town of Montrose, Colorado. Despite warnings about winter travel, Packer and five other men decided to continue their journey. The six men left camp in February, with the goal of crossing the San Juan Mountains to reach Gunnison. According to Packer's later narrative, after about 10 days' travel, they gave up and made camp just above the modern town of Lake City. It was here that Packer reputedly murdered and cannibalized his companions (Curry 2002; Starrs 1990).

In April, Packer arrived at the Los Pinos Indian Agency near Saguache. He stated that he had been forced to cannibalize the bodies of his companions to survive. Over the next few weeks, however, he told several different accounts about how his companions actually died. He was charged with murder and jailed, and in May signed a statement confessing to killing (only) one individual in self-defense. In August a traveling artist for Harper's Weekly discovered five bodies lying near the banks of the Lake Fork of the Gunnison River. The artist sketched the remains as they lay in the open; he returned later with a group of men to bury the remains (Anderson 1990).

By this time, however, Packer had escaped from jail; he was found 9 years later in Wyoming. At that point, Packer signed another confession, was convicted of one count of murder, and sentenced to hang. He appealed, and the Colorado Supreme Court set aside the conviction. A second trial found Packer guilty of five counts of manslaughter. He served 18 years in prison, was paroled, and eventually died in 1907. Obviously, he changed his story repeatedly, and his role in the deaths of the other men has long been debated. Equally obvious is that we will never know for sure whether in fact he actually ate his companions. It is worth emphasizing, however, that throughout his statements his claim of survival cannibalism never changed. He justified his actions by claiming that game was scarce and his ability to hunt was hampered by deep snow, his weakened condition, and lack of ammunition. The variations in his stories as well as his legal convictions concerned only his role in the deaths of the other men; the question of cannibalistic consumption was never seriously challenged (Curry 2002; Starrs 1990).

In 1989 a multidisciplinary group of forensic scientists, including an archaeologist and three physical anthropologists, excavated the historic gravesite to determine if there was evidence to substantiate Packer's claims of self-defense (Starrs 1990). The remains of all 5 victims were recovered and the forensic study proceeded with attribution of age, sex, and also identity of the individuals. A second group of variables concentrated on reconstruction of the death history of each individual—that is, the range of events from the time just before death until the time of analysis, including perimortem trauma and probable cause of death, reconstruction of the characteristics of the probable murder weapon, identification of postmortem cut marks, and those changes that accompanied exposure, animal scavenging, and later burial (Birkby 1990; Fenton 1990; Haag 1990). After analysis, the remains were reburied in the same location as the original group burial.

THE FORENSIC STUDY

The Packer Assemblage

The original study of the Packer victims was designed to investigate whether there was evidence for perimortem trauma to resolve debates about Packer's role in the deaths of the five other men. Specifically, there was debate regarding whether one or more victims had been shot, as Packer once claimed. Although we present evidence regarding perimortem trauma and cause of death, our main purpose in writing this paper for an audience of archaeologists is to examine in more detail the evidence for postmortem processing of the human bone. Because there has been little serious debate about whether cannibalism actually occurred in the historic case, the cut mark data provide valuable baseline evidence of what one type of "cannibalism"—mass murder followed by short-term survival cannibalism—might look like. We hope other researchers can use these data to assist in interpreting

Figure 22.1. Excavation of the Packer victims' burial site in Colorado. Note the demarcation of the grave pit by lines of rock on the historic ground surface (just below the present sod layer); additional lines of rock on the historic ground surface subdivided the pit into five sections that showed the location of each individual body. Note also the degree of anatomic integrity of the skeletons. The individual on the right has experienced some postmortem disarticulation: the cranium has been displaced and is located near the pelvis. The entire skull (cranium and mandible) is missing on the individual located second from the left.

skeletal remains in situations where such additional contextual information is not available—such as one might encounter among archaeological skeletal material.

The remains recovered for study were those of five adult males, here designated by letters A through E. They ranged in age from one young adult (17–20 yrs) to one older adult (50–60 yrs). The others were aged about 30–40 years. Even though the remains were collected and buried nearly four months after the individuals' deaths, the skeletons retained enough integrity so that customary Euramerican burial practices were observed: the two bodies that were still fairly well articulated were-positioned on their backs; side by side but not touching. The three other bodies exhibit a higher degree of repositioning of the body parts. Lines of rock on the historic ground surface marked the extent of each individual's grave within the group burial. Thus, even though one might consider this burial as a mass grave, the bones belonging to each individual were not commingled, and individual skeletons were easily identified during excavation.

The bone itself was well preserved, and evidence of perimortem trauma and postmortem processing was readily apparent. The identity of each individual was tentatively determined based on the comparison of individualized physical characteristics with written descriptions of the individuals and with the drawings that appeared in *Harpers* magazine (Anderson 1990; Birkby 1990).

Only one individual had experienced significant bone attrition (the skull was not recovered). Otherwise, nearly all skeletal elements were recovered for each individual, including the small bones of the hands and feet. There was minimal postmortem carnivore damage to the bone. The minimal disarticulation of bone groups is consistent with a degree of natural decomposition before burial

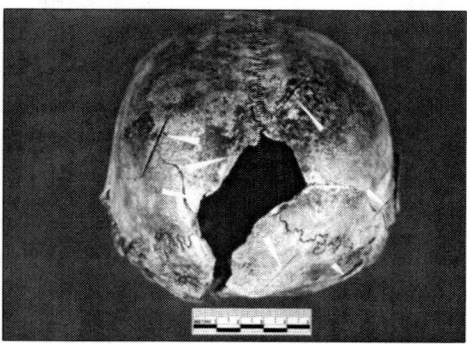

Figure 22.2. The cranium of Individual D, showing extensive sharp force trauma (arrows) and also blunt force trauma.

and also historic disturbance when the bodies were first buried. There is no evidence that any body parts were deliberately disarticulated. It is likely that a certain degree of natural desiccation and partial mummification of the soft tissue before the bodies were buried contributed to the observed degree of integrity of the skeletal anatomy. No soft tissue was preserved on the bone at the time of excavation. The grave site did yield archaeological material such as buttons and fragments of cloth that indicated the inclusion of clothing in the burials (Ayers 1990).

EVIDENCE OF PERIMORTEM TRAUMA AND CAUSE OF DEATH

All five of the skeletonized individuals exhibited abundant evidence of perimortem trauma. All four recovered crania (A, C, D, and E) displayed extensive blunt-force trauma, and all individuals displayed evidence of sharp-force trauma to the skull. Three individuals also exhibited sharp-force and blunt trauma to the arm (humerus and ulna).

Blunt-force trauma appeared as multiple depressed fractures to the cranial vaults, most likely the result of blows from an implement such as the blunt end of a small axe or hatchet. Many of the blows to the heads resulted in fractures radiating outward from the impact sites, as well as concentric fractures perpendicular to the radiating fractures (Berryman and Symes 1998; Galloway 1999). There was also extensive evidence for sharp-force trauma consisting of multiple clefts or notches to each of the recovered skulls. These defects are consistent with hacking actions with a wide blade such as from the sharp end of an axe or hatchet (Humphrey and Hutchinson 2001). This severe cranial trauma is more than sufficient evidence of cause of death for each individual.

There was no evidence of perimoitem gunshot wounds to any of the five individuals. What had previously been reported in the media to be possible gunshot trauma to the pelvic area was, in fact, damage from carnivore activity. The shape and location of large, circular puncture defects in the iliac blades of four individuals (A, B, C, and D) is consistent with bear scavenging (Carson et al. 2000).

The following discussion details the evidence of perimoitem trauma for each individual. Individual A exhibited four apparent blunt-force impact sites to the skull. The left lateral aspect of the skull displayed at least three impact sites, two in the left parietal and one in the left side of the frontal bone. Another impact site is located in the midline of the frontal bone. The right side of the skull shows multiple linear fractures all radiating from the impact sites in left lateral and anterior aspects of the skull. The skull also shows horizontally oriented, hacking-type sharp-force trauma to the occipital, just posterior to the left mastoid process. The same type of sharp-force trauma is also present on the distal shaft of the left ulna. The latter appears to be a type of defensive trauma caused by the impact of a weapon (such as the sharp end of a hatchet) on the raised arm of the victim.

The cranial remains of Individual B are represented by a single bone fragment. Nonetheless, this frontal fragment, measuring 45 mm x 50 mm, also displayed unmistakable evidence of perimortem trauma in the form of four distinct sharp-implement wounds. The implied fragmentary nature of this skull suggests that Individual B also experienced extensive cranial blunt-force trauma that contributed to bone fragmentation.

The skull of Individual C exhibited multiple blunt-force impact sites to the left side. Two impact sites were in the left parietal, and one was in the left temporal. This individual also showed several clefts in the bone produced by hacking blows to the skull. The skull displays at least three clefts: one on the left parietal and two in the region of the coronal suture between the right parietal and the frontal bone. In addition, the left radius of this individual exhibited a complete fracture at midshaft that appears to be the result of hacking trauma. Finally, the left third and fourth metacarpals showed hacking trauma to the midshafts of both bones. The trauma to the radius and metacarpals are interpreted as defensive wounds such as those incurred when a victim raises his hand and arm up to block the blows of the attacker.

Individual D exhibited at least 14 clefts in the skull consistent with hacking trauma from a sharp implement: three on the left parietal, two on the tight parietal, two on the occipital, four on the frontal, one on the left zygomatic, one on the right zygomatic, and one on the right maxilla. A large section of the right frontal and supraorbital region was missing, probably due to blunt-force impact in that region. The left humerus displayed a perimortem butterfly fracture of the proximal shaft. Finally, the left ulna presented with hacking trauma to the distal shaft, similar to the defensive injury seen in Individual A.

Individual E exhibits at least three depressed fractures on the left side of the skull: two to the left parietal and one to the left orbital region. The right side of the skull displays one depressed fracture to the temporoparietal region. Additionally, two sharp-force clefts produced by hacking actions are on the right parietal.

In sum, the forensic interpretation of this peri-mortem bone damage on all 5 skeletons is that the individuals were killed, one after another, by repeated blows to the head with a heavy sharp object such as an axe (Birkby 1990), resulting in blunt-force as well as sharp-force trauma. Defensive wounds to the arms of three individuals suggest that at least three of the men were conscious during the attack and had attempted to defend themselves. There is no evidence of gunshot wounds.

Evidence of Postmortem Bone Modification

Extensive postmortem bone modification was readily apparent, primarily in the form of cut marks, which had been made on fresh ("green") bone soon after death. All five individuals exhibited numerous cut marks on the postcranial skeleton. The number, location, orientation, and distribution of these cut marks provide a means of investigating the death history of each individual, and also of the group as a whole.

If we accept that this murder case is probably one of the best instances of known survival cannibalism where skeletal remains have been recovered and analyzed, we can use this study not only to resolve legal and historic issues involved in the murder accusations against Packer, but also to understand some problematic skeletal assemblages from the more distant past. Our hope is that the data regarding postmortem processing of the bone will provide baseline information regarding what cannibalism of a certain type and under certain conditions might look like. For example, these data regarding the number, location, orientation of cut marks on the bone may help us in distinguishing, for example, defleshing activities from meat removal (filleting) in archaeological skeletal assemblages. This case study thus should be of general interest to archaeologists and physical anthropologists who are attempting to interpret the range of possible cultural behaviors that can result in certain types of observed postmortem bone modification.

The Cut Mark Data

All of the Packer case individuals exhibited numerous cut marks on the axial skeleton as well as on the appendicular skeletal elements. The number of cut marks per individual ranged from 80 to 106, with a mean of 93 cut marks per individual. If indeed Packer were butchering the bodies to obtain meat for consumption, one would expect that he might first remove large muscle groups from the limbs and portions of the axial skeleton. The distribution of cut marks is consistent with this expectation: the vast majority of cut marks are found on bones with the largest muscle units. Cut marks were not found on the small bones of the hands or feet, or on the head, but nearly every other bone that is associated with significant muscle tissue showed signs of postmortem processing.

One might expect that much of the edible tissue of the body would derive from the muscular areas of the arms and legs, and so might reason that cut marks should be located preferentially along

long bones. However, in fact, the incidence of cut marks on butchered animal bone is affected by the location of muscle attachments as well as by the size of the muscle units (Egeland et al. 2002; Hill 2001). The combination of both these factors is seen in this human bone assemblage as well. Long bones exhibited only 40 percent of all cut marks (N= 198), with the other 60 percent of cuts (N= 280) located on the bones of the axial skeleton (ribs, scapula, pelvis, vertebrae, and clavicles). This observed pattern of distribution (see Table 1) could be due to the proximity of several different bones (ribs) close to one another, where one stroke of a knife might easily mark several ribs.

The inferred role of anatomy in affecting the number and location of cut marks on the axial elements is also supported by a strong anterior/posterior asymmetry in cut mark location. On the axial skeleton, the vast majority (77 percent) of the cut marks are located on the back, and only 22 percent on the front of the torso. This anterior-posterior differentiation in cut marks is also seen on the long bones, but it is not nearly so pronounced. On long bones, 62 percent of cut marks were on the back; 38 percent on the front. This difference in the treatment of the axial skeleton and the appendicular elements provides additional evidence that the anatomy of the muscle attachments as well as human selection of specific large muscle units were both important factors in structuring the distribution of cut marks.

There is also clear patterning in the distribution of cut marks on the long bones themselves. The vast majority of cuts (95 percent) were made on the shaft itself, near the proximal or distal end of each long bone, but not in the regions expected in a case of disarticulation. Cut marks were nearly equally distributed between the proximal (N = 89 cut marks) and distal ends (N = 94 cut marks). Only 9 cut marks (5 percent) on the long bones were located in the mid-shaft region of the bone, and none on the articular surfaces, even though these surfaces were well preserved. These data again are consistent with the location of muscle attachments of large muscle units, indicating a cultural strategy of targeted removal of large packages of meaty tissue.

The orientation of cut marks on the bone can also be used to evaluate other details of the death history of these individuals. For example, if one imagines the process of butchering a large mammal such as a deer or antelope, a series of parallel cut marks on a single bone or group of bones suggests that cutting occurred in one event; in contrast, a number of cut marks oriented in many different directions might be more characteristic of an inexperienced butcher, or might represent different cutting episodes with the butcher relocating to a variety of positions around the body, or even more than one individual working at processing the carcass.

Olsen and Shipman (1994:382) make a similar argument regarding the orientation of cut marks in their reconstruction of the process of defleshing human bone for secondary burial. They argue that the orientation of cut marks can reveal the handedness of the person processing the corpse, the position of the corpse (prone or supine) during the process, and the movement of the individual processor around a stationary corpse. They used cut mark maps to argue that each limb was processed as a unit, with the individual doing the cutting then relocating to another position beside the corpse to process the next limb.

A very different pattern of cut marks on the Packer victims indicates that the process of muscle removal was quite different. In the case of the Packer assemblage, it is significant that there is no clear preferred orientation to the direction of the cut marks, and no correlation of cut mark directions even between adjacent bones on the same limb. Olsen and Shipman (1994:382) argue that such random orientations, which they observed only in forearms in their sample (radii and ulnae), were likely caused by the processor's greater ability to manipulate the limb segment—either because it was already detached from the body, or because the cuts were made soon after death, before the body stiffened (p. 382).

In the Packer assemblage, we have the advantage of knowing that the different body parts were in fact *not* disarticulated during butchering, and thus the random orientation of the cut marks on each element cannot be attributed to the processor's freedom to turn and manipulate all these various body parts. Rather, it seems more likely that each segment of each body, or each major muscle group, was processed independently of one another, with the tissue removed by a person approaching the body from a variety of positions and over a period of time. This pattern is consistent with an "as needed" strategy of removing muscle packages, presumably with some time intervals between episodes of processing. In this particular case, this strategy may have been made possible by the late winter context, where the cold would preserve the unused portions of the bodies for later processing and consumption.

Comparison with the data presented by Olsen and Shipman (1994) also supports our initial assumption that the Packer victims were processed for the purposes of meat removal (filleting). Olsen and Shipman (1994:380–381) also describe the appearance and distribution of cut marks that are interpreted as evidence of defleshing. They argue that defleshing, like filleting, results in the production of numerous short, fine cut marks on bone (see also Lyman 1987 and Olsen 1987). They distinguish the two processes on the basis of the location of the cut marks: fillet marks should be clustered at the areas of the bone where muscle and tendons are attached. On long bones, these insertion points are located near the proximal and distal ends of the bone, but not right on the articular surfaces. In contrast, cut marks left during deflesh-ing might be located anywhere on the bone, and cut marks associated with disarticulation should be located on or adjacent to the articular surfaces of the bone (Binford 1981; Hurlbut 2000; Raemsch 1993; Shipman 1980; White 1992).

In the Packer assemblage, the cut mark maps show a well-defined pattern with the cut marks on long bones preferentially located near the proximal and distal ends. No cut marks were found on the necks of the femurs, or on the articular surfaces of the long bones. (Processing associated with the cranium such as for scalping is a completely different issue that is beyond the scope of this paper; no cut marks were found on the crania in the Packer assemblage.) In fact, the location of the cut marks on each bone is logically related to the expected anatomical location of muscle attachments (see Lyman 1987 for an analogous discussion of animal butchering). There is no indication that the body parts were deliberately disarticulated, or that there was any attempt to remove other types of tissue besides muscle.

SPECIFIC INTERPRETATIONS

Several points are relevant to interpreting possibly cannibalized remains from the archaeological record. First, this case study represents a violent mass murder followed by processing of the human body primarily for immediate consumption of muscle tissue. The muscle tissue of the limbs and torso of all five individuals was removed (filleted) as discrete meat units over a period of time, a finding that is consistent with a strategy of meat removal on an "as-needed" basis. There is clear evidence of relatively complete removal of muscle tissue, but no evidence of purposeful postmortem dismemberment, disarticulation, burning, bone breakage, marrow extraction, or other forms of processing that would yield additional calories or nutrition from the bodies. The degree of post-mortem processing of the bone was in fact minimal and represented primarily by cut marks, which reveal the systematic and efficient removal of large meat units.

There are of course other known cases of historic or modern survival cannibalism such as among the historic Donner party (Grayson 1990; Hardesty 1997) and the well-known Andean plane crash case (Read 2002). It is unusual, however, to have detailed contextual information as well as the skeletal remains themselves. Given the many differences in the cause of death of the individuals in all these cases of survival cannibalism, we expect that the most useful comparisons to archaeological skeletal assemblages will come not from the evidence of perimortem trauma, but from the cut mark data that records postmortem processing.

In this respect, the minimal postmortem processing in the Packer assemblage is itself informative. In fact, the food value of the victims was apparently far from exhausted, even if we consider only the muscle tissue. In addition, because we know the approximate time elapsed since death (no more than 60 days), the number of victims (five), and the number of consumer's (one), we could even calculate the approximate volume of meat removed and consumed, as well as its protein yield (Garn and Block 1970) and minimal average caloric consumption per day. Additional food value from the smaller muscles of the hands and feet and from other tissues, including marrow, could have been extracted if Packer had been forced to rely on the bodies as a food source for a longer period of time, or if the bodies had been the primary food source for a larger group of individuals. As such, one can consider this case as exemplifying an initial stage of survival cannibalism, characterized by the filleting of targeted preferred muscle groups for immediate consumption.

The cut mark data also records evidence of postmortem processing that is in many respects comparable to the inferences that archaeologists make regarding animal butchering patterns. If we take this zooarchaeological perspective of the cut marks on the Packer victims, we might compare his butchering strategy to a hunter's strategy of removal of high-utility meat units (Binford 1978,1981; Speth 1983) from the axial and appendicular skeleton of a large animal for consumption. This strategy can be distinguished from the processing of an animal carcass for other purposes, including, for example, drying of meat for trade, storage, or long distance transport

(Binford 1978; Friesen 2001), or for recovery of grease or marrow (Binford 1978; Leechman 1951; Metcalfe and Jones 1988).

The observed pattern of meat removal on the human bone among the Packer victims also contrasts with the extensive processing indicated by highly fragmented animal bone that Turner and Turner (1999:24–37) cite as characteristic for artio-dactyl remains from selected archaeological sites in the Southwest (e.g., Wupatki). Other researchers (e.g., Speth and Rautman 2004) have noted that large mammal bone at a residential site (in their example, a pueblo) exhibits more extensive fragmentation than similar bone from a kill site. This observation indicates that other variables besides meat utility can structure the degree of fragmentation in an animal bone assemblage. These other variables might include the time and personnel available for processing, anticipated use, and so forth. This observation also suggests that the Packer remains might therefore be better compared with animal bone at a kill site rather than a residential site. It is interesting that in fact all processing of the human bone apparently took plate at the Packer "kill site," and that there was no attempt to detach limbs for processing at a secondary location. In comparison, ethnographic studies of deer butchering practices among Southwestern groups (Hill 1938) indicate that disarticulation of limbs commonly precedes meat removal, even when transport of the carcass is not an issue (see also LeBlanc 1999:176).

In this kind of discussion, it seems quite logical to make comparisons with known human strategies of butchering animal carcasses, since of course most of the vast archaeological literature on butchering strategies and meat processing refers to nonhuman animals (see references in Lyman 1987). In addition, one might argue that the basic mammalian muscle anatomy of humans (bipeds) and quadrupeds is very broadly comparable, and so meat removal strategies would also be comparable. Bahn (1991, 1992) uses this line of reasoning when he argues that the apparent similarity of postmortem bone processing between human and nonhuman remains at northern Anasazi sites is due to the basic similarity of human and large quadraped anatomy. Because of this similarity, he argues, there are only a limited number of ways in which to butcher either a large animal (such as a deer) or a human. In contrast, White (1992) and also Turner and Turner (1999) argue that this similar treatment is due primarily to the fact that human and nonhuman remains were viewed similarly (as food) by the consumers and were treated accordingly primarily as a food resource.

We believe that this line of reasoning using butchering strategies and calculating meat yields are in fact potentially useful in accounting for many aspects of the Anasazi assemblages, although Garn and Block (1970) have argued that the nutritional value of the human body is really quite limited. However, as anthropologists, we should also acknowledge that the Anasazi were capable of recognizing a distinction between the consumption of nonhuman animals and the consumption of other humans, and that these acts might have different cultural meanings. (This cognitive and symbolic capability might be more usefully debated in the discussion of cannibalism among premodern humans.) In fact, Turner and Turner (1999:54) also refer to the complexities of reconstructing individual death histories when they note that "butchering is only one aspect in the perimortem history of a carcass." Eutchering, cooking techniques (e.g., Speth 2000), and discard of waste are structured by cultural ideas regarding the ways in which nonhuman animal or human bodies can and should be treated in the postmortem period. It is therefore reasonable to argue that the death history of any given individual (or an osteological assemblage of many individuals) represents a complex combination of factors inch ding both noncultural constraints (such as anatomy), the action of taphonomy or natural processes such as erosion, weathering, and scavenging, and also cultural decisions that may in fact be unique to the treatment of human bone.

In sum, we believe that the Packer study provides comparative data that can help in understanding the highly fragmented human remains in the pre-Hispanic Southwest. In particular, the cut marks on the bone in the Packer assemblage are interpreted as consistent with Packer's claim of relatively short-term survival cannibalism. An archaeologist might phrase these findings as revealing a butchering strategy focused on detaching high-utility meat units for immediate consumption (rather than for storage or preservation). Archaeologists might further note that while the location of the cut marks was structured in part by muscle anatomy, cultural selection also played a role in the butchering strategy. There is no evidence for deliberate disarticulation of the body, either as part of the process of meat removal, or as might be related to the transport of the bodies from "kill site" to "camp site," or for redistribution to other consumers. Lastly, it is obvious that the degree of processing is in fact quite minimal. Had Packer been forced to rely on the bodies for a longer period of time, it is completely possible that he would have resorted to lower-utility meat units (e.g., from the hands and feet, or from the entrails) and to further processing of the bone for extraction of calories from grease and marrow.

Acknowledgments. James Starrs, a law professor at The George Washington University, was the project leader for the Alferd G. Packer Victims' Exhumation Project, which began in Lake City, CO on July 17, 1989. Dr. Walter Birkby' (University of Arizona) directed the study of the human skeletons, with assistance from Bruce Anderson and Todd Fenton. This paper represents a collaboration of efforts of the two coauthors: Fenton (a forensic anthropologist) did the cut mark analysis and interpretations of the Packer victims, and Rautman (a Southwestern archaeologist) is responsible for zooarchaeological comparisons and for considering the archaeological relevance of the case study. A much shorter version of the paper was presented at the 2001 meetings of the American Anthropological Association. We thank Debra L. Martin for inviting us to participate in that session and for inspiring us to join forces to revisit the Packer data in light of current archaeological debates. We appreciate her thoughtful comments, as well as those of T. J. Ferguson, John Kantner, Pat Lambert, Michael Jochim, and our anonymous reviewers. Their collegial assistance in clarifying the organization of the argument does not imply that they necessarily agree with our views. Lori Schiess laboriously checked the cut mark data against the original field and lab notes; Elizabeth Pratt, Jane Wankmiller and Tracey Tichnell helped with the figures. We also appreciate the efforts of our colleague Dr. Helen Pollard, who translated the abstract.

REFERENCES CITED

Anderson, Bruce E.

1990 The Validity of the Artistic Depiction of the Victim's Remains. *American Academy of Forensic Sciences Publication* 90:100.

Arens, William

1979 *The Man-Eating Myth: Anthropology and Anthropophagy.* Oxford University Press, New York.

Ayers, James E.

1990 Archaeology in the Pursuit of Forensic Truth. *Amer ican Academy of Forensic Sciences Publication* 90:99.

Bahn, Paul

1991 Is Cannibalism Too Much to Swallow? *New Scientist* 130:38–40.

1992 Ancestral Cannibalism Gives Us Food for Thought: Review of *Prehistoric Cannibalism,* by T. D. White. *New Scientist* 134:40–41.

Barnes, Barry

1995 *The Elements of Social Theory.* Princeton University

Press, Princeton, New Jersey. 2000 *Understanding Agency: Social Theory and Responsible Action.* Sage Publications, London.

Barrett, John C.

1994 *Fragments from Antiquity: An Archaeology of Social Life in Britain, 2900–1200 B.C.* Blackwell, Oxford, UK.

Berryman, Hugh E., and Steven A. Symes

1995 Recognizing Gunshot and Blunt Cranial Trauma Through Fracture Interpretation. In *Forensic Osteology: Advances in the Identification of Human Remains,* 2nd edition, edited by K. J. Reichs, pp. 333-352. Charles C. Thomas, Springfield. Illinois.

Billman, Brian. R., Patricia M. Lambert, and Banks L. Leonard 2000 Cannibalism, Warfare, and Drought in the Mesa Verde Region during the Twelfth Century A.D. *American Antiquity* 65:145-178.

Binford, Lewis R.

1978 *Nunamuir Ethnoarchaeology.* Academic Press, New York.

1981 *Bones: Ancient Men and Modern Myths.* Academic Press, New York. 2000 Where Do Research Problems Come From? *American Antiquity* 66:669–678.

Birkby, Walter H.

1990 Gravesite and Laboratory Assessment of Skeletal Remains of the Five Members of the 1874 Packer Prospecting Party. *American Academy of Forensic Sciences Publi cation* 90:100.

Bulliock, Peter

1991 A Reappraisal of Anasazi Cannibalism. *Kiva* 57:5–16. Carson E. Ann, Vincent H. Stefan, and Joseph F. Powell

2000 Skeletal Manifestations of Bear Scavenging. *Journal of Forensic Sciences* 45 (3): 515–526.

Chesson, Meredith S. (editor)

2001 *Social Memory, Identity, and Death: Anthropological Perspectives on Mortuary Rituals.* Archeological Papers of the American Anthropological Association Number 10.

Curry, Andrew

2002 Case of the Colorado Cannibal. *Archaeology* May–June: 50–53.

Darling, J. Andrew

1999 Mass Inhumation and the Execution of Witches in the American Southwest. *American Anthropologist* 100:732–752.

Dongoske, Kurt E., Debra L. Martin, and T. J. Ferguson

2000 Critique of the Claim of Cannibalism at Cowboy Wash. *American Antiquity* 65:179–190.

Doyel, David E.

1980 Hohokam Social Organization and the Sedentary to Classic Transition. In *Current Issues in Hohokam Prehistoiy: Proceedings of a Symposium,* edited by D. E. Doyel and Fred T. Plog, pp. 23–40. Anthropological Research Papers No. 23. Arizona State University, Tempe.

Egeland, Charles P., Matthew Hill, and Ryan Byerly

2002 Archaeological vs. Experimental Manifestations of Large Mammal Butchery: Increasing the Reliability of Inferences of Prehistoric Subsistence Behavior. Paperpre-sented at the Society for American Archaeology Meetings, Denver, CO. (forthcoming in *Plains Anthropologist)*

Fenton, Todd W.

1990 Cut Marks on the Recovered Bones from the Packer Prospecting Party. *American Academy of Forensic Sciences Publication* 90:100.

Fenton, Todd W., and Alison E. Rautman

2002 A Case of Survival Cannibalism in the American West: Implications for Southwestern Archaeology. Paper presented at the 67th Annual Meetings of the Society for American Archaeology, Denver, Colorado. Friesen, T. Max

2001 A Zooarchaeological Signature for Meat Storage: Rethinking the Drying Utility Index. *American Antiquity* 66(2):315–331.

Foucault, Michel

1972 *The Archaeology of Knowledge.* Pantheon, New York.

1977 *Discipline and Punish.* Pantheon, New York.

1978 *The History of Sexuality.* Pantheon, New York. Galloway, Alison

1999 Fracture Patterns and Skeletal Morphology: Introduction and the Skull. In *Broken Bones: Anthropological Analysis of Blunt Force Trauma,* edited by Alison Galloway, pp. 63–80. Charles C. Thomas, Springfield, Illinois. Gam, Stanley M., and Walter D. Block

1970 The Limited Nutritional Value of Cannibalism. *American Anthropologist* 72:106.

Ginsburg, Faye, and Anne L. Tsing (editors)

1990 *Uncertain Terms: Negotiating Gender in American Culture.* Beacon Press, Boston, Massachusetts. Goldman, Laurence R. (editor)

1999 *The Anthropology of Cannibalism.* Bergin and Garvey, Westport, Connecticut.

Grayson, Donald K.

1990 Donner Party Deaths: A Demographic Assessment. *Journal of Anthropological Research* 46:223-242.

Haag, Lucien C.

1990 A Toolmark Examiner's Analysis of the Cutmarks on . the Packer Victims' Bones. *American Academy of Forensic Sciences Publication* 90:100.

Hardesty, Donald L.

1997 *The Archaeology of the Donner Party.* University of Nevada Press, Reno.

Hill, Matthew G.

2001 Paleoindian Diet and Subsistence Behavior on the Northwestern Great Plains of North America. Ph.D. dissertation, Department of Anthropology, University of Wisconsin, Madison.

Hill, Willard W.

1938 *The Agricultural and Hunting Methods of the Navaho Indians.* Yale University Publications in Anthropology 18. New Haven, Connecticut.

Humphrey, Joshua H., and Dale L. Hutchinson

2001 Macroscopic Characteristics of Hacking Trauma. *Journal of Forensic Sciences* 46(2):228–233.

Hurlbut, Sharon A.

2000 The Taphonomy of Cannibalism: A Review of Anthro pogenic Bone Modification in the American Southwest.' *International Journal of Osteoarchaeology* 10:4–26.

Johnson, Matthew H.

1989 Conceptions of Agency in Archaeological Interpretation. *Journal of Anthropological Archaeology* 8: 189–211. Kantner, John

1999a Anasazi Mutilation and Cannibalism in the American Southwest. In *The Anthropology of Cannibalism,* edited by Laurence R. Goldman, pp. 75–104. Bergin and Garvey, Westport, Connecticut.

1999b Survival Cannibalism or Sociopolitical Intimidation? Explaining Perimortem Mutilation in the American Southwest. *Human Nature* 10:1–50.

Kelly, Raymond C.

2000 *Warless Societies and the Origin of War.* University of Michigan Press, Ann Arbor.

Lambert, Patricia M., Brian R. Billman, and Banks L. Leonard 2000 Explaining Variability in Mutilated Human Bone Assemblages from the American Southwest: A Case Study from the Southern Piedmont of Sleeping Ute Mountain, Colorado. *International Journal of Osteoarchaeology* 10:49–94.

LeBlanc, Steven A.

1999 *Prehistoric Warfare in the American Southwest.* Uni versity of Utah Press, Salt Lake City.

Leechman, Douglas

1951 Bone Grease. *American Antiquity* 16:355–356. Leonard, Banks L., Patricia M. Lambert, and Richard A. Marlar

2001 Canmbalism, Witch-killing, Parsimony, and Empiri cism. Paper presented at the 66th Annual Meeting of the Society for American Archaeology, New Orleans.

Lock, Margaret

2002 *Twice Dead: Organ Transplants and the Reinvention of Death*. University of California Press, Berkeley.

Lyman, R. Lee

1987 Archaeofaunas and Butchery Studies: A Taphonomic Perspective. In *Advances in Archaeological Method and Theory*, vol. 10, edited by Michael B. Schiffer, 249–337. Academic Press, New York.

Maschner, Herbert D. G., and Katherine L. Reedy-Maschner

2003 Building an N-Dimensional Anthropology. *Anthropology News* December:4–5.

McGuire, James E., and Barbara Tuchanska

2000 *Science Unfettered*. Ohio University Press, Athens, Ohio.

Meskell, Lynn

2000 Writing the Body in Archaeology. In *Reading theBody: Representations and Remains in the Archaeological Record*, edited by Alison E. Rautman, pp. 13–24. University of Pennsylvania Press, Philadelphia.

Metcalfe, Duncan, and Kevin T. Jones

1988 A Reconsideration of Animal Body Part Utility Indices. *American Antiquity* 53:486–504.

Minnis, Paul E.

1985 *Social Adaptation to Food Stress: A Prehistoric Southwestern Example*. University of Chicago Press, Chicago.

Nass, G. Gisela, and Nicholas F. Beliantoni

1982 A Prehistoric Multiple Burial from Monument Valley Evidencing Trauma and Possible Cannibalism. Kiva 47:257–271.

Ogilvie, Marsha D., and Charles E. Hilton

2000 A Case of Ritualized Violence in the Prehistoric American Southwest. *International Journal of Osteoarchaeology* 10:27-48.

Olsen, Stanley L., and Pat Shipman

1994 Cutmarks and Perimortem Treatment of Skeletal Remains on the Northern Plains. In *Skeletal Biology in the Great Plains: A Multldisciplinary View*, edited by D. Owsley and R. Jantz, pp. 377–387. Smithsonian Institution Press, Washington, D.C.

Preston, Dennis

1998 Cannibals of the Canyon. *The New Yorker*, 30 November. 76–89.

Raemsch, Carol A.

1993 Mechanical Procedures Involved in Bone Dismemberment and Defleshing in Prehistoric Michigan. *Midcontinental Journal of Archaeology* 18:217–244.

Rautman, Alison E. (editor)

2000 *Reading the Body: Representations and Remains in the Archaeology Record*. University of Pennsylvania Press, Philadelphia.

Rautman, Alison E., and Todd W. Fenton

2001 Anthropological Perspectives on Anasazi Cannibal ism: From Forensics to Foucault. Paper presented at the 100th Annual Meeting of the American Anthropological Association, Washington, D.C.

Read, Piers Paul

2002 *Alive: The Story of the Andes Survivors.* Reprinted. Avon Books, New York. Originally published 1974, Lip-incott Williams and Wilkins, Hagerstown, Maryland.

Reed, Erik K.

1981 Human Skeletal Material. In *Contributions to Gran Quivira Archeology*, edited by Alden C. Hayes, pp. 75–118. National Park Service Publications in Archaeology No. 17. U.S. Department of the Interior, Washington, D.C.

Shanks, Michael, and Christopher Tilley

1981 Ideology, Symbolic Power and Ritual Communication: A Reinterpretation of Neolithic Mortuary Practices. In *The Archaeology of Contextual Meaning*, edited by Ian Hodder, pp. 129–154. Cambridge University Press, Cambridge.

Speth, John D.

1983 *Bison Kills and Bone Counts: Decision Making by Ancient Hunters.* University of Chicago Press, Chicago.
2000 Boiling vs. Baking and Roasting: A Taphonomic Approach to the Recognition of Cooking Techniques in Small Mammals. In *Animal Bones, Hitman Societies,* edited by Peter Rowley-Conwy, pp. 89–105. Oxbow Books, Oxford, UK.

Speth, John D., and Alison E. Rautman

2004 Bison Hunting at the Henderson Site. In *Life on the Periphery: Economic Change in Late Prehistoric South eastern New Mexico*, edited by John D. Speth, pp. 98-148. University of Michigan Museum of Anthropology Memoirs No. 37. Ann Arbor, Michigan.

Starrs, James

1990 Why Alferd Packer? The Causes for the Dig Fever. *American Academy of Forensic Sciences Publication* 90:99.

Starrs, James, and Katherine M. Ramsland

2005 *A Voice for the Dead: A Forensic Investigator's Pursuit of the Truth in the Grave.* Putnam Publishing Group, New York.

Turner, Christy G., II

1983 Taphonomic Reconstructions of Human Violence and Cannibalism Based on Mass Burials in the American Southwest. In *Carnivores, Human Scavengers and Human Predators: A Question of Bone Technology,* edited by G. M. LeMoine and A.S. MacEachem, pp. 219–240. University of Calgary Archaeological Association, Calgary, Alberta, Canada.

Turner, Christy G., II, and Jacqueline A. Turner

1999 *Man Corn: Cannibalism and Violence in the Prehistoric American Southwest.* University of Utah Press, Salt Lake City.

Tuzin, Donald, and Paula Brown (editors)

1983 *The Ethnography of Cannibalism.* Society for Psychological Anthropology, Washington, D.C. Verdery, Katherine

1999 *The Political Lives of Dead Bodies: Reburial and Postsocialist Change.* Columbia University Press, New York.

Villa, Paul

1992 Cannibalism in Prehistoric Europe. *Evolutionary Anthropology* 1:93–104.

White, Tim D.

1990 *Prehistoric Cannibalism at Mancos 5MTURMR-2346.* Princeton University Press, Princeton, New Jersey.

Received May 10, 2002; Revised January 3, 2005; Accepted January 11, 2005.

Disaster Archaeology on Trial

Forensic Recovery Efforts After 9/11

Richard Gould

EDITOR'S INTRODUCTION

Like most Americans alive in 2001, I remember exactly where I was when I heard the news. I was in my office at the university, prepping for my introductory archaeology course when Jimmy Royce, then a student of mine and now a friend and colleague, walked into my office and asked if I had heard the news about a plane crashing into one of the Twin Towers at the World Trade Center in Manhattan. Jimmy didn't have any additional information and my initial assumption was that it must have been a small private plane and, as scary as it must have been, the death toll would not have been too high. I remembered having read about a military plane, a B-25, crashing into the Empire State Building in 1945. Though the death toll was substantial (three crew and eleven people in the building), and the superficial damage to the building was costly, its structural integrity had not been compromised. So, I figured, there would be a short news cycle for the crash and that would be the end of it. I could not have been more wrong. Soon after the towers came down, I also remember hearing a call for people with archaeological experience to volunteer their skills in the search for forensic evidence and help in the recovery of human remains, especially, but also any other physical evidence that might assist in the examination of what happened on the planes and how the impacts caused the collapse of the buildings. This chapter in archaeologist Richard A. Gould's book, Disaster Archaeology, tells the story of that search.

POINTS TO PONDER

1. What role did archaeologists play in the recovery of evidence from Manhattan following the 9/11 terrorist attack?
2. What was found at the Barclay Street location by forensic archaeologists?
3. Why were so few human remains found at Ground Zero?
4. What lessons can be drawn from the use of archaeology at Ground Zero, even if very few human remains were found?

After 9/11 everyone wanted to help. The nationwide roster initiated by Sophia Perdikaris and posted by the Society for American Archaeology listed about three hundred trained archaeologists. It was a positive and commendable response, but authorities such as the Federal Emergency Management Agency (FEMA) and the New York Police Department (NYPD) were not eager to invite archaeologists—or anyone else without an established relationship to them, for that matter—to come to New York to perform relief and recovery work. The SAA roster was never activated.

EARLY EFFORTS

This was a frustrating time. While the cleanup around lower Manhattan proceeded at a mad pace, opportunities emerged and then disappeared. For example, there was the case of St. Nicholas Church, situated next to the WTC. This tiny church was a historic landmark and the center for the Greek Orthodox community in Manhattan. When the towers fell on 9/11, St. Nicholas Church was obliterated—one of the few buildings aside from the Twin Towers themselves to be completely destroyed. I received a message from Sophia while I was in Australia that the church priest, whom she had known for many years, had asked her if it would be possible to organize an archaeological recovery of objects such as icons and other religious items that were important to the congregation. This was a bit different from what we had originally envisioned, but we agreed that it was an important task and should be possible. I was about to return to the United States, and I said I would call her as soon as I arrived to find out how things stood. We planned to activate both of our small teams of volunteers and combine our efforts at the site.

When I arrived home and called Sophia, however, I learned that this recovery project would not be possible. I was informed that while I was en route, a bulldozer took out the entire site. Since the church was situated within Ground Zero, it was inside the crime scene. Sophia and the priest lacked badged authority to enter and were unable to intervene in the cleanup of this part of the site. Knowing what we know now, perhaps we could have established better contacts with the authorities sooner and persuaded them to allow us to proceed. I cannot say whether our failure in this case was due to the general chaos surrounding the WTC or if it was more a product of the rigid control imposed there by the authorities. It was a missed opportunity that forced me to think carefully about how to anticipate such situations. It was also another case to add to the long and depressing catalog of losses surrounding the WTC disaster.

This experience heightened my awareness of the difference between working inside and outside the designated crime scene. If we were to work effectively in either situation, we would have to be as self-contained as possible. In addition to archaeological expertise and equipment, we would need to have trained site-safety, medical, and security officers—badged officers known to the local authorities and approved by them—with us at all times. After our workshop at Brown this component of the recovery team began to take shape. Security was initiated by Sergeant Napoleon "Nappy" Brito, head of the Bureau of Criminal Identification (BCI) at the Providence Police, aided by BCI Detective Patricia "Patti" Cornell. Hilliary Creeley, then an advanced graduate student in neuroscience at Brown, became our safety officer. She was a certified EMT and had served with her home volunteer fire department from Pennsylvania at Ground Zero along with other first responders. It had been a difficult experience for her and her fellow fire-rescue workers, since no survivors were found. Medical support was provided by James Harper III, head of the Animal Research Laboratory at the Brown University BioMedical Program. Jim was an experienced emergency-services worker who had also been to Ground Zero during the initial response with his national Disaster Medical Assistance Team (DMAT) to aid survivors.

The volunteer team itself consisted mainly of Brown University graduate students with archaeological field training and experience: Jennifer Trunzo, Paul White, Julie Esdale, Leah Rosenmeier, and Brian Gohacki. Another Brown graduate student, Gabriel Flores, with a master's in forensic anthropology from the University of Wyoming, was tasked with assisting the archaeological excavations and, at the same time, making sure we did not miss any human remains. These students, along with Katharine Woodhouse-Beyer, a recent Brown PhD graduate then teaching at Bryn Mawr College, Pennsylvania, formed the field recovery team. Sophia supervised three of her undergraduate students—Jennifer Borishansky, Jennifer Braun, and Matthew Brown—and graduate student Marianni Betti to run the sieving operation. In all, our little band consisted of seventeen volunteers. We met sometime after these trial excavations and came up with the name Forensic Archaeology Recovery (FAR).

As training continued, I contacted Elizabeth Laposata, R.I. state medical examiner. Although the invitation to our team came from New York, I asked her to offer comments and advice and presented her with a summary of our preparations and training. Among other things, we would be representing the state of Rhode Island, and I indicated that we would not deploy until she thought we were ready to go. I contacted her again the following day. She had read our document and simply said, "Go!" We packed the van and departed immediately, with some volunteers traveling by train or bus. The full team assembled on April 1, 2002, at the Vanderbilt YMCA on Manhattan's Upper East Side, where we had arranged for generously discounted rooms and other facilities to house the team. Earlier that day we had taken the van to Brooklyn College, where we picked up sieves and other excavating equipment to add to our own.

EXCAVATIONS AT THE BARCLAY STREET SITE

At 8:30 the following morning we met Ralph Ristenbatt, a criminalist and team supervisor from the New York City OCME, at the Barclay Street site and started work, continuing nonstop until 4:00 p.m. During a break later that day I asked Ralph about his experiences on 9/11. He told me that he had been at the OCME's field office in the WTC towers with two other members of the medical examiner's staff. After helping injured members of the OCME's staff get to the hospital, he and his remaining companion were ordered to Brooklyn Ferry to begin a search for bodies of victims in the East River. They walked across the Brooklyn Bridge, along with thousands of people who were escaping from Manhattan, to Brooklyn Ferry, where they commandeered a boat and spent the rest of the day collecting bodies from the river. As Ralph told me about this, I was reminded of Sophia's account of how she saw bloodstained office papers floating down on her neighborhood in Bay Ridge, Brooklyn, after they had been transported in the air across New York City Harbor in the smoke and heat from the burning towers.

The work at the Barclay Street site took place within a roughly triangular area, measuring about 15 meters on each side, which had a steep, 31-degree slope down to a corner bounded at its apex by brick walls and a high chain-link fence across its top. Our first task was to remove a layer of trash over the site covering the entire area enclosed by the chain-link fence and buildings. Care was taken to recover and record materials resting on top of and in the trash, since it was covered with the powdery gray dust found throughout the WTC area. A line of excavators faced uphill and worked from the bottom up the slope while others hauled buckets of trash and fill uphill along a path at the right side of the triangle and across the top to the sieving station. Because of the steep slope of the site, there was enough level ground for only one sieve, but that was adequate. All the bucketed material was put through a 1/4-inch mesh sieve. At any one time at least three Brooklyn College archaeologists directed by Sophia—all trained in forensic anthropology—manned the sieve and sorted through the debris by hand. They were assisted by Detective Cornell, who was experienced in this kind of work.

The next step was to scrape down the entire deposit within the triangular enclosed area to a depth of 6 cm. This material, consisting of a mixture of soil, light gray ash (the "kitty litter" referred to earlier), and fine debris, was bucketed and sieved. A total of ninety buckets of fill was collected and sieved during this excavation. The site and deposits were photographed before, during, and after excavation. The total volume of surface fill, to a depth of 6 cm, was estimated at 1.070 cubic meters, and the volume of surface fill excavated and sieved to the same depth was approximately 0.937 cubic meters, or 87.5 percent of the total. Even a low estimate of 77.5 percent, however, would provide a better than 95 percent level of probability that our sample was representative of the total components of the surface fill of the site. Considering the difficulties of footing and uneven slopes, obstacles, and some difficulties with measurements, this appears to be a reasonable degree of probable error. In short, we achieved a definitive sampling of the site.

Only ten pieces of bone were found, none of which could be even tentatively identified as human. These biological specimens were placed in evidence bags and entered into custody for the OCME for final determination at its laboratory. Our volumetric analysis effectively ruled out the presence of identifiable human remains at the Barclay Street site at the time of our excavations there. Nonbiologicals were placed in separate evidence bags for delivery via a different chain of custody to the First Precinct Property Office of the NYPD. From there these materials went to the special facility at One Police Plaza, where a massive effort supervised by NYPD lieutenant James Melendez was underway to preserve and, ultimately, repatriate personal effects and office materials from the World Trade Center. All biologicals were placed in labeled and sealed paper bags, and nonbiologicals went into labeled and sealed plastic bags and vials.

Our nonbiological findings included office papers and microfiche documents. The most interesting of these was a microfiche in fairly good condition that listed the FAA registration numbers (N numbers) of every Boeing 767 built until 1991. The document had nothing specifically to do with the attack on 9/11, but this type of aircraft was used by the attackers. The document probably came from the files of an insurance company or some other business and was simply one of those many strange coincidences that can occur at a complex disaster scene. The site also contained smashed computers and computer components. We put these aside since they could not be firmly associated with the events of 9/11. Throughout our work at the Barclay Street site, we encountered the problem of mixed deposits. Perhaps some of these computers came from offices destroyed during the attack, but it was also possible that this location had been used for dumping old computers before the attacks. This kind of ambiguity applied to other materials as well and raised the question, what is evidence? Whenever we found items that were clearly and unambiguously connected to the events of 9/11, such as the office documents, we entered them into custody. We did the same for bones, although this was mainly because we were not expected to distinguish between human and nonhuman bones in the field. That determination was made later in the laboratory as one of the first steps in the forensic profiling that could lead ultimately to victim identifications. Problems of mixed deposits and the determination of what items should be placed in evidence inevitably arise at disaster scenes. Sometimes these problems are linked, sometimes they are not, but they must be addressed as explicitly as possible.

How should we interpret our findings at the Barclay Street site? Given our primary goal of obtaining evidence for victim identification, the failure to find human remains was a disappointment. One possible explanation was that fragmentary human remains may have deteriorated to such an extent between September 11 and our recovery efforts about six months later that they were no longer recognizable. Another possible explanation is that the distribution of fragmentary human remains blown outward from Ground Zero was uneven rather than homogeneous. Both explanations are a function of the passage of time since the event. The first (which I view as improbable) would have resulted from decay, physical damage due to cleanup efforts, or other post depositional factors following 9/11. Although these sorts of factors were evident across the streets and rooftops of lower Manhattan, they were not evident at the Barclay Street site—which is why we chose this site for the trial study.

The second explanation, though more likely, cannot be proved. If our team had been able to conduct a rapid, nonintrusive survey before the cleanup got under way, we would have been able to determine the extent of the debris field in different directions and the degree of homogeneity in the distribution of fragmented human remains. But by the time of our trial excavation, all the results could do was rule out the presence of identifiable human remains at this single location. Whichever explanation applies, we were too late in this case to perform effective forensic recoveries of human remains.

We understood from the beginning that negative results were a definite possibility. For compelling personal reasons, however, I found this almost unbearable. While we were still on site, Sergeant Brito—ever the voice of experience in such matters—sensed how I felt and called to me, "You can't think that way!" He was right, of course, but it was hard not to. I found myself in a constant struggle to maintain an analytical perspective. Sergeant Brito and Detective Cornell pointed out that the conduct of our volunteers was impeccable and that this real-world experience was better than any simulated training. They found this a convincing demonstration of what we could do, and they asked to deploy with us as volunteers if we were called out again. They both continued to play an active role in our training and planning for possible future needs. Part of this preparation was now becoming a process of managing expectations.

We had just demonstrated to the OCME, however, that a team of volunteer archaeologists could prepare for and perform controlled forensic recoveries in debris areas at an actual disaster scene. We had received prior training in skills such as HAZMAT awareness that proved their value at the site, where actual hazardous materials were present. Hilliary, our safety officer, spotted these and called them to my attention, and we were able to redirect the field-workers to avoid them. The personal safety equipment used was generally adequate for the conditions we encountered, although there was room for improvement. Minor injuries such as eye irritation (caused by the dust) and small cuts were treated at the scene by our medical officer, Dr. Harper.

In our first operational foray into moderately ugly conditions, the team members performed well and showed the kind of calm, professional demeanor and meticulous work that is a hallmark of all effective emergency services. The level of team cohesion was excellent. More than anything else, the sight of our wonderful volunteers performing their duties under these difficult conditions reassured me that disaster archaeology was really possible. The complete excavation took only one day, so it was clear that work of this kind can proceed rapidly. This should lay to rest the common assumption that archaeologists always work slowly and would delay other urgent recovery tasks; a team of about half the size could probably have accomplished the task within the two days allotted for it. On the positive side was the fact that a relatively large number of volunteers gained actual experience in performing this kind of work. Although the trial excavations did not succeed in the goal of finding and recovering human remains outside Ground Zero for victim identification, the exercise furnished a clear indication of how forensic archaeology recovery could be accomplished effectively at a disaster scene. The trial excavations at the Barclay Street site were a major step toward proving the worth of the concept of disaster archaeology, even if the results seemed at the time to be disappointing.

WHAT HAPPENED NEXT

On March 26 the *New York Daily News* published an article that contained two graphics showing the GPS locations of human remains found by or reported to a special team of the Fire Department of the City of New York (FDNY) known as the Phoenix Unit. The site of my October 6–7, 2001, sightings appeared in both graphics, which were labeled "As of Nov. 30, 2001" and "As of early March [2002]." The site of our March 2,, 2002, excavations appeared in the second graphic. Whether these GPS locations resulted from my earlier reports and the Barclay Street materials is unknown, but I would like to believe that our efforts were actually noted. Whatever the source, the GPS locations provided independent confirmation that significant amounts of human remains were dispersed over wide areas of lower Manhattan outside Ground Zero. These reports also made the existence of such debris scatters public, precipitating a rush of inquiries by relatives of WTC victims to the FDNY and Medical Examiner's Office.

This publication was followed by an e-mail message on June 17 from Dr. Shaler:

Subject: As you predicted.

I thought you'd be interested in knowing that rescuers have been searching through other buildings near ground zero and have found some, not a lot, of body parts. In one instance they found an almost complete shoulder. Although you guys didn't have much luck, you were certainly on the right track.

After Dr. Shaler's message, additional human remains were reported from rooftops in lower Manhattan, specifically from 90 West Street and 130 Liberty Street—close to where I first encountered fragmented human remains on October 6, 2001. An additional 41 bones were found along West Street and brought to the Medical Examiner's Office. At this point the reports of such finds tapered off, perhaps because they were no longer news. A full two years after the WTC disaster, however, further human remains were reported from another building on Liberty Street. Throughout this period the Medical Examiner's Office continued its tireless efforts to identify remains, relying heavily on both conventional and innovative methods of DNA analysis. Throughout 2003-2004 the number of victims identified fell sharply. Only eight victims were identified after September 2004, and by February 2005 Dr. Shaler announced that the victim identification process had officially ended, with 1,162, or 42 percent, of the 2,749 victims remaining unidentified. Everyone knew this day had to come, but the effect of the news was devastating for many of the families and relatives of these victims. It should be noted, however, that identification work has continued. In addition, the OCME has confronted the difficult problem of common tissue—thousands of unidentified fragments—by placing them in frozen storage to await improvements in DNA and other scientific methods of identification. More than four and a half years after the event, human remains thought to be from 9/11 were still being encountered by workers on buildings outside Ground Zero.

In April 2006 a firestorm of public concern erupted over further finds of fragmented human remains from the Deutsche Bank Building at 130 Liberty-Street, outside Ground Zero. Workers preparing to demolish the building reported finding four hundred pieces of bone on the roof, with the definite possibility of more to come. Graphic accounts of these finds were punctuated by expressions of anger and grief by families that have waited four and a half years for an identification of lost relatives and by public officials' calls for action. Workers clearing the building for demolition did their best to collect human remains under the supervision of an OCME forensic anthropologist and a professional archaeologist. The effects of this disaster did not end in the weeks and months immediately following the event, and one reporter (Greg Smith, of the *New York Daily News)* commented to me then that FAR was "amazingly prescient," calling attention to the problem back in 2001.

In the months that followed our activities at the WTC, we negotiated a cooperative relationship with the Rhode Island Salvation Army Emergency Disaster Services under a memorandum of understanding (MOU). Since this MOU was finalized, we have been supported four times—once for an actual disaster and three times during field-training exercises—by the Salvation Army, which provided meals, hot drinks, and emotional counseling for the volunteers while we were in the field. The Salvation Army also invited us to restock our safety and medical supplies after our return from New York. Most of our supplies (Tyvek suits, rubber gloves, face masks, eyewash, and a myriad of other items) were used up rapidly in the field and had to be replaced. After 9/11 the Salvation Army established a warehouse in Hartford, Connecticut, where it received thousands of tons of donated supplies from around the nation. This warehouse became a major supplier for the emergency services at Ground Zero, and it still contained large amounts of unused supplies after the cleanup was finished.

In April 2002 Hilliary and I drove the van to the warehouse. We were told to take whatever we needed, and we spent several hours sorting through boxes, repacking personal safety equipment and medical supplies, and loading the van. It felt strange and sad to work inside this darkened, cavernous building surrounded by high mounds of clothing, packaged food items, bottled water, and, of course, the items we were looking for. As we opened boxes, we encountered dozens of handwritten notes and cards with messages intended to encourage the emergency workers at Ground Zero. Mike Orfitelli, the Salvation Army warehouse manager there, had warned us to expect these, but even so the emotional impact was overwhelming. Each was like a message in a bottle, cast into this strange, dark place by events that were real but still hard to imagine. For both Hilliary and me, the difficulties and disappointments of the past months became overwhelming. I saved some of these notes and have them with me now as I write.

After we returned to Providence, I read the messages again and responded to those that had included addresses. Among them was a message from the students at the New Canaan (Connecticut) High School. Soon afterward I received a reply from Gary Field, the assistant principal, who had helped organize the packing and shipment of these supplies. He indicated that some of the students had lost relatives at the WTC. New Canaan is an upscale town within commuting distance of New York City, and it suffered losses like those of similar communities in New York and New Jersey. Some of the students, he said, had not been dealing well with the aftermath of 9/11, and the school was looking for ways to help them achieve closure. They organized a day-long assembly for the entire school shortly after the first anniversary of the event on the theme "Overcoming Difficulties." Would I join the other speakers and tell the students about our activities at the WTC? he asked. I jumped at the chance, not quite knowing why.

My turn to speak came in the afternoon session. The morning program had focused on the events of the day at the WTC when the attack occurred and immediately afterward, and the speakers were moving, especially the pastor from St. Paul's Chapel, who was there when the towers fell and described the rush of first responders to the scene. I decided I would try to communicate what the aftermath was like. There were about 1,200 students present plus various faculty members and community volunteers. Microphones were set up at the front of the stage for any students who might want to come up afterward and speak to the others. How does one speak to a group like this? I kept the talk describing our work short. I thanked them for donating supplies and for their messages of encouragement. Then I asked the students how they felt about what we had tried to accomplish. Was this important to them? Did such a major effort to recover and identify remains of the WTC victims seem justified? What about our failure to find such remains? Did this signal to them that such efforts should be abandoned? I made it clear that we needed to know if we were doing the right thing, and they were better qualified to tell us than anyone else.

Earlier I had wondered if anyone would use the microphones, but even before the talk was over, students began to come forward. A line quickly formed, and what followed was a rush of personal and emotional responses that pointed to a clear message. It didn't matter that we failed to find the remains of the victims, one student after another said. None of them had known that anything like our excavations had taken place at the WTC, and they said that just knowing that we had tried was more important than anything else. The idea that I presented of using archaeology to do this seemed blindingly obvious to them. They were deeply moved by the fact that so many of our volunteers were fellow (albeit older) students. They said they would do this if they could. These high school students, some of whom cried openly as they spoke, were actually reassuring me that this was indeed the right thing to do. I realized for the first time with a full emotional as well as intellectual awareness that as an archaeologist I needed closure, too, and that the actions we had taken at the WTC were a good way to achieve it. This was a message I could take home to the volunteers in Providence. It moved our efforts to a new level beyond the proof of concept. Now it was possible to see the conduct of field archaeology as an integral part of the recovery process, for this process did not depend on tangible results alone. Families and friends of victims could understand what archaeologists were prepared to do on their behalf, and simply knowing that made a difference to them. At the end of this highly emotional day I do not know who had benefited more, the students at New Canaan High School or me.

An echo of that moment appeared in a newspaper article describing an emotional meeting between Chief Medical Examiner Charles Hirsch and relatives of 9/11 victims at an interfaith prayer service: "Gordon Haberman of Wisconsin, whose daughter, Andrea, was killed in the attack, recalled ... a moment from the Ground Zero memorial service on Sept. 11, 2003, when he recognized a member of the medical examiner's staff. Haberman saw him stoop down during the ceremony to pick up a handful of dirt and sift it through his fingers. 'It hit me like a shot,' Haberman said, 'that two years later, almost to the hour of my daughter's death, they were still searching.'"

Forensic Finds Add Substance to Claims of War Atrocities

Richard Stone

EDITOR'S INTRODUCTION

In the midst of a war characterized by standing armies as well as guerrilla fighters, it was, perhaps, inevitable that people guilty of nothing more than being peasants at the wrong place at the wrong time would get caught up in the fighting. Perhaps it is sadly predictable that soldiers, many peasants themselves, themselves caught up in the fog of war, frightened for their own lives in the face of a hidden enemy might, in their anger and their fear, turn on innocents and attack them. This happened in 1951 at a place called Bulgap in South Korea. The stories told by survivors and neighbors are gruesome. They remembered seeing dozens of local civilians, including children, executed, their bodies unceremoniously being dumped in a trench, guilty of nothing more than a suspicion that they were in some way connected to a local band of fighters who fought on the side of the North Korean enemy. Though until recently hidden and spoken of only in hushed words and skeptical terms, forensic archaeology is revealing the truth behind the eyewitness accounts describing the crimes committed by South Korean soldiers against their own people during their war against North Korea.

POINTS TO PONDER

1. What do eyewitness accounts describe happening at Bulgap in South Korea in 1951?
2. What forensic evidence has been collected by archaeologists there that support the eyewitness accounts?
3. Was Bulgap an aberration, or is there other evidence of war crimes against South Korean civilians during the Korean War?
4. What lesson can be gleaned concerning the attempt of war criminals to hide their crimes in the face of the techniques employed by modern forensic archaeologists?

Hampyeong, Korea—Early in the Korean War, the South's army was fighting on two fronts: against the North, which had invaded in June 1950, and against homegrown Communist guerillas. In February 1951, the army's 11th Division and police in the divided peninsula's southwest were closing in on guerillas holed up on Bulgap Mountain in Hampyeong County. Operation Full Moon—an assault on Bulgap—was planned for the night of 20 February. But the rebels caught wind of the impending attack and, knowing they'd be routed if they made a stand, slipped the cordon. In the meantime, villagers fleeing advancing troops had sought refuge on Bulgap. When soldiers and police stormed the ridge and found only civilians, survivors claim, they dug a long trench, forced the civilians to kneel inside, and then shot them or thrust sharpened bamboo sticks down their throats. Women and children were among the victims.

That's the story South Korea's Truth and Reconciliation Commission (TRCK) heard when it began to investigate the Bulgap massacre last year. "It was controversial," says sociologist Kim Dong-Choon, a commissioner and director of the Human Rights and Peace Center of Sungkonghoe University in Seoul. Some commissioners, he says, doubted the recollections of elderly survivors who had lived in Hampyeong when the atrocity occurred but had not witnessed it. "A few of my colleagues thought the victims really were guerillas," says Kim.

But the survivors have been vindicated by new forensic finds. Last week, TRCK revealed evidence from an ongoing excavation confirming Bulgap as one of the Korean War's darker chapters. Anthropologist Noh Yong-Seok, who leads TRCK's excavations with help from forensic scientists at Chungbuk National University, says the team has found adult skeletons bent at the knees with finger bones clasped behind their skulls and artifacts that rebel soldiers would have had no use for, such as a woman's hairpin and toys. Investigators here have unearthed bones of several children, the first such verified remains from a Korean War–era massacre site, says Noh.

The Hampyeong dig is one of the more stunning revelations to date from the truth commission, which in the past 3 years has documented mass killings in the war's early years of more than 100,000 South Korean civilians, deemed "traitors," by the country's own military and police. Hundreds of thousands more were slain by indiscriminate aerial bombing and ground fire by U.S. and Korean forces, says Kim. "We know now that the Korean War was like a war with no frontline. Everyone was killing each other, whoever was beside them," says TRCK President A hn Byung-Ook, a historian at Catholic University of Korea in Seoul.

As TRCK rewrites history books, it is rushing to wind up investigations before its legal mandate

Figure 24.1. Digging up the truth. Excavation leader Noh Yong-Seak holds a woman's hairpin, evidence of a civilian massacre.

expires in April 2010. President Lee Myung-bak's conservative Administration has not hidden its disdain for the truth commission, which was created by the liberal government of his predecessor, Roh Moo-hyun. "We would prefer to lay the past to rest and solve today's problems, like our economic crisis," an Administration official told *Science*.

Commission officials insist it will be impossible to wrap up active investigations by April. That leaves sociologists wondering whether South Koreans—especially those born after the war ended—will ever come to terms with the incidents TRCK is uncovering. "I don't blame younger generations for lack of interest," says Ahn. "But I expect them to learn a more accurate account of history."

UNTOLD STORIES

It is monsoon season in Korea, and after an early downpour, wispy fog clings to Hampyeong's hills and rice paddies. Paintings of butterflies adorn bus stops and farm outbuildings, and an entire hillside's vegetation is trimmed neatly in the shape of a butterfly. These days, Hampyeong is known for its annual butterfly festival—that and for onions, umpteen numbers of which are stacked in bales along the roads.

After an arduous half-hour slog up a muddy path on Bulgap Mountain, Chang Jae-soo helps two college-age excavators peel back a blue tarp brimming with standing water. The 74-year-old, who lived in a nearby village 6 decades ago, has remarkable stamina—perhaps, he says, because the exhumation has revitalized him. "I feel like I am getting my honor back," he says.

A row of tarps, each about 3 meters wide, extends for 50 meters or so along the ridge. Noh's team has been excavating here for about a month. So far they have unearthed remains of about 100 individuals from the shallow grave. Noh crouches and reaches behind a skull and picks up a humerus, several centimeters long, that Chungbuk National University scientists estimate belonged to a 12-year-old child. Spent bullet casings lie scattered among the bones, as do some rusted spoons. "Spoons are one possession the villagers surely would have brought with them. They had to eat," says Noh. He lays the bone down gently. Nearby is a tiny pale blue ball—a marble. "This is one of the few toys children back then would have had." They have found bones here of toddlers as young as 3 or 4.

Although some victims here may have been guerillas, forensic evidence of a civilian massacre, Noh says, is now incontrovertible. About a quarter of the dead were women and children. Noh has led TRCK exhumations at 13 sites that so far have yielded remains of about 1700 people; no other site has such young victims. Hampyeong, he says, "is the most tragic one of all."

It's not surprising that villagers would have fled to Bulgap. A month before the Hampyeong incident, troops shot dead Chang's parents, his uncle and aunt, and three younger sisters. Chang, 16 at the time, escaped and later found his way to an elder sister's home across the peninsula. For years after the armistice, Korean society spurned people deemed to be Communist sympathizers—even those like Chang who had nothing to do with the guerillas but were tainted merely by having lost family members in massacres. "People hardly got a chance to get an education or a job," says Chang, who made ends meet as a traveling salesman.

Under the military dictatorships that ruled after the war, Noh explains, "we were taught to not question the government or the army." At one notorious massacre site, Gyeongsan Cobalt Mine, victims were shot and dumped down shafts. Noh's crew there has so far recovered remains of 240 of an estimated 3500 victims. "Many people knew about the cobalt mine, but for 50 years they didn't say

Figure 24.2. Seeking closure. Seven members of Chang Jae-soo's family were killed.

anything. It was taboo," says Noh, who grew up in the area. In the 1990s, a rising chorus called for an investigation into alleged crimes against civilians, ranging from when Korea was a colony of Japan before World War II, the Korean War era, and up through democracy movements lasting into the 1980s. Roh bowed to pressure and established the commission in December 2005. Roh, who committed suicide 2 months ago, apologized to victims on behalf of the nation in January 2008. "It was the first time in our history that the government acknowledged the war's civilian victims," says Ahn.

TRCK's creation opened a floodgate: More than 10,000 petitions have poured in, and several thousand cases are still pending. Investigators have interviewed hundreds of victims and alleged perpetrators; many of the latter have shown little or no remorse. "Offenders justify what they did as inevitable," says Ahn. However, he notes, "our aim is not to put perpetrators on trial. It is to reconstruct the past through the victims' eyes."

Last December, Chang and others formed the Bulgap Mountain–Yongcheon Temple Provincial Union of Bereaved Families of Civilian Victims—one of 100 or so such unions across the country. The union plans to sue the government for compensation once the excavation is finished. But more important than money, Chang insists, is that he and other victims are finally putting the bitter years of postwar discrimination behind them. Using words one would expect from a perpetrator, he says, "We're not seen as sinners anymore."

Section 7

DEBUNKING PSEUDOARCHAEOLOGY

Archaeology certainly attracts some real whack jobs. Okay, most of them are my professional colleagues. And they would certainly include me in that category as well. But seriously, the discipline does tend to attract a tremendous amount of interest and attendant speculation about the human past. Much of that speculation originates in the minds of people who know virtually nothing about the scientific method or actual archaeological evidence. Hi Giorgio. Anyway, I am including here a couple of articles that address some of the more egregious of the unsupported speculations about human antiquity.

The world didn't end on December 21, 2012. Case closed. The great Maya apocalypse fizzled like every other dire end-of-world prediction and another piece of pseudohistory and pseudoarchaeology bit the dust. Well, except for those who claimed the world really did end on December 21, but we just don't know it yet. Or that, because of a math error resulting from the fact that the Maya didn't add a leap day every four years, the end-time is actually still coming up in a few years. Whatever.

Like other varieties of pseudo-archaeology (also called cult- or inauthentic or dubious- or fantastic- and a host of other prefixes), the Maya end-time was nonsense. The Maya did not, in fact, predict the world would end in 2012, the Maya calendar did not end on December 21 of that year, and, even had the Maya predicted that the world would end, so what? The Maya was an intensely interesting and sophisticated culture with an advanced mathematical and writing system, but there's no evidence that they were privy to the secrets of the universe. Just to show you how bizarre it got in the run up to December 21; author and nutjob Patrick Geryl, one of the purveyors of the Maya end-time myth, suggested in a cable documentary that, in order to save themselves, people needed to sail to the middle of the Pacific Ocean in the days preceding the 21st. When asked if he would be leading the flotilla of those escaping the wrath of the Maya calendar, he demurred. When asked why he wouldn't be following his own advice, he admitted that he has a tendency to get seasick. In other words, this loon believed the world would end and the only route to salvation would be to be on a boat but he wouldn't be doing this because his tummy would feel all icky. OMG.

Archaeology attracts a lot of this kind of speculation. Claims that the great leaps forward in technology and knowledge exemplified in the archaeological record (in architecture, metallurgy, writing, math, calendars, etc.) represent evidence of the work of extremely advanced outsiders—perhaps denizens of the Lost Continent of Atlantis or even extraterrestrial aliens—are rife in archaeology. A growing group of archaeologists (Card, Anderson, and Feder 2013) are taking an active role in responding to the nonsense that dogs our discipline. I present two articles here; the first deals specifically with the Maya Apocalypse (did I mention that this did not happen?) and a general piece (written by me), that briefly covers a number of unsupported claims about the human past.

The Peculiar Phenomenon of Pseudoarchaeology

Ken Feder

EDITOR'S INTRODUCTION

This may very well be the best article in this reader. Well, it may be one of the three best articles. Kidding. (I wrote the three "best" articles. Really, I'm just kidding.) I have, for a long time, been interested in popularly promulgated misconceptions about human antiquity. I've written a couple of book-length treatments of "frauds, myths, and mysteries" in archaeology and "dubious archaeology" (I'll let you look up those phrases on Amazon; they're kind of taken right from the titles). I truly believe it's terrific that people are so interested in the human past that they read magazine articles or books, watch cable documentaries, or visit web sites that discuss the human past. I'm also concerned that too many of these sources presented highly speculative claims about the human past that are wholly unsupported by scientific evidence. In this article, I summarize a few of the more common speculative scenarios concerning the human past including the Lost Continent of Atlantis and its role in the development of ancient civilizations all over the world; the assertion that ancient aliens landed on Earth and acted in the way of an extraterrestrial Peace Corps to help human beings technologically evolve; and the belief that Native American civilization was somehow inspired by contacts with African or European people long before Columbus or even the Norse exploration of the New World. For more detailed treatments of these topics, well, go to Amazon.com and check out those phrases I placed in quotation marks before.

POINTS TO PONDER

1. Was Atlantis a real place and did it inspire later civilizations?
2. Did extraterrestrial aliens land on Earth in antiquity and interact with ancient people?
3. Were the earth mounds of the American Midwest inspired by the visits of ancient Europeans or Hebrews to the New World?
4. What lessons are provided by the examination of pseudoarchaeological claims? I mean other than you really ought to buy one or more of my books on the subject.

A vast and splendid civilization is tragically destroyed more than 10 millennia ago in a natural cataclysm of imponderable proportions. Extraterrestrial aliens from a world inconceivably distant and different from our own, land on earth, share knowledge with our ancestors and, in so doing, instigate the evolution of the world's first civilization.

Are these and other equally intriguing tales little more than fantasy, or might they reflect a secret and repressed ancient history of humanity, a past denied by stodgy archaeologists? To be sure, they are compelling and entertaining, filled with adventure, romance, tragedy, and triumph. They are, perhaps above all else, deliciously surprising, we didn't learn any of this in history class. Maybe that's why so many people believe them. These intriguing possibilities about the ancient world provide the raw material for stories far more interesting than the dreary research concerning projectile points and potsherds done by archaeologists. However, though they don't lack for drama, these stories do lack for evidence. The attempt to support these notice with dubious or fake archaeological evidence is pseudoarchaeology.

How pervasive is pseudoarchaeology today? The television listing give some indication. In any given week a viewer can likely find ostensible documentaries that, at the very least, sensationalize human antiquity, Atlantis, Pharaoh's curses, extraterrestrial visitors to earth in antiquity, pre-Norse visits to the New World by various groups, and astonishingly advanced technologies in very ancient times are the usual fare.

INTRIGUING TALES

Consider the claim at the core of the recent popular book, *1421: The Year China Discovered the World* by Gavin Menzies. Menzies proposes that 71 years before Columbus set sail, a fleet of more than 100 Chinese ships carrying 10,000 sailors circumnavigated the earth and explored, among other places, America. The problem with his argument, which is largely based on ambiguous old maps, is that there are no convincing early 15th-century artifacts found in firm archaeological contexts that offer proof of the early presence of Chinese explorers or colonists in America.

Compare this to the analysis of a Norse presence in the New World 500 years before Columbus. Admittedly, many archaeologists were skeptical of finding the Vinland referred to in Norse sagas in the New World. That skepticism disappeared, however, with the discovery and excavation of the L'anse aux Meadows site on Newfoundland, in eastern Canada. The Norse artifacts recovered at the site included a ring-headed bronze pin, a soapstone spindle whorl, and typical house remains. These artifacts and charcoal radiocarbon dated to more than 1,000 years ago won over the skeptics.

Though artifacts like the rune-inscribed Kensington Stone found in west-central Minnesota continue to generate heated debate, the archaeological evidence at L'anse aux Meadows and the scatter of Norse artifacts found throughout the eastern Canadian Arctic have shown conclusively that the Vikings reached the New World.

A precociously sophisticated lost civilization, far older than that of Egypt, Mesopotamia, or the Maya is another common theme of pseudoarchaeology. Atlantis is the best-known example. The literary creation of the Greek philosopher Plato, Atlantis is portrayed by him as a powerful, sophisticated, wealthy, but evil empire. Plato created a warlike Atlantis as a plot device in one of his dialogues in order to test the mettle of a hypothetical, perfect society governed by the rules Plato laid out in his best known work, *The Republic*.

U.S. congressman and prolific author Ignatius Donnelly revived the Atlantis myth in the late 19th century, asserting that Atlantis had been a real nation that had greatly affected all other ancient civilizations. Donnelly's belief in Atlantis was rooted in his insistence that the archaeological achievements of ancient peoples on both sides of the Atlantic were so sophisticated and similar—with pyramids, arches, metallurgy, agricultural systems, and written languages—there must have been a common, highly advanced source. For Donnelly, that source was Atlantis.

Donnelly recognized that archaeological evidence would be needed to support his Atlantean speculations. In fact, in the final paragraph of his book, *Atlantis, The Antediluvian World*, published in 1882, he suggests that in 100 years time, the great museums of the world might be filled with archaeological artifacts and implements from Atlantis. Obviously, that didn't happen. Atlantis was intended as a fiction and the lack of any archaeological evidence for its existence shows that it was nothing more.

Swiss author Erich von Däniken purports that extraterrestrial visitors played a crucial role in human prehistory and history. He advanced this argument in a very popular book of pseudoarchaeology, *Chariots of the Gods*.

I read *Chariots of the Gods* when I was an undergraduate student in the early 1970s. I remember being immediately struck by a peculiar pattern. Von Däniken provides dozens of examples of technological sophistication in the archaeological record of Asia, Africa, and the Americas that he felt were so beyond the capabilities of the indigenous people, they must have been inspired by contact with a higher power, i.e., extraterrestrials. Interestingly, von Däniken seemed reluctant to ascribe any archaeological evidence in Europe to extraterrestrial involvement; I counted only two such examples in the book for the entire European continent. His pseudoarchaeology seems based on the libel that ancient civilizations, especially those outside of Europe, could not have been developed by the people themselves, but must have been inspired by what amounts to an extraterrestrial Peace Corps.

The attempt to deny a connection between American Indians and the more impressive elements of the archaeological record seen in the New World is common in pseudoarchaeology. For example, as European settlers spread across the American Midwest in the 18th and 19th centuries, they encountered the widespread remnants of substantial monuments of earth. Many of these were conical in shape, some just a few feet high, but others towered over the landscape. Within these conical mounds were found human burials, often accompanied by substantial assemblages of artistically impressive grave goods of clay, stone, copper, and mica.

Other earthworks consisted of extensive walls enclosing round, square, or even octagonal plazas of up to 50 acres. Still other mounds had been built as enormous effigies, representing on a monumental scale animals like bears, birds, and even snakes. Larger still were earthen pyramids, truncated at the top as if to provide an elevated platform for a temple or palace.

Who built the mounds and produced the artistic objects found within them? The obvious answer was the ancestors of the native people of America. Unfortunately, many Americans of European descent refused to believe that America's aboriginal inhabitants possessed such capabilities. Consequently, it was thought that some other group was responsible. So was born the myth of a race of mound-builders who had originated somewhere in the Old World.

But scholars, including Thomas Jefferson, excavated the mounds and found no evidence to indicate that the Indians didn't build them. In a project funded by the Smithsonian Institution, beginning in 1882, archaeologist Cyrus Thomas and his crew investigated 2,000 mounds in 21 states, collecting 40,000 artifacts. This archaeological evidence showed unequivocally that the moundbuilders had been Indians.

Nonetheless, the notion that Old World people could have made the artifacts within the mounds persisted. The 1860 discovery of the so-called Keystone in Newark, Ohio, immediately east of a series of substantial earthworks, is an example of this persistence. The Keystone looks a bit like a plumb bob with Hebrew writing on all four of its faces. The writing suggested it had been ancient Hebrews—the Wandering Jews of history—who had built at least some of the remarkable earthworks of North America.

However, the Hebrew lettering was modern in appearance, an anachronism on an object that ostensibly dated to the period of Ohio mound construction some 2,000 years ago. Therefore many people recognized the Keystone as a hoax.

The discovery five months later in Ohio of another anomalous artifact was highly suspicious as well. Called the Decalogue for its inscription of the Ten Commandments, this artifact bore a more appropriate, archaic version of the Hebrew language, dating to a time similar to that of mound construction. As Brad Lepper, a curator of archaeology at the Ohio Historical Society, points out, this "improvement" in the Decalogue probably resulted from its maker learning from the rather obvious inauthenticity of the Keystone.

Despite an extensive program of mound excavations over the last 100 years, professional archaeologists have never found any genuine Hebrew—or any other—inscriptions in association with the mounds. The Keystone and Decalogue are viewed by most archaeologists, historians, and linguists as crude hoaxes.

WHY WORRY ABOUT PSEUDOARCHAEOLOGY

Do people actually believe pseudoarchaeology, or is it all just harmless entertainment? Data on the actual impact of pseudoarchaeology books and television programs is hard to come by. However, I have been polling students at my university for more than 20 years, (the number of students polled is roughly 2,000 to 2,500), surveying their responses to claims about Atlantis, extraterrestrials, psychic archaeology, and America's exploration and settlement by ancient Celts, Phoenicians, Egyptians, Hebrews, and so on. The majority of the students neither strongly agrees nor disagrees with these claims, For example, when I last polled them in 2003, only about one percent strongly believed the ancient astronaut hypothesis and an additional five percent thought it could be true. That's good news. However, I have also found that a disturbingly large fraction of my students—anywhere from one-third to one-half, depending on the claim—are fascinated by these claims but admit that they don't know enough to accept or reject them.

In 1983, I polled archaeologists who taught at universities concerning their views about the impacts of pseudoarchaeology. It was apparent at the time that, while many were concerned about the inability of students to skeptically assess extraordinary claims about the human past, few had the time or inclination to do much about it. Fortunately, this appears to have changed somewhat. For example, in the mid-1980s I first circulated the draft of a textbook that debunked pseucloarchaeological claims. Sixteen publishers turned down the proposal, primarily because they didn't believe that university archaeologists felt the need or had the time to discuss such things in class. That book, *Frauds, Myths and Mysteries: Science and Pseudoscience in Archaeology,* ultimately was published, as was another book responding to pseudoarchaeology *Fantastic Archaeology: The Wild Side of North American Prehistory,* by Stephen Williams.

It is gratifying to report that both of those books have become staples in courses on pseudoarchaeology offered by anthropology departments throughout the United States and Canada. That these textbooks have survived and even thrived (*Frauds* is currently going into its 5th edition) is clear evidence that plenty of teaching archaeologists recognize the challenge posed by pseudoarchaeology and devote some time to it in their introductory classes or even teach an entire course focusing on the issue.

A highly significant difference between the 1980s and today is the existence of the Internet, a virtually limitless, open forum for ideas, scientific and otherwise. Certainly, the Web affords a soapbox for all manner of pseudoarchaeological claims. A Google search of the phrase "The Lost Continent of Atlantis," for example, generates over 84,000 hits. A search of the phrase 'Ancient Astronauts" produces more than 300,000. By comparison, a Google search of the phrase "debunking Atlantis" generates almost 6,000 hits, and a search under "debunking Ancient Astronauts" produces a little more than 4,300.

The "Web also allows archaeologists to get their message out and a handful of them have developed sites responding directly to claims of lost tribes, sunken continents, ancient astronauts, and the like. My personal favorite, in fact, is titled Fantastic Archaeology! Lost Tribes, Sunken Continents and Ancient Astronauts (http://www.uiowa.edu/~anthro/fantasti/cultindex.html), produced by Larry Zimmerman and Richard Fox.

Ultimately, how troublesome is pseudoarchaeology? Consder that a low opinion of the capabilities of ancient peoples—or, at least some ancient peoples—seems to reside at its core, The archaeological record is filled with examples of spectacular architectural achievements, sophisticated technologies, wonderful artwork, and glimmerings of science. Much of pseudoarchaeology is based on the belief that indigenous peoples were incapable of producing these things. Needless to say, this reluctance to give much of ancient humanity its due is troubling to scientists who have devoted their professional lives to illuminating the accomplishments of those people.

Fascination with and acceptance of pseudoarehaeological claims also seems to be part of a broader inability on the part of the public to distinguish science from pseudoscience. The results from my most recent student polling is an indication of this. Fifty-three percent expressed strong or mild belief in psychic power, 25 percent in the claim that UFOs are alien spacecraft, and 18 percent in the efficacy of astrology.

Garrett Fagan, a classical archaeologist at Penn State University, became so concerned about what he perceived to be an insufficient and unsystematic professional response to pseudoarchaeology that he organized a workshop on the subject at the 2003 annual meeting of the Archaeological Institute of America. It was extremely well-attended and even drew the interest of a publisher. Fagan, in fact, is now editing a book titled *Archaeological Fantasies: How Pseudoarchaeology Misrepresents the Past and Misleads the Public,* based on contributions to that workshop. The various articles in the book share a common perspective: it is important, but not sufficient, to be reactive to unsupported claims about the human past as they come up.

Fagan believes that archaeologists also need to be proactive, promoting the discoveries of genuine archaeology to the public, and not just debunk the junk. Indeed he has a point. Archaeologists cannot abandon the public forum to the pseudoarchaeologists. We need to show an interested public—one that supports archaeological research through the purchase of books, visits to museums and sites, and contributions to organizations working to preserve the past—that the true stories of antiquity, inspired by the hard evidence of archaeology, are every bit as intriguing, fascinating, and enthralling as the stories told by the pseudoarchaeologists.

The 2012 Phenomenon

Michael Bawaya

EDITOR'S INTRODUCTION

Well, the Earth didn't reverse the direction of its rotation, continents did not become unhinged, mountains didn't topple, we didn't all burn up or drown or get smooshed by meteorites, and John Cusack didn't get saved from all this drama on a big boat. So the whole 2012 nonsense turned out to be, well, nonsense. However, the phenomenon is still worth looking at as an example of unsupported claims about an ancient culture can be, essentially, made up in a media frenzy that results in frightening not just a few people. It's also worth noting, I guess on the bright side, how absurd claims about the Maya civilization, Maya science, Maya astronomy, and the Maya calendar actually opened to door to a discussion of the real, extremely impressive story about Maya civilization, genuine Maya science, authentic Maya astronomical knowledge, and the sophisticated Maya calendar (calendars, actually). If you had read Richard Bawaya's piece on 2012 before December 21 of that year, hopefully you would have been reassured that nothing particularly bad was going to happen on that day. Reading it now provides context for what all the fuss was about.

POINTS TO PONDER

1. Who were the Maya? Where did they live? What were they all about?
2. What was the significance, from the perspective of the Maya themselves, of the day on our calendar of December 21, 2012?
3. Who benefited from the claim that the Maya predicted the end of the world for December 21, 2012?
4. What lessons are provided from the story of the Maya 2012 apocalypse phenomenon?

Michael Bawaya, "The 2012 Phenomenon," *Archaeology*, vol. 15, no. 4, pp. 12-17, 19. Copyright © 2012 by Michael Bawaya. Reprinted with permission.

Rosario Panti, brandishing her sastun, spoke of "darkness." On December 21, 2012, there will be a series of solar eclipses. Technology will fail. Computers, high definition TVs, cell phones—all of our wondrous inventions will mysteriously shut down.

Panti, surrounded by a number of journalists, including me, held forth in the bar of the swank Ka'ana Boutique Resort in western Belize. Though appearing unprepossessive in her white T-shirt and jeans, Panti has a distinguished pedigree: she is the granddaughter of Elijio Panti, who is said to be the last Maya healer, and she herself is advertised as the last Maya shaman. Furthermore, she had her sastun, a strange object looking something like a petrified mushroom, which apparently invests its owner with oracular powers. It is, she said, 4,000 years old, and one of only 13 sastuns known to exist.

December 21, 2012 on the modern calendar (According to some correlations the date is December 23) correlates with 13.0.0.0.0, the last day on the Maya long count calendar, the fateful day when the world will go dark or, according to some prophesies, meet a fate far worse. The ancient Maya were such a remarkable people that, centuries later, the putative end of their calendar has created a veritable cottage industry of doomsaying. Books (some 3,000 of them by one count), articles, and movies portray a variety of cataclysmic, world-ending events that, it's alleged, the Maya somehow foresaw.

Perhaps the best known of these works is *2012*, Hollywood's depiction of the apocalypse. In this movie neutrinos from a huge solar flare result in a cornucopia of disastrous events: earthquakes, volcanic eruptions, tsunamis, and the like. Los Angeles slides into the Pacific, the President is killed when an aircraft carrier crashes into the White House, and cities across the globe are largely trashed. Myriad other works predict a meteor—or, worse, a mysterious rogue planet known as Nibiru, aka Planet X—will collide with Earth.

Then there's the equally dismal scenario of the sun aligning with the plane of the Milky Way Galaxy for the first time in 26,000 years, which somehow leads to the Milky Way's black hole wreaking havoc with our solar system, a reversal of Earth's magnetic field, hurricanes, massive power outages, etc. These dire cosmic forecasts are so prevalent that NASA saw fit to devote a web page (www.nasa.gov/topics/earth/features/2012.html) to rebutting them.

There is also a kindler, gentler vision of what 2012 will bring. Some forecasters see the start of a period of hope and renewal rather than doom and gloom. Though she says December 21 will be a day of darkness, Panti believes the world will continue on and, come the 22nd, be a better place. Rather than the end, this will be a new beginning, a period of regeneration and love. However appealing this picture of the future may be, Anthony Aveni, a noted archeoastronomer at Colgate University and the author of the book *The End of Time: The Maya Mystery of 2012*, dismissed it as being "terribly naive."

"I see (2012) at this point as crass commercialism," said Arlen Chase, a Maya specialist at the University of Central Florida who was one of the talking heads in "Mayan Prophecies 2012," the History Channel's overheated contribution to the End of the World *oeuvre*. ("They didn't let me say what I really wanted to say, because it wouldn't make for a good show," he remarked, referring to the way some of his comments were edited.)

In addition to individuals cashing in on 2012, Chase noted that Mexico, Belize, and Guatemala, the countries where the great majority of Maya sites have been found, are using it to promote tourism. It was, indeed, at the invitation of the Belize Tourism Bureau that I and eight other journalists visited Belize to familiarize ourselves with the country and Maya culture, and to write about 2012.

One evening we were part of a group that attended a presentation titled "2012 The End … And The Beginning," by anthropologist Joe Awe. The presentation focused on the Maya's many achievements, their complex calendrical system, their view of time, and, of course, 2012. "I think the calendar ends, and then we start again,"Awe concluded. However, he believes the date was somehow significant to the Maya. "I don't know how the ancient Maya would explain it, but they knew something powerful was going on."

MUCH ADO ABOUT NOTHING

Gregorio Valentino lives in San Jose, a village of roughly 1,000 people in southern Belize. "Yes, that's what I heard, but I don't know how true it is," Gregorio, who is Maya, said of the 2012 hubbub. He mentioned the Rapture by way of comparison. "I hear the guy got rich," Gregorio said of Harold, Camping, the American Christian broadcaster who originally predicted, the Rapture would occur on May 21, 2011, and then subsequently predicted the event would take place five months later.

Gregorio, his wife Hermenia, and their children—the couple produced 12, two of whom died— live in two small, Spartan structures that stand side by side. They have scant furniture and lack indoor plumbing and electricity. A number of dogs and chickens wander about. Gregorio owns four acres of land that he farms for corn, rice, beans, and other crops, and he grows almost everything his family eats. His commute (he walks) from home to work is an hour each way.

Despite the lack of amenities he and his family like where they live "because this is peaceful," he said. But there are no jobs, so he farms out of necessity and struggles to make ends meet. Maintaining Maya traditions is also important. "We are forgetting our culture from, the beginning," he said. "Nobody knows it. We want to bring our culture back." He does this by adhering to such ancient practices as growing com, cooking with fire wood, and making a thatched roof for one of his buildings. So he has other things to think about than 2012. That's also the case for his relatives and neighbors.

Justino Peck, a San Jose village leader, said his parents never told him about 2012, but "maybe it could be true." He, however, seemed far more interested in the topic of cacao farming. Most Maya farmers still practice slash and burn agriculture, according to Peck, but planting cacao trees, which produce the fruit whose seeds were used by the Maya for hundreds of years to make chocolate, doesn't require clearing land. That's good for the land, and helps prevent global warming.

Peck led me and the other journalists to a cacao orchard, where he picked a pod from one of the trees, split it open with a machete, and then took out the seeds. The ancient Maya ground the cacao seeds and mixed the powder with water and various other things to make a chocolate beverage, and Peck then invited us to his home, where, after his wife demonstrated this process, we sampled the drink.

Ester Sanchez, an administrator at a school in Blue Creek Village that emphasizes the teaching of Maya culture, called 2012 "a new beginning" and that the school plans to celebrate the event, and they welcome tourists to join them. She criticized the media for portraying it as a time of destruction. Silveno, a middle-aged, weathered-face travel guide who also lives in Blue Creek, gives little thought to 2012, but he, too, would be happy to see more tourists.

Whatever the date meant to the ancient Maya, the typical response today, according to anthropologist Joe Awe, is "What does that have to do with the price of milk?"

So what did the date 13.0.0.0.0 mean to the Maya? That's hard to know, but the archaeological record tells us that they were clock watchers."I think it was about creating a time-ordered universe," said Simon Martin, a curator at the Pennsylvania Museum of Archaeology and Anthropology and a Maya epigrapher. Time and religion were integrated in Maya cosmogony. They devised a system of calendars because, he said, "they saw many forces affecting the world."The Long Count calendar derived from that system.

One of their calendars, called the *Tzolk'in,* consisted of 260 days. Some experts surmise that its length correlates with the cycle of human gestation. The Tzolk'in was combined with another calendar, the *Haab,* a 365-day calendar based on the solar year, to form the Calendar Round, a synchronized cycle that covered 52 Haabs.

The Long Count was another calendar that served to measure longer periods of time and to document when an event occurred in relation to other events. According to the generally accepted correlation between the Long Count and the modern calendar, the Long Count begins on August 11,3114 B.C. which is thought to be a mythological creation date. It's a linear calendar (the Maya generally viewed time cyclically) that measured time predominantly in units of 20. A *uinal* consisted of 20 days; 18 uinals made a *tun;* 20 tuns formed a *k'atun;* and 20 k'atuns a *b'aktun.* So the Long Count date 13.0.0.0.0—13 b'aktuns, 0 k'atuns, 0 tuns, 0 uinals, and 0 kin (days)—is roughly 5,125 years after the initial Long Count date, which is to say 2012.

Here is where the fertile, feverish imaginations of modern minds filled in the blanks with scenarios terrible and tranquil. This is necessary because the Maya made but one known reference to 2012, and a number of epigraphers believe they made no predictions as to what would take place then.

That reference to the portentous date was found at Tortuguero, a small site in southern Mexico. There is an inscription on what's known as Monument 6, which is difficult to decipher because of its poor condition. The 2012 date is discernable,but what comes after isn't. "Even in damaged form, (what comes after the date) doesn't appear to refer to 2012," Martin said. His opinion is based on the interpretation of Maya archaeologist and epigrapher Stephen Houston of Brown University. The syntax and structure of this glyph led Houston to conclude the damaged script "would be a back reference to a much earlier event,"Martin said. Martin and a number of other Mayanists have also noted there's a reference to a much later time, the year A.D. 4772, in an inscription at Palenque, a Maya site in southern Mexico. This appears to contradict the notion that 2012 was a final, let alone cataclysmic, date for the Maya.

Some doomsayers have cited the image of water coming out of a serpent's mouth in the Dresden Codex, one of the Maya's few surviving books, to be a harbinger of a great flood. Martin refuted this, saying "it's not that the Maya didn't have concepts of world destruction," but that these concepts aren't connected to the long count calendar. For *the* most part the glyphs served to record the actions of longs, both historical and mythological. "The calendar," he added, "is a vehicle for royal authority. It's all about asserting their earthly power."

"I think people in general like mysteries," said Jaime Awe, who dined with our group one evening. Jaime, who is Joe Awe's cousin, is the director of the Institute of Archaeology at Belize's National Institute of Culture and History and a Maya scholar. He is untroubled by thoughts of 2012, considering it "the end of a cycle," not the world. "I think it's more about us" than the ancient, or living, Maya, "we make a much bigger deal out of it than the Maya themselves."

"I don't subscribe to the notion that the Maya knew or cared about making predictions in the distant future," said Aveni. "It's about romanticizing the Maya, like romanticizing the aliens." This phenomenon, he added, "comes to the fore at a time of deep concern" about problems such as the great recession and global warming, not to mention American religions' fascination with the Second Coming. "The real story here is about us: American pop culture's love affair with catastrophe."

"What does the Maya calendar have to do with our society?" Chase asked rhetorically. Then he answered the question: 2012 "is sexy," a good way to make a buck. Plenty of money has been, and will continue to be, made. Aveni noted that what he called "sacred travel," which is spurred by the love/regeneration view, is "a very big industry."

Jaime Awe said the famed rock band U2 will be performing at Chichén Itza, one of the best-known Maya sites, in southern Mexico, to mark the occasion. In Belize, on the other hand, there will be a number of small, "culturally sensitive" events. A group of Maya have asked him to take part in a "ceremony of renewal." During this ceremony, which takes place at archaeological sites, the modern Maya "petition the gods that their universe remains in balance, for stability in the world, and for continued sustenance," he said. Belize will also have monthly events throughout the year.

One morning we toured Xunantunich, one of Belize's most popular Maya sites. Our guide was a Maya named Anastacio Bol. People visit Xunantunich for many different reasons, according to Bol. "Some come for energy." One visitor informed him that the "center of energy" was one of the site's ballcourts. Bol said he, too, gets "strong feelings" at Maya sites and he thinks 2012 is "just another cycle we're going through."

We made our way to El Castillo, the site's largest temple, which is wrapped by a refurbished frieze. Bol said it's thought that the east-facing section of the frieze was meant to greet the rising sun, which signified reincarnation. Two days earlier Rosario Panti, the Maya shaman, revealed to us journalists that we, and everyone else, will in a sense be reincarnated after December 21. The cosmic clock will be reset to zero, and in love and harmony the counting of days will continue. As she informed us, "you all have zeroes in you." Thank goodness.

CPSIA information can be obtained at www.ICGtesting.com
Printed in the USA
BVOW06s0652030914

365318BV00012B/9/P